keystone poetry

A KEYSTONE BOOK

Keystone Books are intended to serve the citizens of Pennsylvania.
They are accessible, well-researched explorations into the history, culture, society,
and environment of the Keystone State as part of the Middle Atlantic region.

keystone poetry

CONTEMPORARY POETS ON PENNSYLVANIA

Edited by Marjorie Maddox and Jerry Wemple

THE PENNSYLVANIA STATE UNIVERSITY PRESS | UNIVERSITY PARK, PENNSYLVANIA

Library of Congress Cataloging-in-Publication Data

Names: Marjorie Maddox and Jerry Wemple, editors.
Title: Keystone poetry : contemporary poets on Pennsylvania / edited by Marjorie
    Maddox and Jerry Wemple.
Description: University Park, Pennsylvania : The Pennsylvania State University
    Press, 2025. | Series: Keystone Books. | Includes bibliographical references and
    index.
Summary: "Celebrates Pennsylvania's literary traditions and diverse voices with
    179 poems exploring the state's towns, history, and culture. This geographically
    organized collection offers new perspectives on place and identity and includes
    discussion questions and writing prompts for classroom use"—Provided by pub-
    lisher.
Identifiers: LCCN 2025004430 | ISBN 9780271099903 (paperback)
Subjects: LCSH: American poetry--Pennsylvania. | Pennsylvania--Poetry.
Classification: LCC PS548.P4 K49 2025
LC record available at https://lccn.loc.gov/2025004430

Copyright © 2025 The Pennsylvania State University
All rights reserved
Printed in the United States of America
Published by The Pennsylvania State University Press,
University Park, PA 16802–1003

10 9 8 7 6 5 4 3 2 1

The Pennsylvania State University Press is a member of the Association of
University Presses.

It is the policy of The Pennsylvania State University Press to use acid-free paper.
Publications on uncoated stock satisfy the minimum requirements of American
National Standard for Information Sciences—Permanence of Paper for Printed
Library Material, ANSI Z39.48–1992.

To the Keystone State
and all who call it home

contents

PREFACE xiii

GREETINGS FROM THE KEYSTONE STATE   1
  "A Pennsylvania Journal," *Jay Parini*   3

I. BEGINNINGS: PHILADELPHIA AND ITS SUBURBS   5
  "What Cement Is Made of," *Daniel Donaghy*   7
  "At Schuylkill Park," *Chris Bullard*   8
  "Philadelphia: Early Summer," *Eileen Daly Moeller*   9
  "To the Fig Tree on 9th and Christian," *Ross Gay*   10
  "The Quaker Delegate from Pennsylvania," *Joshua P. Cohen*   14
  "Our Fathers in Philadelphia," *David Livewell*   15
  "December 26, 1960," *Steve Pollack*   16
  "At the Polish-American Festival, Penn's Landing," *J. C. Todd*   17
  "Plinkies," *Peter Krok*   18
  "Elegy for the Science Teacher," *Robin Becker*   19
  "Winter Melon Soup," *Vernita Hall*   20
  "Before He Fell, or Jumped," *Mary Rohrer-Dann*   21
  "One day," *Valerie Fox*   22
  "Giant Heart," *Chloe Martinez*   23
  "Mütter Museum with Owl," *G. C. Waldrep*   24
  "Halfball," *Joseph A. Chelius*   26
  "Walnut Street," *Ernest Hilbert*   27
  "5 South 43rd Street, Floor 2," *Yolanda Wisher*   28
  "Bridesburg," *Leonard Kress*   29
  "Sweat," *Nathalie F. Anderson*   30
  "Breezeway, circa 1964," *Jacqueline Osherow*   31
  "Walking Toward Cranes," *Amy Small-McKinney*   32
  "The Frankford Elevated Train," *Robbi Nester*   33

"At the Crest of the Meadow," *Jan Freeman*   34

"Home," *Michael Quinn*   36

"Passing Through Southeastern Pennsylvania Towns in Winter," *Mark Danowsky*   37

"Linvilla," *Nicole Miyashiro*   37

"Quaker Memorial Service for a Young Girl, Germantown," *Carole Bernstein*   39

"Kitchen Table," *Hayden Saunier*   40

"New Hope," *Julie Standig*   41

"Sleepless Johnston," *Lynn Levin*   42

"A Map of Valley Forge," *Grant Clauser*   45

II. SOUTH CENTRAL: FARMLANDS, BATTLEFIELDS, AND THE CAPITAL REGION   47

"In Amish Country," *Sarah Russell*   49

"Dirt," *Jayne Relaford Brown*   49

"All Day Long There'd Been Papers," *Robert Fillman*   50

"On Passing thru Morgantown, Pa," *Sonia Sanchez*   52

"A Girl, Reading," *Heather H. Thomas*   52

"In Reading," *Sandy Feinstein*   54

"Lost Brother, 2019," *Alison Carb Sussman*   54

"No Wind," *Gerald Stern*   56

"'Swans first, now a fountain,'" *Alyse Bensel*   57

"Gettysburg," *Allison Adair*   58

"Letter to Wemple from Gettysburg," *Matt Perakovich*   58

"Gettysburg Poem #3," *Abby Minor*   59

"Taxidermy in South Central Pennsylvania," *Katy Giebenhain*   61

"Harrowing," *Catherine Chandler*   63

"Keystone Ode with Jane Doe in It," *Nicole Santalucia*   64

"Longfellow Pine," *Judith A. Kennedy*   65

"Election," *Cynthia Hogue*   66

"Why Grandfather Counted the Stars," *Martin Willitts Jr.*   68

"Wintergreen," *Le Hinton*   70

"Bully Pulpit," *Michael Garrigan*   71

"Pennsylvania's Governor Advises Voluntary Evacuation," *Virginia Watts*   72

"White Shore, 1963," *Maria James-Thiaw*   74

"Retail Requiem," *Erin Hoover*   76

III. CIRCLING EAST: MINES, MOUNTAINS, AND MILLS 79

"The Invader Alters Everything," *Ann E. Michael* 81

"The Naming of Bars," *Lee Upton* 82

"The Ruins of Bethlehem Steel," *Joseph Dorazio* 83

"In the Allentown Shelter Kitchen," *Susan Weaver* 84

"Packerton," *David Staudt* 84

"You've Got a Friend In . . . ," *Grace Bauer* 86

"Kempton, PA: After My Death," *James Najarian* 87

"Spring Delivers Us," *Jack Chielli* 87

"Huckleberries and Homebrewed Boilo," *Marianne Peel* 89

"Litany of Dyings," *Lisa Toth Salinas* 90

"Turning Over," *Paul Martin* 91

"My Father's Hands," *Harry Humes* 92

"When they say to leave, she says:," *Amanda Hodes* 93

"Centralia, PA," *Faith Ellington* 94

"The Viaduct," *Linda Pennisi* 95

"Coal Ghosts (Excerpts)," *Stanton Hancock* 95

"the next field over," *nicole v basta* 96

"Wilkes-Barre," *Jerry Wemple* 97

"Christmas in Public Square," *Christine Gelineau* 99

"Immigrant Song," *Angela Alaimo O'Donnell* 100

"Agnes 1972," *Thomas Kielty Blomain* 100

"American Water (Excerpts)," *David Chin* 101

"Susquehanna River Bathers," *Elaine Terranova* 1030

"Gracie's Run," *MJ Moss* 104

"Evening Sky Diesel Blue purple tinge," *Craig Czury* 105

"The Sky Above My House on Johler Avenue," *Brian Fanelli* 106

IV. NORTH CENTRAL: THE SUSQUEHANNA VALLEYS AND THE UPSTATE REGION 107

"Susquehanna (Excerpts)," *Shara McCallum* 109

"Gedachtniss Tag: Remembrance Day," *Rebecca Lauren* 111

"The Urge to Bury," *S. E. Gilman* 112

"At the Riverview Cemetery, Northumberland, PA," *Melanie Simms* 113

"Sodom School, Northumberland County, PA," *Michael Hardin* 114

"At the Site of the Laurelton Village for Feeble-minded Girls of Childbearing
Age," *Deirdre O'Connor* 115

"Lines written in the Walmart Supercenter parking lot, Lewisburg, Pennsylvania," *K. A. Hays* 117

"Alvira," *Micah James Bauman and David J. Bauman* 118

"Still April and No Spring," *Anne Dyer Stuart* 119

"Independence," *Dawn Leas* 120

"Shiners," *Ken Fifer* 120

"Glacier Pools Preserve," *Shanna Powlus Wheeler* 121

"Stepping Stones," *Gregory Djanikian* 122

"Sunrise on a Back Porch in Pennsylvania," *Gloria Heffernan* 124

"Throwing like a Girl," *Marjorie Maddox* 125

"Here, there are Blueberries," *Mary Szybist* 126

"Worlds End," *Barbara Crooker* 127

"Prayer Flags," *Judith Sornberger* 128

"Tioga County, PA," *Robbie Gamble* 130

"Lullaby in Fracktown," *Lilace Mellin Guignard* 131

"Nurse in Need," *Julie L. Moore* 132

"North: 1991," *Bruce Bond* 134

"The Ritual," *James Brasfield* 136

"First Rain of Spring," *Rachael Lyon* 137

"Waking Up with Jerry Sandusky," *Julia Spicher Kasdorf* 138

"Greener Than," *Julie Swarstad Johnson* 139

V. THE ALLEGHENY HIGHLANDS 141

"Settlers in the Valley," *Ann Hostetler* 143

"Jacks Mountain," *Emily Miller Mlčák* 144

"Migration at Jacks Narrows," *Jack Troy* 148

"Poem about the Environment," *Jeanne Murray Walker* 148

"Blast Area," *Dave Bonta* 150

"Skins," *Noah Davis* 151

"Up Myers' Lane, Altoona, PA," *Heather Myers* 153

"Fall, Central Pennsylvania," *Erin Murphy* 154

"The Oldest Roller Coaster in the World," *Gabriel Welsch* 154

"The Dairy Queen in DuBois, Pennsylvania Opens for Spring," *Antonio Vallone* 155

"Toward Pittsburgh," *Matt Hohner* 156

"Windber Field," *Edward Hirsch* 157

"I'm from a one-way bus ticket," *Barbara Sabol*   158
"In the Johnstown Flood Museum," *Rachel Roupp*   160
"Steeltown Girls," *Sandee Gertz*   161
"Arriving in Westmont," *Matthew Ussia*   162
"Somewhere in Pennsylvania," *Charles Clifton*   164
"Two Women Watched by Geese," *Ed Ochester*   165
"Life on the Farm: Things to Count On," *JoAnne Growney*   166
"Flight 93 National Memorial," *Jonson Miller*   167
"Until Darkness Comes," *Todd Davis*   168

VI. THREE RIVERS AND OLD MILLS   171

"Pittsburgh," *Patricia Jabbeh Wesley*   173
"Heart Fire," *Maggie Anderson*   174
"Rivers," *Nathaniel Ricketts*   176
"Some Maps to Indicate Pittsburgh," *Terrance Hayes*   177
"Dreaming Door," *Jan Beatty*   179
"On the Way Up: Pittsburgh StepTrek," *Paola Corso*   179
"Family Reunions," *Mark Saba*   181
"John Kane," *Mauricio Kilwein Guevara*   182
"Cinderman," *Andrena Zawinski*   183
"Nine Irenes," *Jocelyn Heath*   184
"Requiem for the Living," *Joseph Bathanti*   185
"Good Friday, Schenley Park, Pittsburgh, 2020," *Jim Daniels*   186
"Dioramas," *Kristin Kovacic*   188
"Tuesday Morning," *Sharon Fagan McDermott*   189
"Then It Was Simple," *Cortney Davis*   190
"Homage to Sharon Stone," *Lynn Emanuel*   191
"The Great Beauty," *Toi Derricotte*   193
"Doppelgänger," *Judith Vollmer*   194
"Ink," *Yona Harvey*   195
"At the Cathedral of Hope," *Janette Schafer*   197
"A Minyan Plus One," *Philip Terman*   198
"Dear Mr. Rogers Revisited," *Shirley Stevens*   200
"The Jailer's Wife's Epithalamium," *Erinn Batykefer*   201
"Walking in Homewood Cemetery During the Pandemic," *Judith Sanders*   202
"The Lost Continents," *Gary Fincke*   204

"Garlic Mustard," *Sheila Squillante*   207

"The Allegheny River," *Jeff Oaks*   208

"D++ Dek Hockey League Champions (2012)," *Mike Good*   209

"Father Rodney," *Richard Pierce*   210

"First Day of the Hunt," *Paula Bohince*   212

"River of Mantises," *Geraldine Connolly*   213

VII. NORTH BY NORTHWEST: THE LAND OF ELK, FORESTS, AND LAKE ERIE   215

"Where Girls Still Ride the Beds of Pickup Trucks," *Karen J. Weyant*   217

"Sanctuary of Fog," *Byron Hoot*   218

"Antlers," *Patricia Thrushart*   218

"Bird Watching in Bradford," *Helen Ruggieri*   219

"Grove City Morning," *Eric Potter*   220

"Migration," *David Swerdlow*   221

"With Latin Filling the Lake," *George Looney*   222

"O! Erie!," *Chuck Joy*   224

"Sometimes I Forget You Lived in This City," *Corey Zeller*   225

"August: Erie," *Deborah Burnham*   225

"Rapture," *Berwyn Moore*   226

"Wind on the Bay," *Laura Rutland*   228

"At the Rib Fest in Erie, PA," *Sean Thomas Dougherty*   228

"The Catcher and the Sighs," *Cee Williams*   230

"Saw Again the Infamous Owl," *Lisa M. Dougherty*   232

"October Echo," *Marjorie Wonner*   233

"Amphibians," *Tammy Robacker*   233

"Fog Off the Allegheny," *Richard Krohn*   235

"Runoff," *Steve Myers*   236

"The Field Mice of Arneman Road," *John Repp*   237

"Eclogue (Winter)," *Christopher Bakken*   238

DISCUSSION QUESTIONS AND WRITING PROMPTS   239

ACKNOWLEDGMENTS   267

THE POETS   275

INDEX   312

preface

Trying to capture the essence of Pennsylvania in an anthology is a daunting task in large part because there is no one Pennsylvania. There are many. For example, the coal towns of the eastern Pennsylvania anthracite region were settled largely by people of Irish and eastern and southern European descent. They have distinct cultures from those of nearby former railroad and mill towns along the Susquehanna River, towns that were settled by the descendants of Germans and Scots Irish. Language often illuminates local cultural markers, making one region of the Keystone State different even from neighboring towns. The Shamokin-area greeting "Ho, bott," a garbled form of the old miners' greeting "Hello, buddy," seems to have made a recent resurgence, with a younger generation using this term as a sign of "coal region pride." The greeting is not heard outside of the area, even in Sunbury, the county seat only sixteen miles away. In the lower Wyoming Valley, the linguistic tag "heyna" is used as a stand-in for "Isn't it so?" (as in "Nice day, heyna?"). However, the term is not heard even a few miles away. As distances grow longer, contrasts become clearer, often evidenced by language. Philadelphia's "jawn" can essentially mean whatever the speaker (and listener) wants it to mean. "Yinz" is the informal "you" in the Pittsburgh region. And whether one is east or west of Altoona marks whether one will hear "soda" or "pop" as the term for a carbonated soft drink.

Thus influenced by place, words pave our stories. While they often connect cities and counties, they also make distinct the peoples, cultures, and traditions of our commonwealth. Individually and together, we tell the tale of this state. As Jay Parini explains in the opening poem of *Keystone Poetry: Contemporary Poets on Pennsylvania*, "Words are the world's ten thousand eyes: / I opened some of them with my own ink." Indeed, in this anthology, 182 different poets open—with their own ink—diverse worlds of city street and country road, panoramic skyline and hidden trail, mountain ridge and coal tunnel, all within the state boundaries of Pennsylvania.

Keystone Poetry, published on the twentieth anniversary of *Common Wealth: Contemporary Poets on Pennsylvania* (Penn State University Press, 2005), celebrates rich literary traditions, welcoming to its pages a range of established and newer poets exploring the hometowns, history, traditions, and culture of the Commonwealth. In these pages you'll find fresh perspectives on old landmarks, novel reflections on alternate locations, and varied responses by Pennsylvania poets to events of the last twenty years. Ordered geographically, the poems traverse county lines, ancestral lineages, and thematic concerns—as well as gender, racial, and socioeconomic barriers. Wherever you locate yourself within this multifaceted state, we trust these poems will lead you to that river, that ballpark, that museum, that job, that house, that alley, that open field of imagination. But we also wish for you new discoveries of place, broadened perspectives of home, and a deeper understanding of those who share with you this Keystone state.

As poets ourselves, as university professors who have taught *Common Wealth* in introductory and advanced classes, and as educators who present on place-based literature, we also felt strongly about adding an educational component to this 2025 anthology. Drawing on *Keystone Poetry*, high school and college educators can use students' hometown experiences to make such disciplines as literature, writing, history, geography, sociology, political science, and psychology more accessible. Building on the vast viewpoints of the anthologized poets, instructors also will gain a rich resource for teaching research, literary techniques, and interpersonal skills.

To delve more deeply in class discussions, see "Let's Talk About It" at the back of this anthology, which also serves as a helpful aid for individual reflection. To further fuel students' creativity, access "Let's Write About It," a practical guide to inspire writers of all levels to create their own "Pennsylvania Journal" with "words [that] are the world's ten thousand eyes." We believe these prompts will be beneficial in a variety of classes, including literature, composition, creative writing, and Pennsylvania-based course offerings.

For those who have previously explored or are now reading *Common Wealth*, we've included writing prompts and conversation starters to strengthen connections between the anthologies. For another resource, please see the Pennsylvania Center for the Book's Literary and Cultural Heritage Maps of PA: https://pabook.libraries.psu.edu/literary-cultural-heritage-maps-pa.

In addition, we are building the foundation for *Keystone Poetry* podcasts as well as in-person and virtual readings that highlight poets from each section of the anthology. If you are an educator, please consider hosting a *Keystone Poetry* poet at your school, thus allowing students to interact with authors who write about where they live, work, or learn, poets who—perhaps like you—have traveled these Pennsylvania hills and valleys.

One of our colleagues, who had moved from the Great Plains to Pennsylvania, said that he was used to only one road between two points. He marveled at the many winding routes here in Pennsylvania, how there can be several ways to get between points A and B. So, too, the poets featured on these pages know that there are numerous ways to define Pennsylvania. As we did twenty years ago in *Common Wealth*, we celebrate the many voices of Pennsylvania. We are excited to share with you this gathering of familiar and fresh faces. Welcome to *Keystone Poetry*.

GREETINGS FROM THE KEYSTONE STATE

A Pennsylvania Journal

JAY PARINI

I had a mostly silent boyhood,
shifting in the streets that wobbled underfoot.
The coal mines tunneled underneath my life,
and corners of my house would fill with soot.

I listened as the women weaved about me,
offering their stories, naming names.
I didn't always care what they would say
in those repetitive and heated rooms.

The neighborhood was ice or mud or dust
in yards where I would often stop to think.
Words are the world's ten thousand eyes:
I opened some of them with my own ink

in that thick journal underneath my pillow.
All the empty pages meant so much,
could still be formulated, gathered
in my hand, a new life wakened by the touch

of pen to soft, white paper. Year by year,
through seasons of the skin, I wrote my way.
My steps were wandering and often slow.
Time told me gradually what I could say.

I. BEGINNINGS: PHILADELPHIA AND ITS SUBURBS

What Cement Is Made of

DANIEL DONAGHY

The cement plant—where all day wind spirals
aggregate around scaffolds and storage
bins tall as steeples—has only three walls,

so it opens to Route 1 like a stage.
Five o'clock: Dump trucks and conveyer belts
stiffen like workers on washroom stools

who stare into their brown or black hands,
or who close their eyes, savoring already
that lager's cold burn against their throats.

Inside locker doors: pictures of wives, kids,
strippers, stenciled numbers. Crusted cement
on toilet tanks, across the line of sinks.

In shower stalls, concrete mix washes off
like limestone loosened by hard summer rain
under a single, shared fluorescent bulb.

The young supervisor slips off waders
and safety goggles and dreams of softballs
arcing toward the rusted steel of the sun.

Diesel and dust turn to soap and cologne,
the day's heavy falling to rap music,
phone calls, texts, doors opening and closing.

Tomorrow's flatbeds glare from loading docks.
Sea gulls stalk the drum-gray air overhead.
Men ease their wasting bodies into jeans,

T-shirts, ball caps. They wait for each other
to pull on clean socks, lace their boots, then rise
together, laughing, toward their evenings.

■ ■ ■

At Schuylkill Park
CHRIS BULLARD

The raised beds abut
like cell walls
in our divided community
garden where a few
lottery winners are allowed
to hack at the trucked-in soil.

The fencing keeps out
dog-walkers and hooded users,
but does nothing to halt
the jaundiced haze
drifting across the river
from Expressway traffic.

I'm feverish to plant
before the quarantine hits,
as if my tomatoes
might restore me,
and those I'm keeping
at a social distance, to health.

My mind holds two
inconsistent thoughts:
each death is a loss,
grievous and unrepairable,
but a billion of them

might set the planet right.

Outside our locked gate,
two laughing kids
in a white blossoming
fruit tree dance
along a shaky branch
until it snaps.

■ ■ ■

Philadelphia: Early Summer
EILEEN DALY MOELLER

The city is Walt Whitman, sitting like an oracle
in Starbucks, on South Eighth Street, fresh
from the Camden Ferry, and happy to be alive
in this window for all to see, basking in flaxen light.
He revels in this sunlight, eases into reverie,
throwing curlicues of shadow across
the glossy pages of wall and floor.

The city dreams in stanza and verse,
breathing people in and out, burnishing them
till they're lustrous and flawed as angels,
experimenting with the timbre of their voices,
soon to send them out to sing for her,
as they wind through the busy streets.

· · · · ·

The city is a rowhouse dog dragging its owner,
toward every other animal it can find,
all scamper and lunge at the others,
all stalk and bait at the squirrels, and lost,
always lost to the bliss of the scent,

the ecstasy of the random encounter,
until its owner tires, and tugs
the leash toward home.

. . . . .

The city is a sparrow bathing in a fountain's
overflow, as water gushes out to the gutter below,
every time a carriage sidles up, so a tired horse can
lower its head to guzzle what it can. The city spreads
its wings and dips its tiny feet, its feathers, and belly
into excess, then it lights on a brick wall to preen in the sun.
So many are the commonplace blossoms here, opening all at once.

■ ■ ■

To the Fig Tree on 9th and Christian

ROSS GAY

Tumbling through the
city in my
mind without once
looking up
the racket in
the lugwork probably
rehearsing some
stupid thing I
said or did
some crime or
other the city they
say is a lonely
place until yes
the sound of sweeping
and a woman
yes with a
broom beneath

which you are now
too the canopy
of a fig its
arms pulling the
September sun to it
and she
has a hose too
and so works hard
rinsing and scrubbing
the walk
lest some poor sod
slip on the silk
of a fig
and break his hip
and not probably
reach over to gobble up
the perpetrator
the light catches
the veins in her hands
when I ask about
the tree they
flutter in the air and
she says *take*
as much as
you can
help me
so I load my
pockets and mouth
and she points
to the step-ladder against
the wall to
mean more but
I was without a
sack so my meager
plunder would have to
suffice and an old woman

whom gravity
was pulling into
the earth loosed one
from a low slung
branch and its eye
wept like hers
which she dabbed
with a kerchief as she
cleaved the fig with
what remained of her
teeth and soon there were
eight or nine
people gathered beneath
the tree looking into
it like a constellation pointing
do you see it
and I am tall and so
good for these things
and a bald man even
told me so
when I grabbed three
or four for
him reaching into the
giddy throngs of
wasps sugar
stoned which he only
pointed to smiling and
rubbing his stomach
I mean he was really rubbing his stomach
it was hot his
head shone while he
offered recipes to the
group using words which
I couldn't understand and besides
I was a little
tipsy on the dance

of the velvety heart rolling
in my mouth
pulling me down and
down into the
oldest countries of my
body where I ate my first fig
from the hand of a man who escaped his country
by swimming through the night
and maybe
never said more than
five words to me
at once but gave me
figs and a man on his way
to work hops twice
to reach at last his
fig which he smiles at and calls
baby, *c'mere baby*,
he says and blows a kiss
to the tree which everyone knows
cannot grow this far north
being Mediterranean
and favoring the rocky, sun-baked soils
of Jordan and Sicily
but no one told the fig tree
or the immigrants
there is a way
the fig tree grows
in groves it wants,
it seems, to hold us,
yes I am anthropomorphizing
goddammit I have twice
in the last thirty seconds
rubbed my sweaty
forearm into someone else's
sweaty shoulder
gleeful eating out of each other's hands

on Christian St.
in Philadelphia a city like most
which has murdered its own
people
this is true
we are feeding each other
from a tree
at the corner of Christian and 9th
strangers maybe
never again.

■ ■ ■

The Quaker Delegate from Pennsylvania
JOSHUA P. COHEN

Pacific, rail-thin
    John Dickinson
the pragmatic,
    humble Quaker,

pleaded fearfully
in the Great Hall,
    feeling certain
at any moment
    his voice-box
would give way,
his knees would buckle under,
    and that's all anyone
    would remember.

Perhaps he'd slink off,
    like an injured animal,
    into the darkest corner of a barn
somewhere in eastern Pennsylvania,

and just let fat
John Adams win—

though clearly in his mind,
    he saw the Union
as a child's paper skiff,
    sailing swiftly out
to war with the open sea.

Our Fathers in Philadelphia

DAVID LIVEWELL

Our fathers, who are probably not in heaven,
Hollow are your names
As they echo in and out of empty mills
On American Street in Kensington.
Your kingdom's come and gone, your wishes slashed
Here on the streets as they are in the heavens
(Where the milky windows hide your ghosts).
Give us your days like daily bread,
And forgive us for trespassing on your ground,
And lead us not into the temptation
That what you made was for something greater than work itself,
But deliver us from this hell you deserted,
Our fathers, whose art is not in heaven.

December 26, 1960

STEVE POLLACK

My 14th birthday
Early morning 18 degrees, clearing skies
We entered Camac Baths from the alley near 12th and Walnut
Front door conspicuous as a speakeasy
The *shvitz* with Dad and Uncle Shim, diminutive for *Shimon*
Clothes hung in metal lockers, keys hung around necks
Winter skin dressed for sports or undressed for loose fit
Racquetball and skinny-dipping in the painted brick basement
Sips of ice water served every 10 minutes in parched heat
In the steam room, river rocks ladled from Schuylkill River tap
Pine scent not reminiscent of forest after rain
Fluttering like a ballerina, landing like a bear
Russian masseur, *plaitza* slaps, marble slabs
Tender oak leaves bundled to a soapy broom
Pleasures of the frozen old country, citizens in the new
Paunchy patrons draped in sheets like Roman Senators
Cigar smoke wafted across corned beef specials on rye
Vanilla egg cream fresh from the fountain, no eggs or cream
Monday, December 26, 1960
One year after my ceremonial admission to the tribe
Seven seasons before Super Bowl became America's grail
Football waited 'til Monday, the day *after* Christmas
From folding chairs, testosterone shouted at a 21-inch tube
One smooth face among stubbled Caesars in a deli colosseum
At sold out Franklin Field: Philadelphia 17—Green Bay 13
The Eagles, our beloved *Birds,* won the NFL championship
My best birthday gift
Three men at the *shvitz*
No batteries required

At the Polish-American Festival, Penn's Landing

J. C. TODD

West Bank of the Delaware River, Philadelphia

Red and white everywhere, Lech's name like a prayer
at novena, recited over and over as though
to stack it up to heaven. And the music—a bright horn,

off-key, an accordion winging through melody,
cleated shoes, their crisp percussion tapping time.
Swollen from an afternoon of non-stop polka,

our hot heels flatten the stubble of day into dusk,
and still we cannot quit dancing for Poland.
On the river, a gaff rig swivels to its farthest reach

above a girl in a red and white halter
who weights the gunnel until the wood hull heels.
No, I hear her cry as she dips below a slash

of boom, dips and leaps leeward. She's saved her boat
from tipping under. Like a hawk, it comes about,
homing toward the bank's green haze. Wheeling and

lifting on thermals off-shore, a box kite yanks
at its taut tether. I shift my bulk to the riverward hip,
and we high-step into the spin.

Plinkies

PETER KROK

A sound with its own private room
In the home of my mind.

On the meatless day, Friday,
Mom made plinkies.
I peeled out the eyes and brown spots.
Then grated the potatoes on the yellow
Kitchen table. I scraped until there was
The smallest piece, about the size
Of a half-used bar of hotel soap.
Often, I scraped my knuckles against
The grater and traces of blood would ooze
Into the soupy batch. Yes, my blood would seep
Into the bowl and I'd think a part of me is here.

Mom would mix two eggs and flour
In the batter to give the mixture body,
Put Wesson oil in the pan,
Heat the pan until it sizzled,
Then pour the potato mix
Into the pan. When she thought
The underside was rusty brown,
She'd turn the potato pancakes over,
Then put them on a plate.

I'd sprinkle sugar when I was younger
And salt when I got older.
Yes, my blood is back there
In the kitchen of that red brick row house.
It keeps weeping into my words
Until no one will remember.

Elegy for the Science Teacher
(MARIA D. PETERS, 1915–2013)

ROBIN BECKER

Mrs. Peters has died at 98, and I'll never get a chance
to apologize for all the trouble I brought to 7th grade
science, where she demonstrated how the folding-door
spider dug ten-inch tunnels into rotting logs with
spiny mandibles and lined the walls with silk
and left a bit hanging out to form a door from which
it catapulted after dark. In the circus of natural history
I was the class clown, she the vivarium; her faith included

the decomposing log and the chemical chatter of beetles.
Born in Breslau in 1915, she spoke with a German accent
about *British Soldiers*—the red-capped lichen that thrives
on decaying conifer—and the slimy slug that propels itself
with an undulating muscular foot along the forest floor.
Colonies of carpenter ants and bees proved the Quaker
principle of cooperation: her ecosystem, her religion. In London
during the war, she taught Basque refugees by speaking Latin.

Ah, Mrs. Peters, did the inter-relatedness of fungal spore and wind
move you to drive the Schuykill Expressway every Tuesday
to pack up clothes for needy families? I could not appreciate
the watershed you made of your life, linking all living
things by a common course. Twenty years ago at a reception
you told me of your father's best friend, a Jewish scientist who
refused to leave Germany in 1935. *My father begged him to go*
you said. *My father cried* you said. *He never forgot him.*

I failed to plot the simple graph on Darwinian snails.
You pioneered the PA School of Horticulture for Women
where girls kept bees, canned fruit, learned farm carpentry
and soil science, studying the energetic sow bug with seven pairs

of legs and a carapace of overlapping plates. Recently, people
have come around to your belief in conservation, sustainability.
A tiny woman, sometimes for emphasis you would pull
out the bottom drawer of your desk and stand on it. We all laughed.

■ ■ ■

Winter Melon Soup

VERNITA HALL

*For the children of Noy S.H., 90, who immigrated
to Philadelphia from China*

The day you buried your mother I remembered
Mrs. Noy's winter melon soup   each warm swallow
singing in the throat   a small bird

flew from China to dreams America whispered
The world at war   Japanese bombs exploding
on her village   the son, age four, she buried   You remembered

she ran with baby sister on her back   Mastered
sewing   patchworked English   fresh-off-the-boat
the foreign words sparse in her mouth as a small bird's

teeth   Grew three children and giant gourds inside her
patch of city garden   a Cantonese-American pot-
pourri   Your mother unearthed a new culture   You remembered

the rites—bowed thrice, burned incense, Joss paper, preserved
tradition   But even in the afterlife I think she would forego
ghost money   to put yin food in the mouths of her small birds

Dumplings   dim sum   oolong tea   She stirred
worlds together   her winter flesh spiced from the loveliest broth   so
long   ladled the Tao as nectar to her hungry hummingbirds

The day you bury your mother   you remember

Before He Fell, or Jumped

MARY ROHRER-DANN

Before he fell, or jumped, Robby Krawic,
wayward altar boy in black jeans, battered
high tops, Marlboros snug against his bicep,
was going places no SEPTA bus could take him.

Before he jumped, or fell, Robby Krawic
at Jardel Rec dances made Jagger look tame,
made girls cant their hips when he turned
his dark-eyed slouch their way.

Before he fell, or jumped, Robby Krawic
drove Patty home from her special school
days their mother worked, let her crank
the radio, shout the words to "Satisfaction."

Before he jumped, or fell, Robby Krawic
wore a gold Saint Jude medal palmed
from St. William's parish store, sold
smokes lifted from Kresge's.

Before he fell, or jumped, Robby Krawic
could hotwire any car, beat any souped-up
Mustang or Firebird in his gold Barracuda,
Friday nights down Decatur Road.

Before he jumped, or fell, Robby Krawic
sauntered in his Steve McQueen shades
through neighborhood parties at the park.
Fathers frowned, mothers touched their lips.

Before he fell, or jumped, Robby Krawic
sat with a six-pack on his pitched roof.
Something happened to his sister Patty
when he forgot to pick her up from school.

After he jumped, or fell, Robby Krawic
never danced, only hobbled, watched from
his basement room the girls forget him,
guys from school leave for Nam or Canada,

the world spin on without him.

■ ■ ■

One day
VALERIE FOX

you're barreling over the cement median, drunk
in the orange Karmann Ghia convertible
next thing you're married, then still married
careening and declining, going left and going
right, on foot in circles, attending Mass, on a dare,
climbing into the dire taxi

meeting up by the Don Quixote statue in Fishtown
stature all wrong, loping along
beginning again, being less married
donning a paper hat, making your way
into darkening compartments, to you this makes sense
like being a savior, you save—

don't hoard—you appreciate the angularity
of High Modernism and insomnia
you don't discard printed napkins—
Ponzio's, Chanticleer's—
peppered with rhymes and telephone numbers,
dated and signed, punctured by thumbtacks,
having fallen, at least once, abject,
to the floor, see shoe print, size 9
young you, never at a loss for trying, for late nights,
inventing evidence to replace the stolen boxes and
bags of it, noting the smell of the hoof and the horn,
of your own ice age, finding pictures of actual people,
having a sense of conviviality and snow-preparedness
just ask anyone, you'll try anything

one day attracted by the moon, hiding from it
the next, or else you just can't find your true compass
not in this sky, never lucky or believing in luck, one good thing is
no one ever told you what to be, just what not to be,
and they left out a lot
for you to be

■ ■ ■

Giant Heart

CHLOE MARTINEZ

Franklin Institute, Philadelphia

My mother swears it was beating.
School trip, 1958 or so. She swears
she was inside it, following a teacher's command,
making her way through the chambers, and when
she put a hand against its wall,
steadying her small self, she felt

movement, felt a terror,
panicked, fled—

half a lifetime later, my daughter
enters it: echoing plexiglass thing, sticky
with fingerprints, but quite still. A five-year-old
can climb through the middle, a few twists
and turns, and come out the other side
none the wiser. She wanders off
toward the dinosaurs, and what
do all these told and told-again stories

even mean? How to ever really see
what it's like inside each other's
giant hearts? It seems important. It seems
impossible, the past a maze
of arteries, pulsing, dark, from which
my mother emerged once, her own heart
beating wildly—

■ ■ ■

Mütter Museum with Owl

G. C. WALDREP

The museum is meant to overwhelm: the profusion,
the arrangement, precept upon precept, line
upon line. The sheer weight of all those ingested
objects, deformed tibiae, trepanned skulls.
It's not the gore of it that upsets me, my friend
said, *but the rage to classify, to collect.*

Back on the street, or rather twelve or fourteen feet
above the foot traffic, the owl cocks its head,

looks steadily at one of us. Which? We can't all
belong here, language won't allow it, neither physics.
Speech's pathogen public in its wet mount—

.

The virus eats away at the bronze globe's
claustral flank. What's beautiful about corruption
are the maps it induces: clandestine autobiographies
re-inscribed in paler serum, the phantom wings
lifting against the moon's apse. Inside the bronze
a sister darkness grows, just a little closer.

.

The unseen parts of the eye crowd the edge
of the retinal plate—nobody asks what their pulse-
alphabets are busy unwriting. *Dance*,
hisses the body. *Dance*, echoes the absence
inside the globe. You catch this voice in a drop
of blood, suspended within winter's blue throat.

.

Things I've never asked my mother: did you ever
have a miscarriage, cheat on your husband,
see your father naked, dream in another language,
intentionally harm an animal. Is there
an animal you've never seen in waking life, that
you wanted to see. Do you have the falling
dream, do you like it when you have the falling
dream. When were you most hungry.

.

Screech, barn, great horned, saw-whet, barred—
Don't speak, said my friend. A novel clutches
more precisely at what speech is trying to say.
The grapes on the table glitter in the humidifying
pleroma: feast of argon, feast of tin. Tear

the veil away, earth's nude calendar of saints.

*

At last the voice is a fire; it hollows the face
into competing planes, acute angles
down which the living slide. The owl, the branch
from which it hung, one girder grasping another
in the city's doubled twilight, bleached
down to the master tones. Friend or phantom, prey
or predator, appetite has its own small god.

■ ■ ■

Halfball
1960s
JOSEPH A. CHELIUS

Redfield Street, Southwest Philadelphia

In the soggy grass I found it
sprouting like a mushroom, the inside
rank as a sewer or an old shell
that brought me back
to the makeshift diamond on Redfield Street:
home a flattened Frank's soda can;
and the crowd sitting out on row house steps:
kid brothers, fathers after supper,
smoke drifting from Pall Malls and Lucky Strikes
as the stars came out
to take their warmups—boys
with broomsticks and plastic bats,
swatting bottle caps like fungoes,
or playing long toss with a pair of sneaks—
dangling them over a telephone wire.

When the games got underway,
how seriously they comported themselves,
striding like big leaguers, assuming
their heroes' stances in the middle of the street:
Tony Taylor making a hasty sign of the cross
before slashing a single into a flower bed;
the cleanup crew of Callison and Allen,
clearing the bases, sending pitches
off awnings, onto flat roofs,
the runners tagging telephone poles, the fire plugs,
holding up traffic in the fading light.

Walnut Street

ERNEST HILBERT

I dodge down the crowded July street,
Breathing garbage and humid perfume.
The stifling block is wild at noon.
Stores prop open doors to lure in buyers:
Banks of icy air waft out in columns,
And I cross through one and nearly shiver.

As I emerge again to warmth,
I remember swimming in cedar lakes
That flashed like dirty tin in summer,
Buoyed in greasy tea-stained water.
We kicked to keep afloat near the adults,
Then raced past the roped orange markers.

The lifeguard's whistle pierced our splashes.
Undercurrents from freezing springs gushed
On our bellies, then sun-kettled eddies, then cold,

Paddling and lunging for those small islands
That seemed to recede with each breathless lash
Of our arms through the churned, cloudy water.

■ ■ ■

5 South 43rd Street, Floor 2

YOLANDA WISHER

Sometimes we would get hungry for the neighborhood.
Walk up the sidewalk towards Chestnut Street.
Speak to the Rev holding the light-skinned baby,
ask his son to come put a new inner tube on my bike.
Cross Ludlow, past the mailbox on the corner,
Risqué Video, Dino's Pizza, and the Emerald Laundromat.
The fruit trucks tucked into 44th Street on the left,
house eyes shut with boards, fringes of children.
Once we went into a store sunk into the street,
owned by a Cambodian woman. She sold everything,
from evening gowns to soup. Over to Walnut and 45th,
where the Muslim cat sells this chicken wrapped in pita,
draped in cucumber sauce. The pregnant woman
behind the counter writes our order out in Arabic.
We grab a juice from the freezer, some chips,
eye the bean and sweet potato pies.

Back into the hot breath of West Philly, sun is setting.
The sky is smeared squash, tangerines in a glaze.
Three girls and one boy jump double Dutch. A white man
hustles from the video store with a black plastic bag.
We look for money in the street, steal flowers
from the church lawn. The shit stain from the wino
is still on our step. Mr. Jim is washing a car for cash.
John is cleaning his rims to Buju Banton.
Noel is talking sweetly to the big blue-eyed woman.

Linda, on her way to the restaurant. The sister
in the wheelchair buzzes by with her headphones on.

One night, a man was shot and killed on this block,
right outside our thick wood door. But not today.
Today is one of those days to come home from walking
in the world, leave the windows open, start a pot of
black beans. Smoke some Alice Coltrane. Cut up
some fruit, toenails. Hold on to the moment
as if time is taking your blood pressure.

■ ■ ■

Bridesburg

LEONARD KRESS

The neighborhood reeks of T-bone. Alleyways are not
wide enough for two to pass unbrushed, and doves the size
of bowling balls coo behind their mesh. The Legion Post
door is propped open. Inside the twin-spired Polish Church,
unpierced by shafts of jeweled light, a couple rehearses
upcoming vows. At the rec center, little girls crowd
the stage. They are learning how to isolate each hip,
how to shake each ponytail and how to sell each smile.
Chatting between dribbles, young mothers watch from the court
as basketballs fly up from arched fingers. Bare-chested
boys leap and elbow after the rebound like Titian's
shoving figures, reaching high up for the hoop-high hem
of the Virgin's spiraling heavenward Assumption.

Sweat

NATHALIE F. ANDERSON

The slick palm slips its grip and the world
tips on its axis—loose ball, jump ball, screw ball.
The world's gone woozy, peels off its jacket,
smacks the backboard, thwacks the bat, teeters, spins.
The only breeze we've got is the world's swerving.

One palm slicks another out on the dance floor,
the hip hand slips its juicy grip, silk slithers—
couples careening into the spin, spritzing
the muggy crowd. Open-mouthed, panting
its heart out: blue note, blue moon.

One palm washes the other, brother sears the hand
of brother, the wilting overcoat slips
from the shoulder and off the arm. He's shedding
the winter as if there'll never be another.
Sidewalk grit. Sun-scalded skin.

Damp sheets, dank air, a key riding a kite:
crackle and spit. The river gets goose bumps,
the sky claps its hands, the air opens
in a wet kiss. Rainbows slick the ripples.
The ball nests all night in the pitcher's glove.

A man's sweat wringing out of him as he walks,
a woman pooling before the window fan,
and children incandescent, haloed in thick air.
Wet patches on a dark shirt. Steam clouds the sky
where by night the stars are boiling.

Breezeway, circa 1964

JACQUELINE OSHEROW

The leisurely fireworks of fireflies,
The cicadas rattling the trees,
The crickets' slow, relentless high-note, low-note,
All this from a stoop in Philadelphia
In a heat so encompassing, so endless,
The mauve between the power lines is motionless
Though dusk is several evenings overdue.
Still, no mother calls us from a window;
Not even a radio cries out.

Nothing. No minute is allowed to pass.
So how is it that I'm no longer there,
Mistaking the cicadas for a shift of power
Surging through an overhanging wire,
The crickets for some mild, more muffled traffic?
Such lazy stars have settled in our lawn,
On again, off again, until a strange dark moon
Entices them to join the spreading darkness . . .
It's an ordinary evening—nothing mythic,

Not even a memorable neighborhood. Each house
Repeats its homely, semi-detached face
As if the matching street front were a mirror.
I only ever wanted to get out of there.
So what, exactly, am I longing for?
Fireflies? Cicadas? Sultry air?
(I still don't understand. Can it be over?)
The sleek rococo of a passing car.
Another summer night that lasts forever.

Walking Toward Cranes

AMY SMALL-MCKINNEY

Chestnut Hill

The crane reaches to a red wood railing.
What is he doing? Nothing below him
but *Ten Thousand Villages*, wooden benches,
the sun a slap, everything else quiet.
Inside I know there are sequins sewn on fabric;
on paper lamps, fish swim toward an ocean.
The crane turns out to be useless.
The operator inches his way down;
the window ledge will have to wait.

Later, I notice it's gone, the balcony gone,
four iron S's left with nothing to secure, nothing to protect.
Long-necked iron lamps
bend to the door I enter: This is the world.
Blue green glass from the West Bank, mindful pillows
with strips of satin leading to its ocean of a button,
an anchor for stitched branches, songbirds from India.
I want to travel, probably won't.
I want to walk into a village where a woman weaves yarn,
squat beside her, not condescending,
not sentimental, but because I am lost.

The Frankford Elevated Train

ROBBI NESTER

I realized intuitively that the subway was a harbinger of an entirely
new space-time relationship of the individual and his environment.
—BUCKMINSTER FULLER

Boarding,
I am full of voices, turning in my seat
to watch the Delaware's brown flow.

York and Dauphin
The wires stretch like swimmers,
speak a secret tongue, black and flat,
crackling leaves. Though it is summer,
the pool waits, an empty mouth.

Huntington
Here a man boards, without eyes.
His face holds light. Rain falls
in flat wet drops.

Somerset
The name I always read wrong—
Summering, Somerfield, Something.

Allegheny
Banks on both sides. I sit on the edge
of my seat, reading "Dr. Cool #1"
on all the walls. Someone
beside me slips out.

Tioga
Trees. Ginkos' frilled leaves,
a thousand luna moths.

<u>Erie-Torresdale</u>
The day the train fell, it was here.
People clutched at legs, falling poles.
One second before the ground,
the last smoke.

Now when I pass here, the train
shifts and slows. On the track ahead,
workers wave us past.

<u>Church</u>
Broken windows, stained with soot.
A steeple with no bell. The train
screams by.

<u>Margaret and Orthodox</u>
Unloading.
I turn once more, eyeing faces
pressed like wings. No wheels
now. The circling slatted door,
the stairs, then the street's
long spiral, a track.

■ ■ ■

At the Crest of the Meadow

JAN FREEMAN

There is the Liberty Bell
There is the home of the flag
Where is the pledge, the allegiance?
Under the sycamores' bark
Where is protection and safety?
Inside the arms of the barn

Here is the Brandywine River
Here are the turns and the branches
Here are the Lenape remnants
under the houses, the roads
Here are the bones of the orchard
Here are the ashes in currents

No one expected the stone
walls to collapse on themselves
Regal and shining, the floors
The open lake mirrored the windows
Slate roof, Dutch tiles, brown and blue
wedged free and split from the grout

Down spun the wind through the kitchen
Quaker hymns spread the mute silence
sweeping the meadow, the stream
holding the fox in her den
twisting the hay through its mold
Hypocrisy painted on ceilings

The Underground Railroad not myth
passed here in the shape of a shoe
Here the locks turned from the keys
Here the teeth smoothed each rough edge
My home, this serpentine town
watched as the house fell down

Home

MICHAEL QUINN

Villanova
For my mother

The realtor never told you This is
the room your mother will die in,
on the left when you step in the door.
It is the night you are called by the

ashwood trees set in their place longer
than your love. How many branches
will scrape the windows & stretch to
hold the bird claws? It is the night you

are called by a garden of deer, pressing
their noses in the dew & dying on the
pool cover. It is this wooden porch you
turned to cement & this roof you repaired.

You have mended the sinking in the wall
& it is the night you are called by the mice
between floors. Their lives are a long scrape.
What noise have you made? It is the night

you are called by a wheezing & a rattle,
the small sofa pushed against the wall,
the small body held aloft in the soft glory
of an LED bulb. It is the night and you

are called by the harsh life of a house in
the forest, built from wood bred of blood,
holding our crooked bones in the winter
& our satin skin in the pollen air.

Passing Through Southeastern Pennsylvania Towns in Winter

MARK DANOWSKY

Wawaset to Route 52 South out towards mushroom country
I drive a stranger's family, oldest son riding shotgun
Warm Winter through the car's speakers
a stag darts—rack gone magnificent starburst by high beam glare
could have flipped us *Through the Wire*
—we trudge on, pass Lenape Road, wind & wind
feeling the elevation on a one-way road called two

Earlier, Nantmeal Township, then a chopped grain field
entering Lionsville, shades of beige, all the space filled in
with geese—god knows how many—it's sunny
outside today, first in three, I want to say sub-zero temps
but most towns within 25 miles offer a light flurry
—in Nantmeal, trees stilled by ice, the gleam of bare branches
staggers, I roll the window down to photograph frozen wine vines—
roads open up out here, the air more crisp, quiet
it seems easier, hours still, before dusk

■ ■ ■

Linvilla

NICOLE MIYASHIRO

The orchard harvested fresh fires
of red apples to pluck from trees.

Each globe cored into blooms of slices
finger-ready for sampling

syrupy dips. It was a place to meander to
from yards that backed into its fields

when too young to drive, and the boys
flipped open flames,

striking Zippo lighters to a thigh,
and girls sipped glowing

honey from one-way straws. *L i n v i l l a* –
hills rolling onto tongue. A skyward

sprawl in grass and sun. Crackling hayrides
that rocked and hummed into cozy

Halloweens. Rounding the bend, the tractor
lit blades of green and limbs ablaze,

the rest: night. A chainsaw revving,
rollicking shrieks the neighbors recognized

from inside, their windows
sighing autumn. Caramel and candied

apples melting into mouth. Crimson jams
dissolving to black the year

the barn burned down. Those sweet
sweet days of tasting

warm sugars, rebuilt, re-savored.
Every flavor now homemade.

Quaker Memorial Service for a Young Girl, Germantown

CAROLE BERNSTEIN

We are left in this room to sort it out
rows of bare pews   facing nothing
      but each other
faces on either side of me   like something burning

One narrow door stands open
painful blaze of sunlight
      late morning sparrows forage around gravestones
as in a little movie
flickering yellow butterfly
      skims above the ground   vanishes

No voice but our voices   no thought but our thoughts
no guide through the land of the dead
      or the living
but this is not my belief   not my place

Her classmates are seated together
each holding a sunflower
      cut and dying
the giant black center   full of holes
they don't know quite what to do with them
tears drip on their hands

Some are crushed
      some look bewildered   or lost
Some choose to speak   their voices float up   are pummeled by grief
why did she   *how could she*
and God and all
      I am left   *I remember*
they understand just enough   and nothing
like the rest of us

A boy jumps up   face flushed
stumbles over many knees and
                              runs out
did he ever come back in

If I could root her out of their consciousness
All of them   I would
place the flower of her in a clear tumbler
press the dead petals in crumbling book   for them to read
                    when they are older
about something that happened a long time ago

■ ■ ■

Kitchen Table

HAYDEN SAUNIER

Bedminster Township, Bucks County

Our table's made of walls. Wide planks salvaged
from the sagging side of the house we pulled down,

boards that sheathed clapboard, were spared
from dry rot and sanded smooth by the work

of our hands. Our table's made from walls that held
a family of six before typhoid took both parents

and fostered out the children to farm families
needing help. Our table's made of old growth

forests no longer forests but now fields that offer
stone and sinew, antler, bone, tin cans, bottles,

blades, each spring a brand new crop of everything
that's come before. Our table's wood is spalted

through with death, hard luck, and joy. Our table's
made of everything, and us, and ours. Sit down and eat.

■ ■ ■

New Hope

JULIE STANDIG

To go to Bucks County, to your daughter's wedding, to book the most
    charming inn
on the farm, where all the food is grown, and they have a goat.

To know this womanchild of yours desires simplicity and respect, to keep
    your thoughts
to yourself, bite your lip 'til it bleeds, shake a voodoo doll.

To visit the inn and ogle old photos from 1938, George S. Kaufman, Lillian
    Hellman,
Harpo Marx. To learn once it was Kaufman's home. They played tennis, sat
    by the pool.

To write screenplays and Broadway shows that got produced. To return to
    wedding planning.

To acknowledge that some of these bridal shops display dresses that display
    a lot of
skin (a lot) and look like something you would see in Brighton Beach or
    Israel.

To learn that the Hammersteins are still involved with the Playhouse, to
    read Michener
and Pearl S. Buck because they all lived here too.

To not be pissed because your daughter rejects every blessed idea you
     present, to not tell her
you're going to put lavender stress cream in the hospitality bags because
     they come from Peace

Valley and to not care that she does not like lavender.
It's stress cream for Christ's sake.

To step aside because this is her time, you had yours. She danced in red
     and gold feathers to
Hello Dolly, she'll dance in lace and flowered garland here.

■ ■ ■

Sleepless Johnston
LYNN LEVIN

When the city lights came on
and the air turned gray
Sleepless Johnston finished filing through
his bars and ran away.

He flew through Pennsylvania
in a green hot-wired Olds.
He left a dummy on his cot
made of prison clothes.

Had coins to call his cousins
and marathon running shoes—
the gifts of a nurse who loved him
or wanted some of his loot.

Johnston, they said, had millions tied
up in high-tech stocks
or hidden away in Cayman banks

or stuffed in a cardboard box.

But maybe he had nothing left
and was after black revenge
was weary of doing life in jail
and had to go home again.

He dreamed his mom would fry him eggs
let him bathe and sleep
a good long sleep to die for
on daisy-covered sheets.

But Johnston was a menace—a thief
and murderer as well.
He shot three young men at least
and killed a teenage girl.

Forty grand the lawmen promised
a price they swore they'd pay
to any soul who'd help them catch
this cunning runaway.

In a tavern a trooper saw him
having a smoke and a beer
but Sleepless fled like a vision of Elvis
when the cop came near.

Oh, there were plenty of sightings
though most of them were fake.
Line workers called in phony clues
for slippery Johnston's sake.

He haunted all the pay phones
begging cousins for a bed
yet most hung up when Sleepless rang.
At least one kinsman said:

The law has us surrounded.
You can't come over here.
Keep running, man. Wing like a bat
or hide like a deer.

But after twenty years in jail
familiar woods were few.
Developers had subdivided
the countryside he knew.

Patrol cars right behind him
in front the rising sun,
Johnston dashed down a cul de sac.
Folks called 911.

No dogs, no guns, no searchlights,
only rest and peace
were the things that Sleepless wanted
as he walked to the police

and gave up by a bird bath—
exhausted, nearly dead.
Sleepless held out his two hands
for cuffs, some chow, a bed.

He hadn't any millions,
just his pants and shirt
and those fancy track shoes
and the lost hope of the nurse.

A Map of Valley Forge

GRANT CLAUSER

Dug in among mud and farmers' fields,
the new country's army licked its wounds,
and you can hike along the scars
they left, from raised redoubt mounds
to the three-century witness tree
bending by General Maxwell's
adopted quarters (now a site
for rich weddings) past General
Wayne's statue (before he became
Mad Anthony) who took a beating
at Brandywine then gave it back
at Stony Point (earning himself a medal),
so when my dog and I top the southwest
trenches, where recovered cannon
pointed toward the patient British
eating Philadelphia like a three-day leave
while Washington's men battled dysentery
and a farmland too poor to afford a war,
I think about how optimistic the settlers
here once were, like even now, when a sunny
day in winter brings all the brightly-colored
joggers out of seasonal depression,
the trail map of Valley Forge shows
both Mount Joy and Mount Misery
but doesn't tell you where to begin.

II. SOUTH CENTRAL: FARMLANDS, BATTLEFIELDS, AND THE CAPITAL
REGION

In Amish Country

SARAH RUSSELL

six horses,
sometimes twelve,
plow spring fields.
Farmers guide with whistles,
clucks and sweat-soaked reins,
their shirts echoing the sky.
Earth receives the blade,
sighs her musky scent,
reveals hidden stones
and the sinew of old roots.
Sowing will follow
if the rain holds off
a day or two.

Dirt

JAYNE RELAFORD BROWN

Village of Dryville, Berks County

Dirt gives, opens to my finger,
lets my little furrow fill
with butterhead and sugarpod,
Detroit Red and Bull's Blood beets.

Dirt lets last year's leeks emerge
and suffer me their shoots
chopped up for soups, brings
baby greens just lightly dressed
and bitten, tendril down to root.

The smell of dirt can take me back
to trips through woods
where blood-root rose,
unrolling root-balls, yanking
tangled hostas into smaller knots.

Too much to plant's the kind of rich I want—
the celebrations of forsythia,
and building whole new beds
on top of table-scraps and news.

Today's gray—wet window screens,
a six-foot mist, the shock from warm rain
falling on last Wednesday's snow,

but sloshing through the rivers trickling
in the shoveled paths to empty trash,
to feed the outdoor cats, and dump
the compost in its steaming bin,

a loosening beginning underneath my feet
lets me remember dirt, and what dirt gives.

■ ■ ■

All Day Long There'd Been Papers

ROBERT FILLMAN

After Berks County poet and Kutztown University professor
Harry Humes's "Reading Late by a Simple Light"

to grade, students with questions,
travel expenses to file,
faculty meetings. And yet

late in the day, he slipped out
his windowless cinderblock
office hole, tiptoed away
from fluorescent bulbs, the framed
motel art posters. He crept
across campus alone, stopped

at a nearby field, listened
for a crow, the dry crumple
of leaves. A stray vee of geese
winged overhead and out of
view. He then sat by a stream,
thought about Thanksgiving break
as he let the scent of earth
breathe its dim life of decay
into his bones. After that

he turned back, taking each step
a bit slower than the one
before, beginning to hum,
his voice like a radio
almost caught between stations.
He told himself to hold on
to this feeling, the fall term
not quite done. He'd have it then—
for collecting his teaching
things, on the long drive home, when
there was nothing but static.

On Passing thru Morgantown, Pa

SONIA SANCHEZ

I saw you
vincent van
gogh perched
on those Pennsylvania
cornfields communing
amid secret black
bird societies. yes
i'm sure that was
you exploding your
fantastic delirium
while in the
distance
red Indian
hills beckoned.

■ ■ ■

A Girl, Reading

HEATHER H. THOMAS

Mother studies trends in hats.
     Remember, she says, *to have style*.
     The straw brim tilts on my crown.
The grandmothers gather into girdles,
     into kid gloves white and black.
     When they argue, I turn translucent
as a photo negative, and open a book.
     Our sacrifice for beauty, they say,
     if only she would cut her hair.
I memorize everything until I learn to think
     for myself. At the library
     old men in coats stagger in,

sit at oak tables with the *Reading Eagle*.
        Help wanted: hosiery mill knitters.
        Up in the stacks Emma Bovary rots
with desire, Lily Bart loses *The House of Mirth*,
        and Edna Pontellier, shadowed
        by the lovers and the lady in black,
abides the pain of wakefulness. Snug in coats,
        the old men nod heads to their chests.
        My body grows heavy, bones
of my feet chalk blue in the shoe store X-ray.
        Mother says big feet give
        a firm foundation.
At Whitner's department store I stroll
        through Foundations—
        mounds of bras and girdles,
a fresh, white smell.
        A woman in a lab coat dusts jars
        of tinted powders in Cosmetics.
Smoke pours from the stacks at Vanity Fair.
        At Stanley's Bar on Cotton Street
        a man can buy a wafer-thin box
of ladies' nylons, a Polish ham, a Sunshine Beer.
        I ride the bus to Fifth and Penn
        and tie fantastic bows at Feel-Fine.
Miss Schultz and Miss LaMonica wear black
        and stand, matriarchs before the racks,
        necks draped with the dreaded tape measure.
My grandmothers depart on the Queen Mary,
        lean on the deck that carries them away.
        No book ever ruined a girl's life, they sing,
waving handkerchiefs. *You'll never know,*
        they sing, as though they knew,
        as though Edna came back

from her final swim, as though my life was not

   a secret ruin of books, secret joy.

In Reading

SANDY FEINSTEIN

A rabbit stares from the verge
along Neversink bike trail, swollen and cracked
from winter and neglect,
sparse grass tangles with dandelions
amid anonymous green shoots
unaware of where they are—
insufficient cover for a tent of old rags
belted by a bright blue line
not far from a boy on a bench
half-listening to salsa.

We ride under a cement bridge
through which the rough track extends
to nowhere really—
an abrupt drop off, the river.

A small asphalt loop, bulbous
like the bottom of a thermometer,
is our turn around.
We retrace our steps,
listen to the music dissipate,
note fearless fat woodchucks
who've found what's green enough.

■ ■ ■

Lost Brother, 2019

ALISON CARB SUSSMAN

A frozen world, sometimes silent, imaginary snow falling around me.
The brown plastic ice bucket in our hotel room. The scruffy brown
  furniture.

A cowboy hat my husband bought me, unused, on the brown table.

This is the second day without you, Brian.
Shovelfuls of stones on my eyes when I wake.
The cold terror of being left alone.

We drove past fields of corn being harvested by Amish men. I listen to the
soil shuffling on winding back roads. Early autumn in Pennsylvania.

We passed a farmhouse porch. A black sculpture of a woman rocks on a
pedestal,
her arms around herself, and she can't stop.

The slow-moving vehicles of the Amish, families of blonds crushed
into creaky wheeled buggies, the clopping of horses' hooves. Brian's
"Whistlepig Manor" alongside Amish silos, piles of hay, tobacco crops.

I float through dense clouds and unchanging leaves.
Build my nest oh god of demons, feather my will.
When I was seven, my younger brother stole Brian away.
I buried my wet face in the sheets.

I drift back to April, Brian still alive, thin,
eating only a vinaigrette-covered tomato, sliced into tiny pieces.
Every day a preferred morsel.

He sits at the computer console, stubbornly working,
his lips carved in a grim smile.
Why Brother Brian, have our ice-block hearts drifted
so far apart?

That April, bound for home, I stood in Lancaster station,
the steel rails below the six-o'clock sun drew me down—
A robin flew up to the station's roof where her chicks waited.
Oh why Mother Robin, did you make your nest
in the center of everything?

No Wind

GERALD STERN

Today I am sitting outside the Dutch Castle
on Route 30 near Bird in Hand and Blue Ball,
watching the Amish snap their suspenders at the sunglasses.
I am dreaming of my black suit again
and the store in Paradise where I will be fitted out for life.
    A small girl and I recognize each other
from our former life together in Córdoba.
We weep over the plastic tote bags, the apple combs and the laughing
    harmonicas,
and fall down on the hot carpet
remembering the marble forest
of the Great Mosque
and the milky walls
of the Jewish quarter.
    I will see her again in 800 years
when all this is sorted out.
I give it that much time,
based on the slack mind,
the dirty drinking water and the slow decay.
I give it at least that much time
before we lie down again in the tiny lilacs
and paper love houses of the next age.

"Swans first, now a fountain"

ALYSE BENSEL

York Daily Record, August 31, 2014

After the swans the city released
to decorate Kiwanis Lake

were found the next morning
with their necks broken,

the parks director replaced
their bodies with a fountain

and a cheap replica
of the Liberty Bell

that is now in ruin, once
a lovely thing easily

replaced to repeat
history. A man was found

floating underneath the ice
so thin with chemicals

it could dissolve like the piles
of morning newspapers

littering the banks
as poor substitutes for nests.

Gettysburg

ALLISON ADAIR

The peacock's spurs are caught again
in the diamond chickenwire of his low
slanted pen. Nobody bothers anymore
to hammer the sagging barn.

Summer visitors regard the old farm from cars
without chrome, up on the hastily paved path—
if they look at all. There's so much
else to see, burnished things, and battlefields

all look the same. But it's here, this land,
where the war's easy sepia finds an end
and a form: like us, the shallow rust-red soil
blows off for York, for Philadelphia, the coast,

and pasture erodes to bone. A black walnut's roots
pierce the buried limbs of our grandfathers' fallen
spruce grove. The caterpillar inches along, lost
in its sad accordion hymn.

■ ■ ■

Letter to Wemple from Gettysburg

MATT PERAKOVICH

After Richard Hugo

Dear Jerry: It's the offseason and still this town's in love
with itself. The war left everything, left ghosts and an economy,
clapboard siding and period fare, bullet holes enshrined in brick,
men in muttonchops and women dressed in layers despite the heat.

Fallow fields undulate in late summer sun and historical markers
invite us to imagine blood on the battlefield, stumps, and lungs
screaming out. The forecast: near 100 in September, and it feels
like the world tipping us off to some instability at the heart of it all.
On my walk this morning, I pass a military tour guide speaking
to a busload of successful American dads, short hair, good posture,
reverent toward Buford's vision and the bravery of the 20th Maine.
I scan for red ball caps. I wonder how many of them long
to "Make America Great Again." What I wouldn't do
to have you here, with your renegade histories and hard stare.
At the Blue & Gray Bar & Grill, they name their burgers
after generals and I order the Longstreet medium rare
and watch the Orioles with the locals in high def.
I haven't written a poem in months and I'm afraid that
none of it matters, not the poems or whether they come again.
But this is an improvement from not that long ago
when it wasn't a fear: I knew for certain. I'm better now
and I hope you are too. It's true what they say about the vultures,
that they still circle the battlefields, some rumor of decay hardwired.
My new wife and I lay on the grass this afternoon
watching their dark-winged parade over our heads.
It'll do for a honeymoon until the money's better. Your friend, Woody

■ ■ ■

Gettysburg Poem #3

ABBY MINOR

I daughter of a mark-
less foothill, a series of windowsills filled
with wasp wings, I who know truly
nothing re. relativity, gravity,
or the science of sound or
light so thoroughly & trans-

parently cannot get it
up for thought or
exchanges about tactical triumphs or
errors of the civil
war. Not sure

where to break in along a fish
hook shape sharp
shooters from Maine taking
the high
ground on this ground I
get a dark, easy shot—
little roundtop, buzzards coming in extraordinary
sunlight, round light, but
which is still not
an argument about the
hook of the union. Part of their black

    linen wings up
  close are paler, part of my
    ghost shuffles away into the gold
grain and stones. Men, & all those of you
  who know how sound & light
    travel, I love you. Nothing big
like a movie wants to happen. Plus the confederate
  flag is just what happens
    to the American flag
      when you wash it.

Taxidermy in South Central Pennsylvania

KATY GIEBENHAIN

I.
It's a roadside faux-Bavarian restaurant
with decent beer, fat gravy,
postcards from Munich and Oberammergau
shingled above its cash register.
Here starts the parade of heads
mounted in intervals
like past presidents,
or kindergarten alphabets
in wood and brass, hairy things of all sizes:
deer to squirrels, to small
creatures of uncertain origin.
It's the turkey, though,
at the far end of the dining room,
harpooned behind the bear
onto the knotty paneling,
the turkey that keeps me looking up
from the table, the entire bird, head high,
legs splayed, asking
with every rotation of our jaws:
How did I get here?

II.
Army canteens, wool rugs,
ladles old enough to have dipped soup
for Gustav Adolf himself
line the backyard sauna.
From his pine-planked shoulders
a caribou presides
over these shared meters
of recreated Sweden.
I stand released from the vice of heat.

I inhale, my ribs slick
and heaving, brows knit in half-pain
at my searing earring posts.
In lantern-light his eyes of glass sparkle,
his nostrils flex. We are someplace
other than this place.
I would answer any question he asked,
my pelted priest.
I haven't felt this unalone in years.

III.
A second-hand store in Carlisle
is not the worst place
for a thirty-year-old, three-point buck
with a lovely neck to land.
It beats the laundry basket
in General Shearling's garage (whose kids
unhooked and brought him here
after the General's funeral).
He'd like a room with rocking chairs,
with whisky decanters
and *Playboys* from the '6os
stacked between *Life* and
North American Whitetail. He'd like
to be near Tuscarora again.
Mainly, he wants to avoid
being driven across state lines
in a rented Lexus, and hung
in a flat with chandeliers,
brass doorknobs and a cat. A cat.
He can face anything
but a weekend antiquer
with scopes for eyes.

Harrowing

CATHERINE CHANDLER

Non est ad astra mollis e terris via.
—SENECA
For Pennsylvania

Her teeming, fertile acres may supply
the world with barley, winter wheat and rye;

but there are other, barren, untilled lands,
for reasons every farmer understands.

It's best to let the bullets, blood and bones
lie undisturbed beneath the soil and stones;

to let the buttercups and meadow-grass
blanket the savagery as seasons pass.

Harvest time in Shanksville, Nickel Mines
and Gettysburg spills over county lines—

no fences here to keep one out or in,
no gleaners search for hair or teeth or skin;

yet constellations nightly sow their light
on heaven's fallow fields of anthracite.

Keystone Ode with Jane Doe in It

NICOLE SANTALUCIA

Shippensburg

So she didn't have anything
wrapped around her throat
So she didn't have a brass
lump instead of a heart
So her breasts were gone
So her right eye was a bullet
So she did have a toe tag
So her fingers dug a tunnel
So her name is dirt
So there was a witness
So she did build a fire
So it wasn't enough
to make it out alive
So her girlfriend was murdered
So her grocery list blew away
So she didn't go to buy milk
So the wind inside her throat
activated a blessing
So the Appalachian Trail
is her gravesite
So she was a lesbian
So she swallowed a peach pit
So she did stay on the trail
So the crickets
sound like can openers
So little shards of metal
dig into flesh
So there are bears
and sandwich meat
and chewed fingernails
So there's a forest

with broken crickets
So it sounds like a leaky faucet
So all women are sinners
fixing the rainbow
So this is the sermon
So in the last scene
a white man waves
at the camera
in the background
everything empties out

Longfellow Pine

JUDITH A. KENNEDY

Something happens to the blood
in April, a million cells scream
to run the Indian paths
along the river, past corn and wheat fields,
over Blue Mountain and northward
like a wild horse ripping
the hemp cord loose,
to get back to the oldest trees
where history remains,
off the tarmac
of Lincoln Highway,
onto old running ways
of the Pennsylvania Wilds,
to nuzzle the face against the trunk
of the Longfellow Pine
that reaches to a narrowing gaze
of blue at one hundred eighty feet,
to hemlocks that have stood here
before William Penn, before

the Spaniards closed in
on what became Florida,
standing now, no roads in,
only foot path, deer path,
curling, no straight way,
then lying belly down
on the cool, sweet darkness,
the ground of the dead and the broken,
the place of the risen,
the blood of the vanquished,
the return of the lost ones,
to hear their stories in the stones,
in red-dirt melodies
with climbing vines of ghosts,
to feel them dance,
the ground respond,
the farthest branch
quiver.

■ ■ ■

Election

CYNTHIA HOGUE

Ephrata

Depending on what sect you hew to,
you're born into or may choose election.
I did not know about such particular
doctrinal distinctions because basically,
I never remembered when told them,

but I'm curious, and when Max—the lovely
Presbyterian missionary attending a Mennonite
intensive in conflict resolution for non-Mennonites
(as was I)—asked me if I wanted to hear his life story,

I said yes. It was a long summer's eve among rolling

> green hills. Max told until dusk
> what I later learned was a Story
> of Faith. Writers love stories,

though I'd never heard one with such seeming
designs. I was all ears, and when Max asked
what I'd do if a king came to my cottage in the woods,
I was game. I'd ask him in, I said, invite him for tea
and crumpets. *Crumpets!* Max murmured. Then—

as if a part of the play about me and a king—
When you're ready, we'll pray. Polite,
I nodded and he was dropping to his knees,
eyes closed, hands clasped, thanking the Lord
for the privilege of bringing this soul to Him.

> Was I that soul? *Oops.* I'd no idea
> what Max thought had happened,
> but knew we'd told different stories.

Max was fighting cancer as well as saving souls.
Mornings he'd go into the Mennonite fields of corn,
pick the ears to eat raw, *for the enzymes,* he'd intone
like a psalm. At week's end the charismatic Catholic
lawyer from Pittsburgh translated Max for me, why

his thanks in the beginning, after which, eager hope,
since I remained courteously clueless of having found
God. There are, he said, three levels of conversion.
I was at the lowest—those who did not know it.
Will you write me when you know? Max, I couldn't

> tell you that nothing ever changed, how
> long before I knew that as breath filled
> my lungs, spirit balanced, opened heart.

Why Grandfather Counted the Stars

MARTIN WILLITTS JR.

The cows clang in Lancaster County's faltering light.
Grandfather checks, once again, the back-fence line
where winter always brings intruders
wearing vests with pockets for shotgun shells
and carrying wire clippers to hunt illegally
on his prime forest land stocked with deer.

He cleans his glasses to see into the future,
to see he won't always be around
to prevent the inevitable. The silent way
of his Mennonite life is weighed
in invisible scales, his good intentions against
the odds of his age. His glasses recall
the two robin nests, their tiny babies
begging to be fed.

A noisy world is edging nearer.
He feels people taking pictures.
He wants his old farming ways, leading a plow horse,
trying to keep silence close as suspenders.

He lingers for a while,
both well into the splurge of stars
and cricket-burst.

Grandma watches him approach, a leaping lantern
light bobbing over the uneven rut fields
in a cloud of fireflies and miller moths.

He returns dew-stained, creasing his way,
wordlessly stamped with a fiery spirit,
thumping into his wooden chair,

because the cricket music stirred his eyes.
He warned the deer in the back acres,
before the hunters can find them.

Even during the Depression,
he never found a day bad enough
that couldn't be overcome by hard work,
reflective prayer and determination.
His glasses still contained images of robin's nests.
Days always begin and end with cows
following the same worn-down path.

His way is the hard way,
the old, slow way,
a horse pulling his buggy
on the side of a road
on his way to Bird-in-Hand,
while the anxious drive past him.

He counts on the familiar stars
like baby robins count on being fed,
like glasses need to see clearly
the end of sadness, like deer
testing winds,
like crickets warning of more heat.

Like the lifeline in his palms,
prayer is always there.

Wintergreen

LE HINTON

Lancaster County
After Robert Hayden

I sit on the screened-in porch, loosen
my black tie, then wipe this day from my eyes.
The chocolate, cemetery mud on the sides

of my black wingtips stare up at me.
My father would have cleaned and polished
them by now, buffed them to a mirrored

shine. In the yard, the paper birches
seem lost tonight. Their mid-summer leaves
drop like indifferent rain. Their bark
curling more than my sisters' hair.

I tasted my first sip of birch beer in Lancaster
at the Central Market, a few blocks

from the clinic's office. The liquid mint
flavor and the hot dog with mustard still linger
in my tongue's past. A bouquet of shoofly

pies and sticky buns mingle with the pleasured
hum of shoppers. Satisfaction floats among the stands.
Every month my father drove this son 40 miles

to a clinic to fix his flawed voice.
Every month after third shift, every
month before sleep, every austere
month he drove his son in a black-heavy Dodge truck.

In this night's regret, mixed with the mud,
and the tie and observant birches,
I peel the curly bark
from these trees and write
thank you on its parchment skin
a thousand, wintergreen times.

■ ■ ■

Bully Pulpit
CONESTOGA MASSACRE, DECEMBER 1763
MICHAEL GARRIGAN

Marietta, Lancaster County

Reverend Elder preached at the pulpit
with a rifle in one hand, a bible in the other

that they were good men in private,
>*they heard his sermons, got drunk, went downstream*

they were virtuous and respectable,
>*they found the Susquehannock at daybreak*

they were not cruel or mean, no,
>*they scalped and killed and burnt their homes*

they were mild and they were merciful
>*those that survived were put in the local jail*

the barrel always angled up to his heaven,
tracing the oak rafters in its crosshairs
as he slammed psalms and scripture
down with his fist into the hard
backs of his pews and his congregation
as his Lord & Rifle Cloak shook

these Paxton Boys were men that tilled their land
    for protection from the Paxton Boys
that only wanted to protect their family and their God
    but two days after Christmas
that simply rode the storm that had been gathering
    they broke in and found the 14 taking refuge
for quite some time just like anyone else would
    they chased down families with Tomahawks
they wished not to be taken by the thunder
    they split heads and scalped and cut off hands and feet
and lightning but to give it, to control it.
    and then finally a bullet in each mouth.

with praises of the Almighty, Amen.

°Reverend Elder's sermon paraphrased from William Buell Sprague, *Annals of the American Pulpit*, vol. 3, *Presbyterian* (New York: Robert Carter & Brothers, 1858), 77–79.

■ ■ ■

Pennsylvania's Governor Advises Voluntary Evacuation

VIRGINIA WATTS

Fifth Period
Honors English Grammar
Miss Betty Bartels

Class, can someone think of a sentence with a dangling participle?
Yes, Virginia?

Sitting at our desks, the Three Mile Island Nuclear Power Plant is melting
    down to its core.
Excellent. What's wrong with that sentence?
Three Mile Island is not sitting at a desk.

Half the high school is missing.
Along hallways: crudely sketched skulls and crossbones
mar glittery posters: *The Class of 1979, Senior Prom,*
Stairway to Heaven.

At the cafeteria table, my jokes fall flat:
What's the only kind of pizza you can buy at DeAngelis now?
    Mushroom
Get rich quick scheme?
    Lead ovary shields

My father appears, and just like that
I am on my way to my brother's house
in Maryland. On the truck radio,
the Bee Gees harmonize their top hit "Tragedy."
I turn around to home ground sliding away
behind exhaust pipe and rusted bumper

One last glimpse of Hershey Park:
the first giant hill, the Comet Coaster,
no car at the top.
Empty backyards, still swing sets,
cows corralled inside barns,
black tarps smothering crops,
stoic tractors abandoned midfield.

My father's voice:
There's a Hires Root Beer Stand
just across the state line
Hungry?

White Shore, 1963

MARIA JAMES-THIAW

Harrisburg
Dedicated to professor and activist Ann Lyon

Our new home, west of the river,
was called *The White Shore*—
"White" and "colored" fountains,
"colored" backdoors in restaurants,
or no service for Negroes at all.
The Susquehanna served as tracks
others knew not to cross.
River water walled us away from
people that might dare us to
look at ourselves.

> *It's in the deeds—*
> *You must agree—*
> *that no colored persons*
> *will frequent your home,*
> *live with your family*
> *unless, of course, they've been*
> *hired as a domestic—*
> *White gloved, uniformed,*
> *smiling, acceptable.*
> *They can wash your cars,*
> *cook your food, even nurse your babies,*
> *but never look you in the eye*
> *or, God forbid, call you friend.*

Mid-September, time to party!
It was a gas! Groovy music and more than
100 of the East Shore's finest and funkiest
black, brown, and tan

activists, artists, and orators
scaled the Susquehanna River,
that preverbal wall,
forgot the tracks,
and boogied down at our house.

Chubby Checker, Sam Cooke—
We twisted and twisted again,
records spinning half the night,
but as car doors opened and guests
spilled out—
long haired with peace signs,
braided in bell bottoms,
bouffant and blown out—
eyes bulged behind thinly
veiled neighbor's windows.

The calls began at nine.
Complaints became more shrill as time
went on,
nasty insults, threats, slurs,
every hour till three.

Morning rose as it does
and the news man delivered a blow—
a barbaric bombing back home in Alabama—
four little girls lost.
Our thoughts succumbed to whys and woes,
not the hateful calls from the night before,
but the angry caller was now at our door.
My husband politely poured a drink
and asked,
What did we do to offend?
Park on your lawn?
Music too loud?
Cigs in your grass?

No, no, no!
It was the color of some of your guests!

We had broken the White Shore's de facto law,
blurred the line between East and West.
Bad enough, we were Jews, but we
welcomed "colored people" in our midst.

He dropped his hateful Pennsyl-bama bomb
as if we would receive it in shame,
crushed like that ravaged Baptist church,
apologize for defiling his perfect little street,
with Black folks, feminists, hippies and Jews.
Instead, we showed him the door.

For years following
our kids were punished on playgrounds.
But as the Beatles sang, we taught them
Let It Be—
No one's going to stand between
this family and a great party.

■ ■ ▥

Retail Requiem

ERIN HOOVER

Requiem for Ames, markdown chain rolling
high through the eighties, for fading brands
bought up and Frankenstein-fused, for stores
finally shuttered, their doors pasted with bright
commands, everything must go. Requiem
for People's Drug, for Hills' firetruck
of a toy aisle, for the hamsters balled up
in the pet section at Woolworth's, for Hess's

junior clothes corner, all the places I knew
were sick before they died. Requiem
for Wanamaker's and G. C. Murphy, brands
whose Harrisburg fronts I glimpsed like cathedrals
from a car. Requiem for Phar-Mor, the discount
drug-shill whose rocketing growth, 300 stores
out of nowhere, turned out to be criminal,
and for that particular Phar-Mor I shopped
as a teenager, where in the makeup aisle
at the zenith of my insecurity, I learned to
sip generic diet sodas and dream. Requiem
for Encore Books and for Blockbuster Video,
those places I worked and whose registers
I know in my sleep—you haunt me. Requiem
for Montgomery Ward, grandpa that slumped
through the century but whose anchor location
in the mall had, no shit, a kick-ass electronics store,
bravely carrying on until the Christmas
the corporation called it. We mourned the old,
historic ones, Ward, Sears, we launched
their kayaks on fire, kept their corpses standing
as the analysts screamed their doom. Requiem
for family shopping day, for the trip into town,
for the blow-out, the blaring commercials,
holiday discounts encircling us like hugs,
perpetual, near-constant sales, for President's
or Labor Day week, the frantic Christmas rush,
your season, Lord, for months. Requiem
for Pomeroy's, survivor of the Great Depression,
whose elegant tags I still find on inherited
clothes and furniture. For the Bon-Ton,
who bought Pomeroy's and then closed in 2018,
including my store, whose ladies' fashion buyer
pegged my style—where is she now?—the building
still vacant, a restaurant's overflow parking lot.

Eternal rest grant them, O Lord, the businesses
begun and finished, warehouses scraped out
but aisles marked in masking tape on the floor,
the haphazard fragments of signage and shelving.
Requiem for the people we were as we loitered
through those aisles, browsed and tried on
and rung up, for our credit cards, and for the people
who unlocked the glass doors in the morning
and locked them again at closing, the people
who lost their jobs, in many cases us.

Requiem, too, for the people who made the goods
we bought, the means of production bone-close,
most likely overseas, the slashed-through
price tag signaling deals that were too neat,
slave labor, subject of Sunday news shows,
conditions we could protest if we would only agree
to see them. May we guard against those forces
shuttled through their online replacements;
may we one day understand the psychosis
that built then eroded what it built, that was us.

III. CIRCLING EAST: MINES, MOUNTAINS, AND MILLS

The Invader Alters Everything

ANN E. MICHAEL

Lehigh Valley

I killed them, the spotted lanternflies,
beetle-like, bright red,
and blotched with black and white,
in their fourth instar stage
before they reached
true form, their moth-like adult
phase, winged leaf-hoppers prepped
for reproduction.

I stopped them from flight,
from sex, from passing along
genetic strands that could result
in many thousand future insects
of their ilk. I called the state
agricultural department,
reported entomological findings—
hoping to learn how to
avert infestation of vineyards,
forests, my own back yard—

but what I know from both
experience and metaphor is:
The invader alters everything.
We must adapt to what we
resist; there is no going back.

The Naming of Bars

LEE UPTON

In memory of Drinky's, which closed after
thirteen years in Easton, Pennsylvania

And someone sat at a kitchen table and said
I've got it: the name for your bar!
And so there are bars named
Otto's Shrunken Head and The Surly Wench and
The Stumble Inn and Dutch Kills and
Please Don't Tell and No Fun
and Mother's Ruin and Old Man Hustle,
and The Tipsy Cow and The Pine Box,
and my personal local favorite: Drinky's.
Because that's what it's about and that's honest,
and after a good night you maybe want to
spray yourself off at a car wash.
And whatever you name your bar
make it easy to remember
because even if people are there to forget things
they need to remember what to call your bar.
You're doing God's Work.
Which is the name of a bar,
the bar in my head,
and because of the sadness of last call
and because someone at the end of the bar
looks dicey I mean threatening
I mean, by now, pretty good,
and because I feel like a Mudslide tonight
and because some drinks have even better names like
Same Day Delivery and Gecko Tail
and Hats on Tight and Little Bunny Foo Foo and
because I like when a cocktail comes with a toy
like a Happy Meal,

not so much a parasol but maybe a tiny sword,
like I'll need that in the depths
of the dangerous world inside my glass and
outside my glass every night when
the bar goes dark.

The Ruins of Bethlehem Steel

JOSEPH DORAZIO

*We live underneath the debris of institutions that fell
into ruin long ago, and whenever we find a way out
there may be the pure sky above but still no order around us,
and then we stand even more isolated and threatened
by the daily danger of sudden new collapses.*
—RAINER MARIA RILKE

Men made things at the mill: armor plate, battleship guns,
girders that gave rise to the Empire State Building
and span to the Golden Gate Bridge. "Tell him of Things,"
Rilke wrote. "He will stand astonished, as *you* stood
by the rope-maker in Rome or the potter along the Nile."
To forge iron is to win the favor of Hephaestus—a chance at godhood.
But the fume-belching blast furnace has expired, its lungs
succumbed to a carcinoma of rust; steel's improbable obsolescence.
Even the slot parlors with their promise of glamour and bling are
devoid of the clinking of metal falling on metal.
The humiliation of a company once powerful, now spent & exhausted,
is all that remains—
along with offers to treat addiction to casino games.
And yet, it's *here* that they come
to once again press their luck: a new rank and file
whose ferrous blood obeys the ore's magnetic tug—
the faithful summoned to Bethlehem.

°Written on the occasion of the opening of the Sands Casino on the site of the former
Bethlehem Steel Mill.

In the Allentown Shelter Kitchen

SUSAN WEAVER

It's weird. After midnight, everybody else in bed, we're talking about
Charlie's death threats, the other girl and me. She goes, "Take them
seriously. He might do it. Like when that guy on 12th Street strangled his
wife and their two kids." I remember in the papers that brick row house,
yellow police tape wrapped around the front porch like his extension cord,
squeezing life out. It put the fear in me.

Then in the kitchen's quiet, we hear a thump. A silvery thing rises up. We feel
a damp chill hang there like the spirit of the shelter, warning: "Believe it."

I still got the creeps this morning. Guess it takes a while for something
to sink in. I don't waste time looking in the mirror at this shiner here.
Yet I wonder about the house on 12th Street. Did his eyes get mean, like
Charlie's? Did he ever say in a flat voice, "I wish you were dead. Right
now, if you were dead, I'd laugh"? And did she let it in just a little at a
time?

■ ■ ■

Packerton

DAVID STAUDT

Pain is not the river sliding black and gold
below Packerton mountain's dark back.
Pain lingers in blue snow backwaters,
the deeper, permanent cold of ground
stinging back the open hands of ice.
The township's last black bear, oiled fur
drilled by parasites, crouches in terror
of daylight in an ash can under the Conrail
trestle. White rails ring hunger and rabies
prowls the Long Run dump in packs of stray

white dogs. Dump trucks rumble down sandy
state roads, too heavy to brake for deer.
Their partial carcasses, frozen,
remind us of doomed stone ovens
Iroquois abandoned. It is a pain
of slate blue hills, their forests of stone.

Snow won't stick to the white tin backs
of our houses. They withstand each evening's
slap of cold, like faces of teenage
daughters, indifferent, eyes open. I nail
a strand of colored lights in coils
of barbed wire around my parents' doors.
Their faded faces stare from within,
convinced I'm good inside. Moored in salted
driveways, Chryslers' lacquered hoods endure,
polished and brittle as each father's
sense of his own guilt. I stand in my
parents' front yard, hammer in hand.

Backyard beagles curled into springs of bone
die in their coops another night. In their dreams,
tremendous snapping turtles crawl, driven
by hunger, up the thawed banks from the river.
Christmas lights stop blinking, buoyed in wind.
Tonight the deer, who live a thousand years,
come down from their country to watch us.
In fields behind factory parking lots
they turn to stone, their eyes wicked opals.
Only the river still moves, bright through black
land bared to a golden sky. Cold and slow
as our gestures toward any neighbor.
Golden and wide as the feeling we're
sure we've offered, sure we deserve.

You've Got a Friend In . . .

GRACE BAUER

After the 2020 election

It's not often the eyes of the world
are laser focused on the state I was born in,
but for days its name was chanted like a mantra:
Pennsylvania, Pennsylvania, Pennsylvania—
until its syllables became a kind of song
summing up a nation's hope and rage.

O Quaker State now Swing State!
O Keystone State now key!
O State of Independence
so much was depending upon—
for days, a week, the world waited, pondering
the purple conundrum of your melting pot
like a coven of witches trying to read the future
in your roiling reds and simmering blues.

And I waited along with everyone else,
while you counted, and counted, and I recalled
this one time when I was a kid, and found myself
in the middle of the Lehigh, treading water
in a panic, and some boy I didn't even know
swam out, grabbed my hand, and dragged me back
towards the bank, until my feet could touch bottom again.

Kempton, PA: After My Death

JAMES NAJARIAN

Slow down. The turn in from the valley
will be as blind as ever. The tracks
no train has troubled for decades
will make you brake for them even now.

There still won't be a church in town,
and the houses, all forty of them,
will seem to want to shift their places,
like children in school. The post office,

built in 1985, will still be "new."
The sign-painter's will be there,
the feed mill, the hotel-and-tavern,
the long-shuttered farrier's, and general store.

Will the hills be greener then? I promise you
nothing. When you drive up to the old trails,
the mountains—Hawk and Pinnacle—
will stand like cast-iron cutouts on the sky.

Spring Delivers Us

JACK CHIELLI

Long before the snow began melting
on this mountain, there were deer paths
etched through the thin forest
and the fragrance of a distant fireplace filled the valley.
Be still here long enough
and one begins to believe
they can be awakened.

Down from the slopes of the Kittatinny Mountains,
the northeast winds rake through the fields
of broom grass, brushing aside the leaves
that cover the shallow graves of small animals
—exposing the alchemy of turning bones into dust.

This is where the dead leaves are pushed
from awakened branches
into the awaiting flames
of the green ferns.
Where time becomes timeless.
My darkness endless.
Where a cold rain falls.

To be reborn into this sunlight
is to shed the woefulness that infects my mind.
It is to die before my death.

Spring snakes across the Appalachian Valley
through these mountain paths
lined with crimson underbrush
—it's no secret,
spring comes prepared to deliver us,
and we,
surprised as always,
succumb.

Huckleberries and Homebrewed Boilo

MARIANNE PEEL

Mahanoy City

Her fingers always smelled of cabbage
when she made the Halupkis on Saturday night.
She'd plunge her hands into that boiling water
slivering out the core of the cabbage,
unafraid of the blade.

I used to think her fingertips
must be callused hard
scalded beyond
all sensation
the way she manhandled those cabbage leaves.

Her fingernails were stubbly squares and I wondered
how she managed to wrap them around that bottle of homebrewed Boilo,
that Boilo that burned my nose hairs when I took a whiff
that Boilo that she slugged down between folding the ground pork and
     sticky rice
into a cabbage bundle, raw pig in a blanket.

Long ago she was a young widow,
a dress shirt presser whose heavy steel iron
smoothed out the blood clots her husband hacked up.
The checks for the Black Lung came on the first of the month.
I used to find them, damp, in her apron pocket.

She told me it was *damn hard to fall asleep once he passed.*
She used to parcel her going to sleep
into measures of his wheezing.
She could count on that syncopation
to soothe her off to sleep.

She became an insomniac after he was dead and buried,

recycled his handkerchiefs into rags
 to polish the toaster,
 to spit shine her shoes,
 to dab at her lipstick that oozed the corners of her mouth.

They found her
one fine summer morning
when the mountain laurel was in bloom.
She'd gone picking huckleberries up the side of the mountain,
collected them in a rusted tin coffee can.

She used to like the sound of the berries clanging in that can.
Counted them till the sun made her dizzy
and she climbed back down the mountain.
Her old sundress, all covered in closing-go-to-sleep flowers,
was hung on the bathroom door over her acetate powder blue nightgown.

They found her in the bathtub all sunk down and comfortable
with a cigarette still burning on the edge of the tub
and a glass of Boilo rippling through the bathwater,
her fingers still stained bluish purple,
the huckleberries still on her hands.

■ ■ ■

Litany of Dyings

LISA TOTH SALINAS

My mother spent her summers in Mount Carbon.
Each year, on departing, threw her shoes
into the dam: each flung farewell repeating
like a refrain throughout her childhood.

By the summer of '46, her Uncle Brose had
explored its woods, mountains, waterways

for more than 60 years, could teach a young
niece what in the great green world was
worth tasting, what could poison her.

One year she watched her grandfather put up
storm windows, closing his family in for winter.
Sometimes you hide in order to survive.

At his death, relatives filled the dining room
at 141 Main Street with mourning, sorrow
spilling into the next room: mother's youngest
sister hid inside grandfather's casket. A small
child's way of saying goodbye.

Those who love this one-street town and
return to it start at the base of the hill.
They pass the remains of the Mount Carbon
Brewery. Pass the closed Catholic church.
At the top of the hill: Calvary Cemetery, still open.
Main street, its own litany of dyings.

In Eastern Pennsylvania we cannot bury
our winter dead until the ground thaws.
In the meantime, we wait, digging for answers.

Turning Over

PAUL MARTIN

In zero cold the engine's slow
to turn over, coughing
awake like my father sitting on the edge
of the bed staring at the blue linoleum floor,
coughing again, lifting his heavy body

into another day on the railroad section gang,
the icy wind through Lehigh Gap blasting
down on him as he raises the spike hammer
and strains against the crowbar.
But now he's drinking coffee,
looking toward the dark window,
thinking of what?
Maybe watching Friday Night Fights
or ordering tomato seeds,
maybe the ghostly face in the window
staring back at him.

My Father's Hands

HARRY HUMES

Girardville

They brought him home, sleeves still smoking
from the flash fire in his mine, our mother's lips
a thin line of grief, Dr. Murray arriving
minutes later, peeling back skin from knuckles
and palms, greasing the wedding ring,
the Masonic ring with its red stone and diamond chip,
dropping it to the floor, the injection
not helping my father at all, who groaned
and cursed the tunnels, the Welsh bosses.
He was home for months, his hands great wads
of cotton and tape that stank when we got too close,
trying not to let him know, trying not to imagine
what was under the bandages that no longer fit anything,
all of us trying to avoid them the way we avoided
Skipper Todd who hiccoughed questions about our father
through a tube in his throat, none of us ever

saying more than our mother told us to say, never how
we'd suddenly awake and find them hovering over us,
never about how he'd sit for days in the coal cellar,
our mother feeding him down there, never about
the pounding that echoed up through the house
on Ash Alley, the house that began to fall down.

When they say to leave, she says:

AMANDA HODES

Centralia

Memory is held down by rocks, like a windy sheet,
       in all four corners.

Memory becomes my house, which won't blow away.
       Initials in the rocks from our daughter.

The house morphs to a ship with memory sails,
       mast white wood speckled by rain.

The hemlocks are sentinels, but roots dance all night
       sidestep flames and tip-toe coals.

Chalk doesn't wash away in this place. Stays tattooed
       on the blacktop and bark.

Too windy to play outside with the paint,
       and the swing-set uproots a hemlock.

Its tentacles grip to the brick of our house
       until they grow upward like ivy.

Centralia, PA

FAITH ELLINGTON

a god's honest ghost town on fire beneath my soles on
grimy layer of graffiti over cracked asphalt road over
coal seam enflamed and predestined to burn for
oh, the next several hundred years (or so)

pass mailbox mouths agape
as houses relent into earth all the while
rocking chairs rot & porch lights are hanged from solitary chains

dwindled down town dissolved by overundergrowth
& still I see a man mowing the lawn though no
one is supposed to live here. Population: 5
(I read online)

coal country is coalfire country is sinkhole country too
area supposedly secured after sinkhole exhaled hot air
into Centralia's streets, citizens made aware their land
was on fire right beneath them:

this is coal country and we know the risks even more
than we know the process of eminent domain and condemnation
limestone sacrificed to oxygenation

that forced flight—I walk around in it
roads paved through an empty zip code
eyes alert to toxic smoke & we know the rumors-turned-fact
some places are uninhabitable after human error
coalfire raging already for sixty years apocryphal
town suspended over uncauterized coal vein

(place palm on earth &
expect the earth to be warm but it is not
expect the earth to scorch you but it will not
fire embedded far below, danger still)

The Viaduct

LINDA PENNISI

Mount Carmel

It separates her town from the rest, so without realizing it, she grows up
with the word. It doesn't scare her like *bridge* scares her, the Susquehanna

rushing beneath Sunbury and Danville, carrying branches and leaves
from their trees into foreign places. Beneath the viaduct, Mr. Hildenbrand

welds parts for lawn mowers and cars, and just beyond, Savitski's Coal
snakes its way into the ground near the house her father was born in.

Though she rarely walks from Maurer's Dairy to the Avenue of steeples
and crosses, and rarely looks beneath to the paths and tires and crows

among the weeds, on game weeks as the boys stay celibate
and practice passes, she and the other girls tie white and red

streamers to the viaduct's rail, so the away teams understand
whose territory they are crossing into.

■ ■ ■

Coal Ghosts (Excerpts)

STANTON HANCOCK

Walk the streets of Wilkes-Barre,
hear echoes of other Main Streets

in Ashland,
in Shamokin,
Girardville and Saint Clair,
in the smoking ruins of Centralia,

her fires burning for nearly 60 years,

each steaming crater a silent dirge.

Listen carefully:

the ghosts of Centralia moan a lament
for lost lives,
loves,
and limbs.

On midnight walks in Bloomsburg,
past the courthouse where they hung the last of the Mollies,
listen closely,
hear the last defiant declarations
and the taut snap of the rope,

feet kicking midair,

then nothing.

■ ■ ■

the next field over

NICOLE V BASTA

Wilkes-Barre

you might as well call it tender—the bridge
downtown climbing the dawn like morning

glory on a trellis. i have found joy where i was told
there could be no joy. sometimes that is my home

the soot-throated sighs and the valley they hover
over; where my dead lie in pine on a miner's

pension, broken-backed or bent spirit.
this is where i was young, knowing little

of history, crawling into what only looked
abandoned. every fence jumped in the diamond city

named *the most unhappy place in america*
since i've moved away.

they don't use the affirmative
but i've been sadder everywhere.

the susquehanna remembers before the earth
was tapped, when what we had was promise.

the river has never known its own name.
only tied to bone, out here, on this farm, a ramshackle

bridge to get us from one side of a rain to another.
i'd like to carry a body across like that—tender

but i am more like the gathering of rain
a muscle of clay arching beneath the current.

■ ■ ■

Wilkes-Barre

JERRY WEMPLE

Each day you buy the newspaper with pocket change, scan the classifieds in
the back, circle a few to call. It takes a little while, but you catch on. Joey, a
stoner metalhead kid who works in the office, too, makes it clear when you

return from not viewing the third "just rented" of the day. He phones the numbers you called and they all say, *come over, still available, nice place especially for the money.* You are still young. Two years at a college that didn't fit, so back home you find a decent job for the times, which were hard all around. But it's near an hour's drive each way so you look for an apartment. Nothing much, you think, just a place to stay during the week with winter coming. Thinking it over, it is all obvious: the older woman who spoke through a cracked door, the knock that no one answered while a man sat watching in his car across the street, the woman who says her husband just called, their friend's kid is looking for a place. *Sorry about that,* she says, turns her back and walks away. Your mother always urged you to get an education: *It's something no one can ever take away from you.* That was true, regardless of what she meant. By then you'd learned some lessons. You mostly did not have to study on them too long. Your world was small, and like an Amish horse with blinders, you stared ahead, kept following a narrow road. Then you began to enter bigger worlds with harsher lessons. Standing on those porches in early November, the wind coming on, you wonder who they saw? It took years before you saw yourself: a half-breed kid born in a coal-town orphanage. It doesn't matter all that much by now. You've done well enough. You worked that job for a year, about as long as you could stand it. You tired of having your sub-shop order taken after everyone else in the place, of the clerk eyeing your license plate through the convenience store window like you were going to run off with five bucks' worth of gas, of people asking if you worked in the store when you were wearing street clothes like them, not a blue smock and a name tag. A couple months after you left, in the worst mass murder in the state's history, a mixed-race man from that town shot and killed thirteen people including his own five children. He said he wanted to spare the kids the affliction of growing up half-caste. The sole trial defense offering was that the racism of the town had made the man insane. You wondered which slight, which slur it was that made him shake off lassitude, caused mad ire to rise and burn. When you read a newspaper account about the man and what he did, you were saddened but not surprised. The weariness had begun to close upon you.

Christmas in Public Square

CHRISTINE GELINEAU

The electronic bird calls of the blind
crossing signals carol the Christmas tree
guy-wired to the hardwoods in the center
of Center City: a misshapen dowager
of a spruce bespangled in rumpled rows
of colored lights, her tiara star askew.
In her heyday Wilkes-Barre had been
the Diamond City, black diamonds
of anthracite coal. Over time oil and gas
siphoned off much of coal's kingdom
but it was the Knox Mine disaster
of 1959 that sealed things.

Are we surprised to hear how old
the story is, how often we repeat ourselves?
Mine officials sent the miners down to burrow
illegally beneath the Susquehanna.
When the riverbed caved in it took three days
of jamming railroad cars, culm, whatever debris
came to hand into the voracious whirlpool that opened
before the wound could be staunched but by then
twelve miners, and the fortunes of Wilkes-Barre,
had been swept into the web of mines now irrevocably
plugged by ten billion gallons of river water.
O Shepherds, o silent night, beneath this tree,
in the hollowed-out heart of one more
once-prosperous American city, as evening
settles into night, a lone policeman
in his idling patrol car watches
wreathed in silvery exhaust.

Immigrant Song

ANGELA ALAIMO O'DONNELL

Pittston

There you go wearing your dirty heart
on your sleeve again, your mining men
and breaker boys' faces smudged with coal,
lunch buckets open, sandwiches sooty
with the prints of their blackened hands,
telling the story of their sorry
days, years spent in darkness while the sun
tried to shine through thick clouds that part
only rarely, so unlike bright Sicily,
its sapphire seas and fields of gold,
Etna's rich volcanic sands,
fishing boats skirting the vivid land
rife with life and color, all you lack,
how much they would give and give to go back.

Agnes 1972

THOMAS KIELTY BLOMAIN

More than a summer job for the federal government
Riding a bus each morning to sites of destruction
Where we would shovel out mud dredged up
By the friendly Susquehanna River driven to unfamiliar rage
By days of angry rain from the basements of homes and stores
For three dollars an hour tax-free

Our own family cabin terraced on the bank in Meshoppen
Was taken whole along with the boats and canoes

Bikes and dock and appliances and all the neighbor's places
And we were accused of being looters as we rummaged through
The puddles for relics after the flood

I should have seen it coming
Not that I could have done anything about it
Swimming there just days before
A fearless and foolish teenager
In a current more swollen and dangerous
Than I'd ever seen

I knew this river very well and it wasn't mean
The cliffs and swells and stilted cottages along the shore
And I believed with all the innocence I still held back then
That you would never be betrayed by something you loved
And left there with only recollections and ruin

■ ■ ■

American Water (Excerpts)

DAVID CHIN

6

During the depression, she found work
in a knitting mill—-ten cents an hour,
ten hours a day—thirty years. Single mother
of three young girls, she feared hobos
and slept with a loaded pistol under her pillow
and loaded shotgun under the bed.

Her silver spoon won shooting clay pigeons
with her sportsman husband before he left her
hung on a nail over her stove:

    Rose Belle Carpenter 1916

Passed down to me, her double-barreled
twenty gauge leans against my bedroom wall.
After the third call, I hesitated,
then bought shells—light load for an old gun.

7
Passed to me also, the small vest
sewn for my father seventy-three years ago—
blue pinstripes on white cotton,
deep inside pockets for his travel papers,
and a black cloth pouch, the size of a teabag,
tied with a red string for luck.
Chiu Gnor, his mother, filled it with sand
scooped from their village well.
She told him, "If American water
upsets your stomach, dip this in it to feel better."
Twenty-nine years must pass
before they speak again, face to face.

8
Vancouver-bound, he steamed third class
on the Empress of Asia, crossed Canada by rail,
then steamed down the Atlantic on the Yarmouth
to Boston to be grilled under Chinese Exclusion.

Names of passengers flicker, flutter
before my eyes. Microfilm unreels. I stop
at August 4, 1936 and search for my father's name:

> *Langford, Beatrice*
> *Chinaman*
> "
>
> "
>
> "
>
> *Manzer, Fred*

Chin, Gwing Guey, Chinaman, my father,
has a name not worth recording, too hard to spell,
too alien, other, foreign, even now,

under the index finger
of my southern caller tracing the listings,
finding my name, reaching for his phone.

9
Tendril, leaf and stem unfurl faster,
almost, than I can weed, stake, and tie.
My cucumbers, squash, snow peas, tomatoes,
peppers, and bok choy make a reply
my father would have understood.
"It's ignorance" he'd say, hold back the rest
and have me work my garden.

Near summer's end, at the wetland's edge,
goldenrod shudders and bobs with bees.
I balance, steady and weigh. I don't forget.
I dip my grandmother's sand in American water and drink.

■ ■ ■

Susquehanna River Bathers
ELAINE TERRANOVA

This was no paradise.
The road bristled with ferns.
A tree threw its shape, headfirst
out of the shadows, so I saw
that there was water. We undressed
and went in. The human smell
fell away. Our limbs moved out
from the hub of the body,

so simply connected. Our skin
was a jumping off place for light.
You could make a moral of this,
like the dazzle spinning off
Prometheus' hand: that water
completes us, that without it,
an animal is dust. From the far shore

rose factories and resplendent dumps.
I held up my head. I scissor-kicked,
remembering to take in breath enough
to get me through. Climbing out,
I passed bushes and vines
looking themselves as if they had just
stepped out of the water. And on
the closest lawns, strange flowers,
cannas and dark dahlias, circled
the grass and rusting iron furniture.

Gracie's Run

MJ MOSS

Currents carry us. Currents marry us.
A love affair with water may begin and end
in currents. It was swimming in the river,
there was no pool at camp, that made us all
companions as we spat and blamed the currents.
We lugged the Old Town canvas, a heavy
bastard bitch, paddles, floats and gear, and set out
to beat the current. For three days on the river,
two nights on the banks, Susquehanna
had her way with us. Capsized, soaked,
and cursing we learned respect and in learning, loved.

Ten years later, a winter flood, Gracie called
*There's a loose gas tank; it's running down
the flood.* Hooded and gloved we launched,
rode the winter river. We knew we'd never
find the tank. And the river didn't care.
Faster than a summer run, we flew
with paddles dripping.

Evening Sky Diesel Blue purple tinge
CRAIG CZURY

Dimock

last of the sun burnt white through a stand of maples past the drill
rig then rolled down over the hill

Hayfield mowed into rolls slit up its gut deep through the shoulder
pipe lined

Tomorrow this gaping trench will be backhoed shut
leaving a long blood-rose stem after bypass

If you were to tell me the patient has 100% chance of recovery
I'd plant carrots and onions

a long corridor of sweet corn and cabbages in this scar

End to end the cemeteries are a feeding tube of bones
blanched in the vapors of black poppies

What I want is what others around the world wanted
and gave their lives for

to drink from your mouth and say this is good

The Sky Above My House on Johler Avenue

BRIAN FANELLI

Scranton

is pregnant with inky clouds in early March,
Blizzard of '93. I'm snowsuit yellow,
two rubber boots, gloved hands.
I'm waist deep in walls of white,
red-cheeked with chapped lips.
I'm pulling the frayed string of a toboggan
and then zipping down Prospect Hill near Weston Field.
I inhale the bite of late winter,
suck cold into my lungs,
raise my fists into the air because I did it,
conquered the biggest hill.
I spit out a mouthful of snow
and then lug that trusty sled home.
I retrace my path, still unplowed, as children's laughter
echoes in the nip of night
like a cocksure army cheering victory,
claiming the neighborhood at least for an evening
until the inevitable roar of snow plows and salt trucks come morning.

IV. NORTH CENTRAL: THE SUSQUEHANNA VALLEYS AND THE UPSTATE REGION

Susquehanna (Excerpts)

SHARA MCCALLUM

I stand on the cliff overlooking the confluence
of the river's branches.

I have come to witness its grandeur.
But not much here wants to deliver.

Not the chain-link fence stopping my fall.
Not the butterfly flitting on weeds.

In every direction, hills rim the horizon,
sloping down to muddy water.

Across the surface, a skiff skitters,
spume in its wake.

At this juncture, the current's slight shift
confirms the river's indifference

to our demarcation of North and West,
to bridges connecting island and mainland.

Beauty is part fiction here. I conjure it
by not seeing:

the way as I drive along the river
on Route 15 I blot out

rusting gas pumps,
crumbling farmhouses, and barns;

the way I turn from the wreckage
of human industry to study an oak—

upper limbs steer me toward a sky
so blue it tries belief.

~

In this watershed, time is a pendulum,
swinging backward and forward as the mind directs.

Amish buggies clacking on asphalt collapse
three centuries. Almost.

Steel rails leading from town
signal that other Railroad:

fugitive mother and child racing night,
reversing the river's course

from Columbia into Lewisburg,
where a stable next to the creek and tracks

flickered refuge on their journey north.
Today, a train drags along this site,

trailed by its whistle.
Like that ricocheting sound, memory

wants to invoke the past, asks us to hear
an infant's cries, a mother's hushing reply,

gives body to our wounds,
as if we could commemorate the dead.

Gedachtniss Tag: Remembrance Day

REBECCA LAUREN

Isle of Que, Snyder County
                              your curse
will be to ache as you've never imagined:
your limbs will long for the scent of this ridge.
—JULIA SPICHER KASDORF

At home the Susquehanna River
wears our mountains down to shale;

hills limn boundaries; warm milk
and honey drip like the setting sun.

When the sky was large and gray,
my ancestors arrived here brave

birthing babies to the Atlantic, sailing
from Silesia to America, native land looming

rivers with unfamiliar names, valleys
the hulls of great ships. I am only a child

of their dreams. I have no story to skip across
the ocean-bound water. So I fling stones against

lapping wakes, dream of homemade paper sails
that could coast as far as the Chesapeake.

If I squint hard enough, I can almost see
their wooden crates bobbing in the distance—

spiraled mountain laurel climbing
the sides in red and white, splitting

with the weight of their new world.

The Urge to Bury

S. E. GILMAN

Lost Creek in Monroe Township

It was a raccoon on the side of the little run, little
Lost Creek that dries up in summer and flows in spring,
and the flow has gone after life had run, turned
fur into yellow rushes, skull flat with ears that used
to stick up, plastered down. The tail you could tell
was ringed, blends in grey with the stones that line
the soaking bed, the patient lying off to the side.

I wanted to clamber down the ravine to the culvert,
dig up the tender corpse and give it to a grave proper.
In these times of so many passing, the culling that started
in emigration and war, now in the grocery store,
each one of us a vector, a suspicion, some already dead
and no one can come to the hospital, no one to the wake.

Like we are sleeping, nightmaring and waiting because
it's too soon to wake up now, too soon to tell who remains
to grieve, to hold the hands of the dying, to say goodbye or
see you soon or never. We who uncorked royal tombs of Egypt
and simple belongings of the frozen men and women of Thule,
uncovered bits of their lives, stone points, a Viking
brooch prized and wore. What we leave behind besides a shell
is desire to bury to rest and say they were worthy of earth
left in all ground, but not abandoned, all ground hallowed.

At the Riverview Cemetery, Northumberland, PA

MELANIE SIMMS

Bones stretch out
across the graves of Northumberland
crowned by stones, by words,
pronouncing their lives
as memorable.

Bouquets and Walmart wreaths
adorn markers while
dates mark passages
of time. Lilies and roses fragrance the air
where souls lay quiet
beneath weeping willows.

But I hear ghosts whisper.

I find myself each Sunday,
walking the cobbled path to console them,
offering daffodils or lilies to unmarked graves.

The nameless markers blink in recognition.

As I walk, I think of my own death,
and of how they might welcome
me more kindly if I remember them here and now;
that, in my own passing, they might greet me
like old friends reunited.

Sodom School, Northumberland County, PA

MICHAEL HARDIN

In the early 1800s, a village blooms
between Appalachian ridges
and the Susquehanna's West Branch.

Sodom, the farmers name it—
they aren't wicked, just Methodists—
more warning than affiliation.

After two hundred years, only
the hexagonal school remains,
as if God had rained brimstone.

A single room, one door and seven
windows, limestone walls. Big enough
for thirty students, although

books claim one hundred
squeezed inside. Lot's wife
looked back and turned to salt.

The town has vanished. A vacant
school reminds us what we've lost.

At the Site of the Laurelton Village for Feeble-minded Girls of Childbearing Age

DEIRDRE O'CONNOR

No ghosts. Only witness trees
　　　　casting dark on lawns. Cool nets.

　　　　　　Rustles above, alongside.
　　　Where the fields were, maybe,

green beans, cukes, tomatoes.
　　　　Where the grass now sways hip-high,

　　　　　　hips in cotton dresses swayed.
　　　Where the orchards: pear, plum, apple.

Baskets of them in arms.
　　　　Where stone was lifted and made

　　　　　　an institution.
　　　Porches painted white.

Can't you see the ones called morons
　　　　mending dresses,

　　　　　　idiots shelling peas,
　　　the deviant

berry-pickers, water-fetchers,
　　　　milkers of cows,

　　　　　　and those incorrigibles
　　　who couldn't be trusted

with a shovel,
      weeding the long rain-loosened rows

          on hands and knees? Scrubbing floors,
      hanging sheets to flap

and then by supper
      spread again on beds.

          Can't you see yourself
      standing inside the corn

grown higher than faces?
      How you might watch the whores

          and nulliparae dance
      like boys and girls,

music drifting
      from open windows, curtains wafting

          as if in a film and you alone
      in knowing what you were

missing? No one seeming to notice,
      no one bashing through stalks to lead you

          back by the ordinary arm.

Lines written in the Walmart Supercenter
parking lot, Lewisburg, Pennsylvania

K. A. HAYS

My child wants Pokémon cards, the most rare and evolved creatures a nine-year-old's birthday money can buy, & I want a store with no crowds, so together at 6:41 a.m., we drive Route 15 North to the Walmart Supercenter, the semis asleep in the lot, fog blurring the massive structure where something about the dawn or the fog lights up all eleven security cameras silver on the Supercenter's roof, attending like the eyes of a Madonna to a field of empty shopping carts. Inside the store, my child debates: is the Charizard EX tin better than the MewTwo EX tin, since if your health points are high but you can't do as much damage, you aren't that useful. Is it better to be able to do more damage with less health? This is unclear. But since each tin is on Clearance, the decision is moot—*both* the flying lizard & the bipedal humanoid with feline features can belong to my child, & as we sweep through self-check-out, the store's music switches on out of the silence (7:00) & the store aubades out, *Are these times contagious? I've never been this bored before. Is this the prize I've waited for?* When we walk from the fluorescent-lit body out to the body of Planet Earth, the fog has gone, & the light makes the wet lot into a mirror. The trucks still doze, but with clarity: a logging truck, a car carrier stacked with Hondas, a Dole fruit truck. Inside each truck, it occurs to me, beats a living heart, a person who'll wake the engine: a bipedal humanoid sticky from sleep, with lines pressed into the face where the pillow folded. A human whose damage-capacities and health I cannot know. I know only that the truck—the larger body to which the human tends—holds serious damage power. I climb into my car & strap my body to its larger one. I can hear from the backseat the crackle of a shrink-wrapped package opening. Eleven eyes watch us from above, eyes that could show us to ourselves: our exit from the car ten minutes ago, our entrance to the Supercenter, and our emergence with two tins depicting fantastical species now clutched by the common invasive species in the backseat—the same species serving as conductor of an entire ecological collapse—& the two of our bodies, like the bodies of the drivers of the trucks, have been swallowed (three times already this morning) into damaging structures that they did not construct, but to which they faithfully attend.

Alvira

MICAH JAMES BAUMAN AND DAVID J. BAUMAN

. . . in the spring of 1942 the federal government seized the small village of Alvira, Pennsylvania, and after kicking out the populace, razed almost every building in the village to build the Susquehanna Ordnance Depot.

—ATLAS OBSCURA

Below Bald Eagle Mountain you can find
what remains. South of the old church,
a few stone walls, three cemeteries,
and one hundred forty-nine bunkers.

Ordnance, a variant of *ordinance*,
cousin of *ordain*, a carefully chosen word.
The townsfolk were assured they could
come home when the war was over.
Eighty years later, almost no one has,

the soil no longer fit for farming.
A state game land sign tells a disarmed
version of the truth. The whole operation
was shuttered eleven months after completion.
These concrete igloos lie mostly empty,

taken over by brush and brambles, buried
and crowned with a tangle of trees,
territory of turkeys and hunters. Inside
these hills are cacophonies of echoes,

stacks of steel and lumber, a broken
rocking chair, charred wood, ash
from a fire ring. Not all these heavy doors
are welded shut. Scraps of stories now

scrawled on inner walls and entrance ways.

Drooping bows of rhododendron hide
a blank slab and a crumbled foundation.
Who knows what once was or who lived here?
High in the forked limbs of a maple hangs a new
woven nest where an orchard oriole sings.

■ ■ ■

Still April and No Spring
ANNE DYER STUART

Jerseytown

Now in the country of lost dogs, smashed cats
Deer baked flat on the side of the road
Brittle last grass of winter
Husks of brown
Brown days and brown shoes and felt-tip pens and worry
Spring is a season of indomitable rage
If you're young
If you feel young
If you feel sure you will feel young again
Now on the ribbon of black tar
Dazzle of bright orange warnings
Before the abandon of Easter's tease
Before the sweet pained trill of a house finch
Whose sweetness makes you sad
And how little those birds are
In the yard in the air in the trees in the rafters
Of the back porch
With their insistent optimism
With their industry and might

Independence

DAWN LEAS

The rain comes every day for weeks. Sometimes in giant bursts, droplets breaking on tree branches. Often in drenching curtains the wind blows west to east. The water pools muddied in the construction site outside my office. I'm quickly giving up on summer. You're saying you'll never let go. On the eve of the Fourth of July, it's dry. We drive over an hour to the middle of nowhere for a softball game. There's a tractor parked outside the Turbotville Great Valu and marked spots for buggies. A young couple climbs into one. He's suspendered and bearded. She's white-capped and long-dressed, unwrinkled. They look full of hope. I think there's a poem here. I try to take pictures, but my memory is full. You refrain from a lecture. My niece throws strike after strike after strike in the bottom of the sixth. The stands cheer. The next day we wake to more rain.

■ ■ ■

Shiners

KEN FIFER

Ricketts Glen State Park

At Waters Meet it's no breeze
rising from stones after falling asleep.
Silence grows unthinkably thin
while shiners flash and fan their fins
for the least of things in the water's dish—
lines and circles, indecipherable signs.
I have a thought but waters cloud it.
I have a thought but can't pronounce it.
Waters Meet collides steep creeks,
pooling dark around downed pine
in shallows waterstriders glide
when all their legs can't bring them ease.

Glacier Pools Preserve

SPRING 2020

SHANNA POWLUS WHEELER

Hughesville

We'd rather quarantine on trails
through fern and mountain laurel,

tracing moraines, ridges of glacial debris,
both gaining and closing distance.

Allegheny acreage seems the only safe place—
a sense deep in the genes of amphibians here,

who know these vernal pools, glacial thumbprints
filled by rain and snowmelt, bear no predators.

Salamanders, fairy shrimp, and wood frogs
feast on swarms of mayflies and phantom midges.

The reckless spawning weaves rafts of eggs—
cotton clouds that hover just below surface.

Deer sip respectfully along the edges
glorious with scum. We, too, perch and peer

into leafy, tea-brown shallows teeming
with the frenzy of metamorphosis:

spotted salamanders with frilly gills
wriggle legless through the murk.

A fairy shrimp swims the backstroke
with a brazen ripple of her twenty-two legs,

as if she knows our world has upturned
and any strangeness, like the wood frog

calling across the water with the voice
of a duck, is no longer strange,

at least for the mysterious time being—
may it be ephemeral like these waters.

■ ■ ■

Stepping Stones

GREGORY DJANIKIAN

Montoursville

You're standing beside a stream in Irasburg, VT
feeling how quiet your body has become,
how your shadow floats on the water like an invitation
to everything below it, rainbow trout, brownies,
maybe some mayflies skimming above them,
making the whole scene livelier and creaturely

and given the convergence you've noted now
of human, fish, and insect, you might desire
some knowledge about fishing, what flies to use,
how to assemble your grandfather's vintage gear
which happens to lie in its case beside you
though you know little about the parts,
how they all fit together

but you remember your friend in this very stream
whooshing his bamboo rod back and forth
like a pendulum marking time and place
feeling the water against his calves
the joy of the line thrumming in his fingers

and wouldn't it be fun to skip a stone
across the water counting the splashes
as you did across Loyalsock Creek one afternoon
while your girlfriend clicked your picture
which still hangs on your living room wall
and reminds you of how it feels to let go

like the kite whose line snapped in a gust of wind
as your children watched in amazement
to see such a light thing soar
toward the cumulostratus gray

but those two crows squawking from a topmost branch
are diverting your attention now, enough to make you think
of the cawing you heard years ago at 4 AM
outside your window, loud and raspy

like your old tenor sax which has been collecting dust
and which you played with a certain vigorous flair in jr. high
marching in parades like a little tin soldier
wailing out "The Victors" and "On Wisconsin"

and shouldn't you grease the cork sometime,
suck on the reed to make it wet and pliable
as if you were sucking on the elephant grass it's made of,
Arundo donax, which is not unlike bamboo, or reedy papyri by the Nile

along which, coincidentally, you were born
though you've never stepped in its waters
or fished it, or floated on it even as a shadow

as you are floating now on this stream
standing still and thinking how long it took you
to get here in your incidental life
episodic, syncopated

hopping as if from one stone to another
across the wide and continuous waters.

Sunrise on a Back Porch in Pennsylvania

GLORIA HEFFERNAN

Montoursville

Bald Eagle Mountain is fringed with mist
hovering over the trees
like furrowed eyebrows,
wispy and white,
as morning yawns over the valley.
The back porch reverberates with the music
of wind chimes, blue jays, and a pick-up truck
roaring down Warrensville Road.

I sip cinnamon-scented coffee
perched on the porch swing,
listening to the *caw-caw*-caphony
of crows bickering in the pine trees
and the improbable crowing of a rooster
echoing over suburban rooftops
where only last year a cornfield swayed.

The empty coffee cup is still warm in my hand.
In the kitchen, the sound of slippered feet.
Soon the cracking of eggs.

Throwing like a Girl

MARJORIE MADDOX

Williamsport
Mo'ne Davis, pitcher for Philadelphia's Taney Dragons, who repre-
sented the Mid-Atlantic team as the 2014 Little League World Series
Pitcher, Williamsport, PA

Seventy-miles Mo'ne style,
fast ball, curve ball, flashing into-the-future
ball, every which way but
losing.
                    Batter's up,
            so we chant
                    "Mo'ne! Mo'ne!"
awake, sleeping, warming up
for the life worth stealing
in this home run of a series
we call "team,"
                    we call "You go, Girl,"

braided phenom with an arm
that hurls hope way past today's
whirl of photo ops and change-ups,

all the way to a close up
of two T-ball boys playing the part,
debating, voices escalating
            "I'm Mo'ne."
                    "No! I'm Mo'ne!"

and a summer of daughters
leaning into the pitch that blasts the phrase
      "throwing like a girl"

into the All-Star compliment
that it can be,

that it *is*

when lean machine Mo'ne
takes the mound,
smiles as wide as a long drive,
then delivers the dream
we braided girls of
baseball,   basketball,   soccer,
business,   science,   writing
still need in whatever
and every season.

Here, there are Blueberries

MARY SZYBIST

Lycoming County

When I see the bright clouds, a sky empty of moon & stars,
I wonder what I am, that anyone should note me.

Here there are blueberries, what should I fear?
Here there is bread in thick slices, of whom should I be afraid?

Under the swelling clouds, we spread our blankets.
Here in this meadow, we open our baskets

to unpack blueberries, whole bowls of them,
berries not by the work of our hands, berries not by the work of our
fingers.

What taste the bright world has, whole fields
without wires, the blackened moss, the clouds

swelling at the edges of the meadow. How changeable I am,
how subject to every shift of light.

You must live for something, they say.
People don't live just to keep on living.

But here is the quince tree, a sky bright and empty.
Here there are blueberries, there is no need to note me.

Worlds End

BARBARA CROOKER

We were sitting on the rocks, my husband
and son, down by the Loyalsock Creek,

in a stone cabin built by the CCC. Back
home, my mother cannot sleep—her recliner's

too small, the hospital bed's too hard—
like Goldilocks in the bears' cottage,

nothing is just right. Nothing will ever be
just right, as her body fails and fails

some more. Up on a ridge above the Loyalsock,
the trees are at their peak. Even the creek water

burns red, orange, yellow. The cell phone
in my pocket in case hospice calls thumps

against my thigh. It's one of those brilliant
blue days you think should last forever,

the trees glowing redder, starry asters
lining the rocky path. Back in the cabin,

pork and cranberries have been slowly cooking all day.
I boil wild rice, add toasted pine nuts, yellow raisins.

At home, my mother lifts a bowl, fills her nebulizer,
inhales the hot steam, breathes more easily for a little

while. I throw more wood in the black iron stove,
whose hunger is insatiable, whose belly can never be filled.

■ ■ ■

Prayer Flags
JUDITH SORNBERGER

I see now why each line of wash
in a backyard makes me want to drop
down on my knees, that I am witnessing
the prayer of t-shirts, blue jeans, sheets
and underwear—the prayer flapping
below terra cotta rooftops in Siena
repeated in the same tongue right here
in Tioga County, Pennsylvania.

Don't tell me those women don't know
they are praying. Have you ever
watched even a busy woman hanging
out the holy ghosts of her family?
Seen her stand there afterwards,

her empty basket resting like a child
on her cocked hip, as she adored
the spirit of the wind tossing them
into the deep blue mind of heaven?

Even a grieving woman feels her feet
lift from the earth when the breeze
kicks up the ankles of her drying khakis,
feels her shoulders sprouting wings
as her blouse takes flight. I don't know
if she is grateful as she clips each
garment to her line, or if each one
bodies forth a precious worry.
Maybe her clothesline is one long wail.

But watch her hours later
when she goes to bring her wash in,
leaning into the warm scent of sun
woven with birdsong, closing her eyes
for just a second as she guesses
this must be how God smells,
pulling each piece into an embrace
of folding, settling it in her basket,
and giving the whole stack a final pat.

Tioga County, PA

ROBBIE GAMBLE

Roadkill: deer carnage
everywhere, a half-skinned badger
skeleton, canines askew.

At the Burnin' Barrel Bar
big ballcapped men push back
on stools with surgically repaired knees,

licking their chops
at the new bigscreen crop
of pro fantasy rookies.

Bridge construction on siesta,
the transports sigh
and heave on the gravel lot outside.

Behind the bar
a bank of bourbons flanked
by Stars and Bars, and a Terrible Towel.

North out of town toward the New York line
a parish billboard proclaims: Don't wait
for six strong men to carry you into church.

Lullaby in Fracktown

LILACE MELLIN GUIGNARD

Tioga County

Child, when you're sad put on your blue shoes.
You know that Mama loves you lollipops
and Daddy still has a job to lose.

So put on a party hat. We'll play the kazoos
loud and louder from the mountain top.
Child, when you're sad put on your blue shoes

and dance the polka with pink kangaroos,
dolphin choirs singing "flip-flop, flip-flop."
Hey, Daddy still has a job to lose—

don't be afraid. Close your eyes, snooze,
because today our suns have flared and dropped.
Tomorrow when you wake, put on your blue shoes.

Eat a good breakfast. Be good in school.
Good boys go to college goody gumdrops
so someday too you'll have a job to lose.

Waste trucks clatter by as the gray bird coos.
Flames pour forth when the faucet's unstopped.
Child, when you're sad put on your blue shoes.
For now, Daddy still has a job to lose.

Nurse in Need

JULIE L. MOORE

Perhaps she arrived as the water rose
    to the lamp posts on Main,
        flooding the first floors of stores

like Western Union and Treadeasy Shoes,
    sending a canoe with four souls downtown
        past the clock stopped at 11:49 the morning

after St. Patrick's Day in 1936, when someone
    from behind, someone from on high,
        took the photo I now see online.

My grandmother left home at sixteen,
    sick and tired of being the eldest
        of a dozen, diapering babies, wiping

faces, scrubbing clothes and dishes and floors,
    living poor on a farm where her father—
        he was mean, she'd told me once—

blamed Jews for their bad lot.
    She got out. Lived with an aunt
        and went to nursing school.

When the call for help came, she trekked
    with the doctors and other nurses
        to Lock Haven, town between the Poconos

and Appalachians, where two feet of snow
    had fallen in the coldest February ever,
        then thawed—so fast!—in a 50-degree,

Leap-Day melt. The unlucky flow of liquefied snow
　　　slid down the mountains, rushing
　　　　　into the Susquehanna that long ago

carved out the Anthracite Valley, a ship suddenly sunk.
　　　And there she was at eighteen (I was capable
　　　　　of nothing heroic at that age!),

no stranger to suffering but still, so young,
　　　donning her newly sewn uniform
　　　　　from McCall's, crisp and white, buttoned

to the V in its neck, collar set, cap pinned,
　　　not sure at first what to do with her hands,
　　　　　slipping her right one into her hip pocket

as she awaited instructions. Soon enough they came.
　　　And she metamorphosed into nurse in need,
　　　　　resuscitating a coal miner who'd nearly drowned,

bandaging a teacher who'd cracked her head open
　　　on brick, or pulling mud from a boy's mouth,
　　　　　then hearing him cry for his mother

who'd let him go as she was washed away.
　　　Maybe. I don't know, really.
　　　　　I never asked till now, as I hold her gold pin,

inscribed, "Service of Honor,
　　　St. Luke's and Children's Hospital,"
　　　　　nearly a century later, decades after her death.

I want to think it was great,
　　　this thing she did that she never talked about
　　　　　in the countless games of Pinochle we played

as she smoked Marlboros in her dusters,
    laughing at our penny-ante antics,
        a widow by then, steeped in grief and alcohol.

My father, even now, doesn't know the details
    as I raise the memento in conversation
        and the thank-you note by Dr. C. Dudley Saul,

founder of the first-ever A.A. treatment center.
    I read aloud his words,
        which reveal all we'll ever know:

"You were everything a nurse should be."

■ ■ ■

North: 1991

BRUCE BOND

Bucktail State Park, Highway 120, Clinton County

In the euphoria that followed
the American air strike
when the New York Exchange soared

over the smoldering cities
and hovered there, a frail spire
aimed at heaven, I was driving

North, like so many who work
in town and live in the canyon.
It was the one road along the icy river

through the narrow tunnel
of my light, the radio cupping
a last match of news in its palm:

I live so close to nowhere.
I've driven this route ten winters,
and never was it so difficult

under the tallest trees,
ice-shagged, splintered,
holding up all of January

as if to give it back.
The highest branches rose
like the antlers of a startled elk.

There was no other way
but up, past the bent girders
over Cold Fork, through the small

fires of snow, layer after layer.
Winter's vault closed without a click.
Higher still where the road turned

into dirt and stone, tapering,
I got out to open the driveway gate
and felt my body grow tight

against the cold. There would be chores,
kindling to gather, a day's weather
in the satellite dish.

But for the time I stopped everything
to stand in the distance
of myself, turning white,

and could hear the thin ecstasy
of saws, the rise and fall,
a crackling in the hard wood.

The Ritual

JAMES BRASFIELD

Miles Township, Centre County

I stood holding a rope end
at a barn the morning
my grandfather,
the county veterinarian,
made me one of the tribe.

We brought the colt down
gently by the galvanized tub
on the grass. Grandfather
shredded sheets, dropping strips
into a milky antiseptic.

As if to draw an arc, pencil
on paper, he drew the scalpel
over the scrotum. Blue veined,
bloodless as a boiled egg,
a gray testicle was born.

Ball in hand, he cut the muscle.
All the while the horse was walleyed.
Staring, I pulled the rope end
tighter, hopeful that holding down
the horse was not dependent on me.

When the next testicle
was taken, I wanted to let go,
but we all held taut while Grandfather
stuffed wads of sheet into the cavity.
He stitched the loose skin.

He patted the horse.
We dropped our ropes.
In that way a horse will stand,
he stood, still at first
to gain his bearings.

Being tamed as he was,
he walked within
that mute circle of the ritual.
I was listening to rags
slopping the emptiness.

First Rain of Spring

RACHAEL LYON

State College

Everywhere the earth breaks open.
The smell of wet dirt fills my house and bleeds
into my dreams. Worms crawl up
from rain-soaked ground and lift
their heads, blinking their worm-blinks,
full of the wisdom of winter.

Toddlers from the daycare down the block
hold their handled rope and shriek
beneath a covered walkway,
practice outside voices, delight in raw sound.

What hope is stirred by the promise of spring,
by the growth coming up underfoot? Though
I know in my bones what the months ahead hold,
the back-breaking worry and work,
their laughter contaminates my mouth,
eats away like snowmelt, like wet sun.

Waking Up with Jerry Sandusky

JULIA SPICHER KASDORF

Centre County

He snores beside me naked, so I play
possum, tell myself he raped boys

from over the mountain in gym showers
I'll never use, that a person is innocent

as long as he sleeps. Then he shifts, sighs.
I feel the pulse in his pelvis beside

my pelvis. When he stands up, his legs
are in great shape for a man his age.

It's a dream, oldest trick in the book
yet I lie in the dark telling myself

Sandusky is a town in Ohio named
for a Polish fur trader or else

the Wyandot word for "here is pure water."
Sandusky is a town in Ohio known

for roller coasters and a killer whale
trained to jump for dead fish. Sandusky

is a football field next to Brownson House
in little Washington, where Jerry grew up

in a flat above the rec center, and also
Jerry's dad, Art, the athletic director.

Sandusky's in solitary in Greene County,
23 hours a day, three showers a week.

Sandusky is the Germanized spelling
of Sandowski, Sedowski, names lugged into

mills by men who worked 16-hour days
then built homes, a church, the Polish social club

up the hill. Don't let me get sentimental
about the workers and go soft on Sandusky

whose dull face in the newspaper the day
of his arrest made me think of a mill hunk

who hasn't yet learned enough words to speak
in the blast furnace of his new language.

Greener Than

JULIE SWARSTAD JOHNSON

State College

How to explain it, except to say
I couldn't understand how there wasn't
another Ace Hardware until Lewistown,
and Lewistown was an unfathomable name
at the bottom of the mileage signs along one of maybe two
main routes through this central Pennsylvania town.
How to explain, except to say I came
from a place where the big-box stores are legion,
where the Arizona desert was bulldozed over decades
to make mile after mile of intersections

that repeat themselves with only minor variation,
a geography of void and plenty, anything available,
if not at this store, then the next or the next. How to explain,
except to say I thought someone had cut off part
of the sky, what was left a small, drab covering
that had me in tears when the rain didn't stop
for a week. And those hills that they sometimes
called mountains, the trees obscuring everything underneath
into ominous shade. How to explain: when one day
what was at first a bird with a rust-colored chest
bounced through the grass and the word
robin lit up in my brain, some wire falling into place
between description and experience,
the joy of it flashing madly like bulbs
on an old movie theater sign. The local words
ridge and *gap* and *run* became little maps,
rudimentary phrases I could repeat to myself
the way I'd once learned *bongiorno* and *per favore*, beginner words
that could act as charms in a new place,
magic keys that sometimes open doors and sometimes
do nothing at all except give you a reason
to keep on going. *Run* and *ridge* and *gap*:
all that water alive in the landscape, all those strange,
long hills shouldering through the dusk
and the places the water cuts through them,
the highway on stilts high above the houses in gray twilight
and the solitary owl—wild, hurtling form—merging
with the solid absence of the trees.

V. THE ALLEGHENY HIGHLANDS

Settlers in the Valley

ANN HOSTETLER

Kishacoquillas Valley, Mifflin County

The records tell us little of what it was like
to travel with families with wagons and horses
along footpaths worn into anticline ridges—

they testify to faith and endurance,
the cruelties of settlement—ambush,
displacement, captivity, death—

but not of what it was like to carry
an infant in a sling over rocky ground
on horseback, or give a hungry child

sassafras bark to chew on when the food
was gone, or for the nursing mother hollowed
out by her empty belly's ache.

Or how a boy learned to hold the cool flint
in one hand, chisel in the other,
shape it with the grain—

how quickly the arrowhead could slice
a man's chest, cause him to drop on
the rock that smashed his skull.

When they crested Stone Mountain,
the settlers were astounded to see smoke rising
from Indian settlements, rows of corn

planted in the already cleared farmland.
A hundred years or more later, an arrowhead
rises to the surface of a furrow. Pocketed

by the farmer, it marks the beginning
of a collection my Amish uncle will inherit
from his grandfather. He opens

his palm to show us the leaf-shaped stone,
its edges finely toothed, and tell us
the story of discovery.

"Where did the Indian children go?"
my sister asks me later. "Who made
that arrowhead? Was it just for hunting?"

■ ■ ■

Jacks Mountain
EMILY MILLER MLČÁK

i

The mountain folds back
on itself, a pinch between
the sky's fingers.
The Juniata follows
bending into
Jacks Narrows.

Where one man killed
another over a horse,
stolen or owed. Where one
body would become namesake
for another's land.

There is no word
of the horse.

ii

The Standing Stone—a pillar
inscribed with the history of
the Juniata people, that too is
gone, left only in accounts
and forgetting. The Juniata—
river of many sorrows—
each a tear, hardened
into fossils, riverbed
made up in brachiopod shells
curved oil lamps,
marking out the ghosts.

Like the quarry men walking up
Jacks Mountain for work.
Pick axing the ganister
ripping seams of stone
loading the daily quota
3 tons into the dinky cars
sending them down the mountain
to Harbison Walker,
to be pressed into bricks.

One story pressed against
another in stratigraphic layers
of words & absence.

iii

Sandstone ridges and limestone floors
standing in for the absent
ocean. The ocean once pulled over
the land like a salty sheet, then
folded back into ridgelines and gorges.

Jacks Mountain parts valleys,
the Dry from Kishacoquillas,
whose name means
the snakes have gone into their dens.
Rattlers, copperheads & garters alike,
massed and coiled, stilled for a moment.
Springtime will see them unfurling
like the ghost horse's mane, its name & fate unknown.

And stilled for the longest moment
the crushed-up bones
of my father, the box folded
into the open space of the cemetery.
The next day we walk
the 1,000 steps up Jacks Mountain
alongside unseen and unremembered men
their lunch pails bumping our water bottles.

Counting the steps together
986, 987, 988, 989, 990
each step holds its history.
My skeleton a brief speck of time in
motion, the horse whinnying, the
men calling out, the forgotten ocean's
rush into tongues.

iv

A second standing stone at the Juniata
with the names of settlers &
surveyors—not history but
ownership—that too has gone—
and the man who killed to get his
horse back, hung in Philadelphia
far away from this landscape, curved
and folded and snaked.

Mushemeelin
let me write his name at least once.
In death, the stealer of his horse still names
the mountain and river-bed.

The horse's hooves leave fossil prints.
Curved lamps of the sea light its mane.
Everything that we own will eventually
be stolen, will be lost, will be left nameless.

Ghost ocean
Ghost horse
Ghost mountain
And sooner than that
My own.

Migration at Jacks Narrows

JACK TROY

Had it not been for hundreds of vultures
—no acre of sky was empty of them—
circling river and town, how could I not pull over,
quitting human traffic to marvel at theirs.

I watched them glissading thermals,
swooping down slopes they'd found,
miming slipstream tides,
quartering over water, giddily off kilter
while the highest hung motionless as kites,
correcting for gusts, heads steady,
fronting visceral machinery of wing-sockets.

They figured the wind, made visible
what I had not seen. One watched me
watching through the windshield,
rocking as if bored by his own miracle.

Poem about the Environment

JEANNE MURRAY WALKER

I have written the awful poem to rescue nature,
a poem that starts: *Alaska's melting.*

The poem walks like a toddler wielding an axe.

It exaggerates. *After which our houses will burn.*

The poem becomes a stunt woman, changing shapes
and definitions. It wants to be all things to all

people. It becomes an ancient seeing-eye dog,
trembling and sniffing methane that escapes
the permafrost like a serial murderer
we can't ever call back.

Are you listening yet?
the poem asks. *By the time we see*
it's personal, we'll be doomed.

The poem sees a beautiful hill in Pennsylvania, napping
like a woman sleeping on her side after a bath.
Behind her a steel tower lurches to its feet and comes for her.
No bigger than a thumb, the poem calls out to her,
throwing its tiny voice. *Wake up!*

All day the poem wonders who will take care of
the baby planet they have discovered
in the womb of the Milky Way.

Attention, the poem calls. *Attention.*

The poem wants to be a book of safety matches.
Drag your match across its gritty strip: a blaze
of worry leaps in you, enough to start a forest fire.

But the poem is all faithfulness. It believes
in miracles, the budding of a lily in the human heart,
the mountain moved, one spoonful at a time.

Blast Area

DAVE BONTA

Tyrone

The blast was larger
than anticipated: beds
of limestone can dip
in odd directions.
The ground shook with release.

In the yellow house
next to the quarry,
the crash of a plate rolling
off a plate rail
and onto the tile floor
was followed by a couple
seconds of silence,
then the trucks
yelping into reverse.

The windows were all open.
Raindrops began to blow
against the curtains.
An index finger
resumed its pilgrimage,
dipping into
the hollow at
the base of a throat
too frozen with joy and terror
to make a sound.

Skins

NOAH DAVIS

Tipton

In this valley, where mules catch pigeons
in their mouths, women wrap rattlesnake skins
around their daughters' thighs while babies
wail out from their red rooms.

   Come wailing out and away
from these snake skins with the fear strongest
when we can only see shapes.

   And the fear lives
in these shapes until one day in January
these babies, who have grown into children carrying
their own fear, hike to a talus slope and with axes
chop away a chestnut stump,

   where they find thirty rattlesnakes
curled in cold and kill every one of them.

   These babies, grown large enough
to carry dead snakes in their hands, lay the snakes on the snow
in shapes only hawks can read.

·

In this valley, where bees build honeycomb
between railroad ties, women wrap rattlesnake skins
around their daughters' thighs while babies
wail out from their red rooms.

   When the babies are teething,
these mothers lay rattlesnake skins
on swollen gums.

These babies grow into children
who know what it means to have rattlesnake skins
in their mouths, which they remember as they hike through groves of bear
    oak

    and hear the snake's metallic buzzing
and speak to the snake in a way only bodies who have been together
since breath began know how.

    .

In this valley, where bears walk upright
on the road, women wrap rattlesnake skins
around their daughters' thighs while babies
wail out from their red rooms.

    The mothers wipe mucus and blood
from their babies' cheeks and bellies
with the rattlesnake skins and because the skins

    of these babies are new
the scales mark their cheeks and bellies
until fathers come and scrub away the divoted prints.

    When these babies grow
into girls and boys who want hands to touch them,
they recognize who else was born in this valley

    by rubbing their hands over cheeks
and bellies and finding the keratin-memory of rattlesnake scales
left by mothers.

Up Myers' Lane, Altoona, PA

HEATHER MYERS

This poem is gutted, like the first day of buck
brought back by my father—

the residual smell of cold air and woods
bound to the distant echo of loss.

I'm devoted to this place, to all of the faces
on the walls: wood-grain, antler mounts, fractured frames.

.

Home appears homely, peeling red and white,
where the heart has been tested.

There is nothing wrong with this ugliness.
Appearance is a matter of surviving.

A door is held open, ivy wrapped around
this doublewide where we 3, once 4, loved.

.

Despite all those odds, we are still here.
Roots bind where they must;

trees push through the foundation, beginnings unharmed.
There's nothing to be afraid of here—not anymore.

I fill towels with crab apples,
snap dandelion heads in a basket.

.

Inside, it's safe. Look at what I've kept—
take it as an offering of faith.

Fall, Central Pennsylvania

ERIN MURPHY

Altoona

Twang of a basketball
on the street, teen dribbling
his way to a pickup game,
the sky a bruised backdrop
for barren trees, cracked
macadam court lacquered
with golden ginkgo tears.

The Oldest Roller Coaster in the World

GABRIEL WELSCH

Lakemont Park, Altoona, PA

Embalmed in chipping paint, its spars yawed
with each bump and shimmy of the cart
that clattered down the slopes with all
the excitement of gravity. The biggest thrill
and scare was watching loved ones slide
down as the whole structure lurched
and groaned, as boards popped out
of their joints and snapped back, as metal
whined with strained age, as the operator—
a shambling fleshy boy doomed to a register
life or to be shot dead in a desert—
pushed each cart the first few feet,
to let it latch the pull chain
and lumber and clack up the first incline.

What it must have been like before flight—
when sixty miles per hour was enough,
we knew, to tear flesh from a face,
when the moon was still made mostly of myth—
to climb in a cart and creep up, to feel
for perhaps the first time, the way
the planet pulls you back, how long a falling
rush can last and not kill you, how the heart
can yearn to be yanked down. How clever
we've become to trick a body with mortal fear,
and to set it up so you can do it every day,
and pay for the privilege.

■ ■ ■

The Dairy Queen in DuBois, Pennsylvania Opens for Spring
ANTONIO VALLONE

The line of trucks and cars for the drive-thru
stretches out of the parking lot
down along the gravel berm of State Road 219,

windows rolled up tight
against the frigid air,
engines idling to run heaters.

We wait a half-hour or more
just to reach the speaker,
so we can place our first order in months.

Wearing winter coats,
our breath steaming the windows,
we need to park in neighboring dealership lots,

spooning the sweetest Blizzards ever
into our mouths, flakes floating out
of the cloudy sky like coconut or powdered sugar confections.

■ ■ ■

Toward Pittsburgh

MATT HOHNER

Night falls between mountain ridges,
open car windows & headlights on,
lullaby of tire song beside cow farms,
faded Mail Pouch Tobacco billboard
painted on the side of an old barn.
Fragrant alfalfa breath of summer
darkness settles like gossamer hands
enfolding a postage-stamp grass meadow,
edge of the woods by the interstate
south of Breezewood and the Turnpike;
U2's "Promenade" pulses low on the car stereo,
and you, behind the wheel, steady as years.
Light by quiet light, Edward Hopper's America
nestles into its small, white, box houses,
blue glow of computer and TV screens
spilling out through upstairs bedroom curtains.
Slide show, seaside town. Coca-Cola, football radio,
radio, radio, radio, radio, radio. . . .
Thin fog hugs the farm fields' edges;
fireflies glitter the treetops:
hold this moment, a little longer.

Windber Field

EDWARD HIRSCH

I don't know why
I thought it was a good idea
to bring Wilfred Owen's poem
on the colliery disaster of 1918
to that tiny high school class
in western Pennsylvania,
but soon they were writing
about smokeless coal
and black seams
in the ground, the terror
of firedamp, the Rolling Mill
Mine Disaster in Johnstown,
the closing of Windber Field,
the memory of standing
in a wide ring
around a mine shaft
to watch a man emerge
from the earth
like a god, a father
in an open cage
sailing across the sky.

I'm from a one-way bus ticket

BARBARA SABOL

Johnstown

straight out of that town—factory whistle, iron works,
a dusty smoke stacked skyline. The overheated river's hiss
beneath the Allegheny ridges. Percussion of jake braking
down the mountain's grade.

I'm from rock: granite, limestone, the grainy quarry water
that floated us anywhere else under the blossoming stars.
I'm from watermarks outside the 12th floor of Swanks,
cipher for the city's resilience—rising from two
flooded centuries; citizens still treading water.

I'm from the stone angel who guards the graves
of the unknown drowned at Grand View Cemetery;
from grandparents, never known, who rest there, too.

I'm from compound bow versus five-point buck; hunting season
trumped school. Back pocket Skoal halo. Red neck, blue collar,
pink collar, orange vest, my scratchy Catholic uniform.
Mass every morning. I'm from *O Sacred Head*—

we intoned the crown's piercing meanness, knelt before it
in clouds of frankincense. From the busy confessional—
a tether of venial sins: the cuss, stolen change, the hand
down there. Eve and her serpent; benign Blessed Mother.

I'm from nickel-a-prayer votives and the sanguine back of God
walking away from long unemployment lines—fathers, brothers, sons—
after the mill shut down. Labor unions fisted with dues.
I'm from too-proud-for-welfare, for food stamps.

I'm from green stamps, back yard gardens, sheets on the line,
the ham steak special at the Tick Tock Diner. St Casmir's, St Clement—
babushkas bent in prayer. From hand-rolled pirogie,
kielbasa reek, cold bottles of Pabst to cap long days.

I'm from the incline plane ascending from factory grind, up
to scrubbed suburbs then down again into the foundry's belly.
I'm from hand-stitched, home-cooked, nothing wasted.
Streetlight curfew, Archie comics, penny candy, four-square.

On frosted mornings, the dairy truck's clink announced the frisson
of ice-cold whole milk. From the bakery van still warm
white bread, Banana Flips; from canned goods stacked
against atomic fall-out. From the nimble illusion of safety.

I'm from Bob Prince's *swing and a miss,* from the hockey puck's slap
across War Memorial ice. JFK and Jesus, framed. I'm from whatever
is not polished, high falutin', not some Emily's idea of etiquette.

I'm from the sparking trolley that ferried us into town (antique traction token
still in my jewelry box). At home on wheels, I jumped its grooved tracks,
motored past the city's strict boundaries. Their alarm at the threshold;
no backward glance.

I'm from a country of regret, of missing that gritty Shangri-La where
no one left and I returned as guest. Now an exit off the turnpike,
between Lake Erie and the coast. The place a vapor, thick as myrrh,
a recurring dream.

In the Johnstown Flood Museum

RACHEL ROUPP

I walk along the wall of wreckage
with Abby, my former professor, now a friend.
I mirror her softness, following her slow steps
as she takes time to look at every piece of debris.
Among the broken boards, we find a wagon wheel,
twisted remnants of a porch, and several feet of fence.

When Abby told me about her mission
to learn all there is to know of the flood,
I invited myself on her trip to the museum—
secretly eager to learn from her again.

Leading me as if she is the museum's docent,
Abby points to a black-and-white photo of men gathered
in front of the South Fork Hunting and Fishing Club.
Shakes her head disapprovingly when she names them,
tells me they are the steel barons whose dam
caused the disaster. Overhead, whistles blow,

echoing the warning that came too late for so many.
We circle a model of the Conemaugh Valley,
tracing the path of the flood as sections of the little river
light up in time with the audio of water rushing.

We talk about another flood back home,
the Austin Dam Disaster, and how the valley
we are standing in now is so much like the one
200 miles north where we both grew up, 50 years apart.

Together we read the names of everyone lost.
I move closer, taking in the lavender scent that follows Abby,
the fluorescent light reflecting off her blond bob,

and the gentle jingle of her bracelets as she notes
the remarkable resilience of an unbroken plate.

We examine a quilt in a glass case. A group of women
worked on it just before the flood. When one was swept away,
the survivors made it a memorial to her. I take a picture of Abby
as she leans in, looking intently at the cactus flower pattern.
The label says the woman's name was lost. But all of her stitches stayed.

Steeltown Girls

SANDEE GERTZ

Johnstown
For Karen

Each day came down to an hour snuck behind
Stofko's alley, knelt on sagging concrete steps
while you rolled strawberry papers
and city boys rode bikes in Mad-Dog blush.
Other girls held flutes on stadium fields,
but we were left to watch the steel sky turn
its silver shades—the soap opera time
before parents came home from market or work.
In brutal cold, we'd walk straight into stiff wind,
hands cupped around our lighter, staring up
into stripped winter trees. Sometimes we'd pass
the hockey player with brown eyes and a stick—
a decent Catholic boy I'd lost to our madness.
As a mother now, I marvel at how we roamed
those cracking sidewalks, not much older than my son
trading baseball cards in his room.
I never told you that sometimes, in the seconds
before that first drag, I felt like running

home to stop the buzzing of the timer on the kitchen stove,
to wrap myself in the scent of mother's dough
rising there—her dishcloth folded perfectly
over the porcelain sink. Instead, we stepped
over hopscotch diagrams and planned
out lives with chalk left on the alley floor.
When I go back, Karen, I see those steps
and worn-out convenience stores.
I see toddlers who could be yours spinning
on playground swings.
New girls, in skirts too short for the chill,
cross corners of Messenger and Horner.
I see their eyes, slits of rainbow glass,
a sheen too bright to look into.

Arriving in Westmont
MATTHEW USSIA

My grandparents always wanted
to move up here, become Hilltoppers,
a nickname to show the millrats below
who won't be drowning in the next flood.
But for the looming fear of seasonal layoffs,
the closest my grandparents ever got
were graves in Grandview
I could never find on my own.

Settling for a West End duplex,
my grandfather worked first shift,
waiting for the bus before dawn,
losing his hearing in a shower of sparks.
My grandmother got bit by a rat
at the bakery where she worked.

I lost the socialist campaign buttons
I found in their attic.

On my way to pick up a dinner
that to them, a wedding feast
for me, is boring Saturday night takeout,
my un-calloused hands
sign away what would have been
a week's wages after the tip.
I've worked hard to get here
but never at the mouth of a blast furnace.

I was born during the last great flood,
a long-distance call from my mother
as she was going into labor
followed by catastrophe—

a local call three weeks later,
a ham radio operator
from Perth Amboy
talking to someone in Morrellville
claiming he was a friend
of my grandfather
who wanted to know if I was a girl or a boy.

His health failing,
they had to bring his first grandson
as soon as I was ready to travel.
When my parents called
from the opposite end of the turnpike,
he turned his chair around
with his back to the television.
For five hours, he stared at the door
waiting until he could hold me for the first and last time.

Somewhere in Pennsylvania

CHARLES CLIFTON

Upper Yoder, Cambria County

I decided to call myself
On the telephone, a black, heavy
Bakelite object fastened
To the kitchen wall, a coiled
Looping cord hanging down.
Slowly, I dialed my number.
The thing rang, and a person
Unknown to me answered.
"Hello? Who is this?"
For a moment I could not tell
Whether the words took shape
In the air or in my head
Or where it is that words
Are born, in the earliest light
Or in the questioning of the dark.
Do they flood up in a dream?
Do we only remember what
We think we say? I had not
Thought far and deep enough
To answer, but I held
The instrument close and
This time because there are
So many voices inside me
I heard a woman's voice,
Urgent and distraught—
"My God! Where in hell
Are you?" and I calmly replied,
"I am in here. I am just calling out."

Two Women Watched by Geese

ED OCHESTER

Armstrong County

in the lowlands, in the valley
of the Kiskiminetas: three geese,
white ones, silent and still, as the young women
stare at their chimney, or the blue November sky,
or the sun, one with her hand cupping her breast
as I drive by with boxes of books in the back seat,
Jerry Lee Lewis singing "It'll Be Me."

I wanted to tell you this, I think it may be
a love poem for prestidigitations
of this world and for you, for the plain
secrets we stand in and sometimes give way to,
loving for once where and what we are
like those women staring at loose bricks
or God, the geese too in their dim
imprinted lives thinking "mother!" and
that's ok, let them wiggle their tails,
they think they're happy but
they're happy. Love's in the saddle
sometimes, that dumb rider
that ties us to earth, like a thumb rubbing
the amethyst in my pocket or the Swiss coin
I've carried for years. "Don't speak" I'd say
if you were here. Years ago I threw
the gold ring into the corn on rock hill
and that's what I meant, I think: "be
the crop growing," though that was portentous—
it was the 70s, honey—and now I'd say, ok
love is a relative value but that's not bad
if you don't have any absolutes around and

anyway what do I have but the things in this world,
two women staring at the sun, three geese
enthralled as I ride by in the sealed car
and a mile or so down the road understand
for once and hit the horn and honk
and honk and honk.

Life on the Farm: Things to Count On

JOANNE GROWNEY

Meadow Lane Farm, Indiana County

I want to say how beautiful it was—but it was not. Each animal, each shed, each acre was useful; we kept them with good care and counted them, counted on them. One hundred forty acres, seven sheds. A white frame house, eight tall rooms and bath, a cellar with a dozen shelves for canned goods and four lines for laundry, a truck room for junk. We five in three bedrooms, four beds. One extra room for guests—my aunts. Our dining room with seven doors plus closets. A shed beside the corn crib with space for three wagons and a Plymouth. The barn with two mows for hay, a third for straw, a granary, a bathtub for livestock drinking, and six private stalls. Nine cows with two for milking, which I did. In seven days no minutes to be happy, no hours to be sad—not even when my father died. My mother's a good woman, worth three good women. For sixty years everyone has thought so, and more than a hundred have said. I've stopped counting.

Flight 93 National Memorial

JONSON MILLER

My not-yet "Nanny,"
not yet great-grandmother,
still a little girl
in bare feet
in the family fields
two miles east of Lambertsville.

Sometimes she shook her feet,
kicking off pebbles and clods,
before stepping.
And sometimes she swatted away
a skeeter or fly.

And sometimes she looked up.
But no jet or airplane
traced her sky
in those days.
But there were clouds
and rain.
Sometimes too little.
Sometimes too much.

What had some corner
of the Ottoman Empire
to do with her
and her potato patch?
And what did her corner
of Somerset County
to do with it?

Did her fine white house
rattle as the engines fired?

Did the ground bounce
beneath her?
Did she feel
the thump
across a century?

■ ■ ■

Until Darkness Comes

TODD DAVIS

*A 100-year-old gray and ductile iron foundry in Somerset, PA, has
issued a closing notice to workers, according to local reports.*

The white blades turn the sky: red-
eyed turbines blinking away the danger
of flying things. Small children float up
over the Alleghenies, parents chasing
the dangling ropes of weather balloons.
It's hard to predict when a storm may blow through.
A boy huddles by a bedroom window, wonders
if his father knows where every deer hides
on the mountain. It's his job to pull the sled
when his father makes a kill. He's been taught
in school the wind that circles the blades carries
electricity to the towns where steel was made.
Three years ago his sister disappeared in the clouds,
heat lightning like veins in the sky. She sends a letter
once a month with a weather report and money
their mother uses for an inhaler. Most of the coal dust
has settled, but fires burn on the drilling platforms
and the prehistoric gas smells like the eggs that spoil
in the hutch when the hens hide them.
The boy never wants to leave this place. Everything
important is buried here: his grandparents; a pocket knife

he stole from his best friend; the eye-teeth of an elk
he found poached at the bottom of a ravine. Yesterday
in the barn a carpenter ant drilled a hole. The boy bent
to the sawed-circle and blew into it, breath forced down
into darkness. He dreams each night of a horse galloping
from a barn, mane on fire like a shooting star. He prays
for a coat sewn from pigeon feathers, for small wings
to fly over the tops of trees where the children land
when their balloons begin to wilt. On summer evenings
barn swallows careen like drones, gorging dragonflies
that skim the swamp. The birds' blue shoulders cant
and angle, breast the color of the foundry's smokestacks
as they crumble beneath wrecking balls and bulldozers,
extinguishing the mill fires the boy's grandfather
never dreamt would go out.

VI. THREE RIVERS AND OLD MILLS

Pittsburgh

PATRICIA JABBEH WESLEY

This city of hills and rivers and steel,
always, the slant in the road,
the winding, falling cliffs, bridges, the escape
route, through which I come to find myself.
The city where, if you can cry loud
and hard, all you'll do
is replace river.

So, when the land comes sliding down
with house, pot, and pan during the rains,
you may not need to swim.
Your tunnels never lead me to the other place
I have lost, and in seeking to find
that place, I spill poetry
in small bits of broken crumbs,
in between the burnt metal pieces
of the past of my own city.

When I was a child,
I used to hear of this faraway place
where my people came to drown
themselves in search of America.
Pittsburgh, I do not know
if they found America, or if like me,
they came and went
away still longing for home.

Sometimes, for me, your roadways
lead to the Strip District for cassava roots
and fish and *gari* and sweet potato greens,
or sometimes, I find all the condiments
we could not bring with us

when we fled Africa.
So, I come to the Strip, where streets
are so jammed, if you do not pinch
yourself hard enough,
you might forget
you are not in an African market.

Pittsburgh, maybe someday
I may discover why you do not go away
even when I drive away to the small
town where I have buried myself
like a seed all these years.
Whether it is your merging rivers
or your hills rising into other hills
or your tunnels, or the ghosts
of my people who once lived here,
or just the wandering in my feet
looking for home,
I do not know.

■ ■ ■

Heart Fire

MAGGIE ANDERSON

Three months since your young son shot himself
and, of course, no one knows why. It was October.
Maybe he was following the smell of burning leaves
or the warmth of the fire in the heart, so hard
to locate in a country always readying for war.

One afternoon we sat together on your floor, drinking
tea and listening to Brahms on the radio. He would
have liked this music, you told me. He would have liked

everything I like now and what he wouldn't like I don't
like either. He has made the whole world look like him.

Today, driving into Pittsburgh, I see you are right.
The sky is cold blue like a shirt I once saw him
wear and the bare trees are dark, like his hair.
I see how vulnerable the grasses are, pale and flimsy
by the roadsides, trying to stand straight in the wind.

At Canonsburg, all the pink and green and purple houses
have the same slant of roof toward the hill, like toys
because I'm thinking about children, how sometimes
we want to give them up if they seem odd and distant,
yet even if they die before us, we cannot let them go.

I see your son in landscapes as I drive, in a twist
of light behind a barn before the suburbs start,
or under a suburban street light where a tall boy
with a basketball has limbs like those he had just
outgrown. Because I want to think he's not alone,

I invent for him a heart fire even the unenlightened
living are sometimes allowed to see. It burns past
the white fluorescence of the city, past the steel mills
working off and on as they tell us we need, or don't
need heavy industry for fuel or war. Your son

keeps me company, driving down the last hill into
Pittsburgh, in the tunnel as I push for good position
in the lanes. He is with me as I spot the shiny cables
of the bridge and gear down, as all the lights beyond
the river come on now, across his safe, perfected face.

Rivers

NATHANIEL RICKETTS

After Julie Swarstad Johnson

This story will end in sadness, the heavy flow's confluence at the wide
Ohio's mouth. The rivers of my childhood speak the same tongue
they did a hundred years ago. Flood to the roadside, freeze in
ice sheets thick enough to drive on. We've drowned these bodies
of water in shit and sulfur. I learned to backflip at rope swings tied
to train trestles that knew not to touch the water. We didn't know what
red lights flashing on the pylon meant—too much shit dumped to swim. That
red reflected instead in a rash that spread from my brush-burned knee
to my heel. *Antibiotics should solve this* said the doctor. *Not all rivers are*
meant for swimming. I didn't shit or swim for a week. Rivers are meant
instead for waste from mills, prisons, factories upstream. It all trickles down and
seeks its level. The water isn't water. You float a little bit easier. It retains its shape
a little longer than it should. It retains more than shapes between retaining walls.
It retains Lenape names, like *Oolikhanna: best flowing river of the*
hills, and *Menawngehella: ever washed out, ever collapsing river.*

Some Maps to Indicate Pittsburgh

TERRANCE HAYES

After Michael Baldwin and Mel Ramsden, the artists
who make up Art & Language

THE GREENFIELD MAP TO INDICATE PITTSBURGH ACCORDING TO
PENETRATION BY WORK BEYOND THE OBJECT

When I lived there a woman appeared at my stoop ruffled as someone
pulled from a nightmare. The rope burns were like burning bracelets on
her wrists; the blood in her blush gave her cheeks a sad sunset tint. She
was from a mill town, a desolate suburb of basements and cookouts, but
I let her in gushing, "Okay, okay, okay," with a sliver of pity. And later
when she put her fingers in my mouth, I tasted pepper. Nothing is sure
struck with darkness. No one's grief is ever as profound as your own.

THE HILL DISTRICT MAP TO INDICATE PITTSBURGH ACCORDING TO
DEVELOPMENT OF AN EVERYDAY CRITIQUE OF FALSE UNIVERSALS

It is perhaps impossible to have a neighborhood without neighbors and
a market, but the ghosts believe otherwise. Dust on the theater mar-
quee is undetectable in the twilight. Stand in any district cemetery and
there will be a low singing though there will be no singers. The faint
stain on the library steps may well be blood, but there will be no corpse.
Place your ear to the road and you will hear someone screaming below.

THE NORTHSIDE MAP TO INDICATE PITTSBURGH ACCORDING TO
DEVELOPMENT OF THE POLITICS OF REPRESENTATION

Let us look at the North Shore's modernity as would a boy sitting on
the bottom of the Monongahela, a muddy word that means "soft, col-
lapsing slopes." Gravity is the only true geography. Rachel Carson, Andy
Warhol, Roberto Clemente, no one lives forever here except as bridges
under which boys hide from authority and rainfall, the downpour of sta-
dium banter and rebuke. If you fall into the water, you will climb out of
the water blacker than you used to be.

THE SOUTHSIDE MAP TO INDICATE PITTSBURGH ACCORDING TO CAPACITIES TO GLIMPSE THE POSSIBILITY OF THE ABSENCE OF PRESENCE, AND THUS THE POSSIBILITY OF CHANGE

After two or three rivers and bus transfers you arrive at a boulevard of dive bars with scarred tabletops. You find patrons with mouths stretching literally ear to ear. They have an absurd number of imperfect teeth and miniature noses. They want to tell you immigrant tales featuring steel, steamships, and orphans. When they invite you to brawl at two a.m. do not refuse. *Brawl* is merely another beautiful word for *dance*.

THE LAWRENCEVILLE MAP TO INDICATE PITTSBURGH ACCORDING TO UNDERSTANDING REALITY AS HYPERREALISTIC

Borders make no sense, but are as familiar and awkward as one body entering another. Imagine a future in which all bridges must be rebuilt and the fundamentals of making an ax from a sharpened stone or making fire have been forgotten—can you make fire or an ax? If you are to live here on out as a bridge, you must never say, "Get off my back." You must say what the water says, "Everybody sing to me, everybody sing with me," and sing.

Dreaming Door

JAN BEATTY

For Don

You brought donuts in the morning of our first days and
we watched the great rivers through my South Side windows/everything
swelling, we ate in the turquoise kitchen and opened the dreaming door:
our Pittsburgh rolling by on the coal barges, the P&LE carting steel
to the still-rising cities of the West, a couple speedboats
running the dirty summer Monongahela,
you on your way to work. I said *no one's ever*
been this nice to me as I walked you the 52 steps down
from my third-floor apartment, you tilted your head,
looking at me in a way I'd never seen:
like I was the most sublime person,
your blue eyes seeming truly puzzled:
I haven't even started to love you yet,
and at the door the world barreling through—
this time with gifts, fierce fires,
and planets of luck.

■ ■ ■

On the Way Up: Pittsburgh StepTrek

PAOLA CORSO

In memory of Antonio Calderone

As we climb these steps
look out on our city
ribbons of river
bridges arching their golden spines
duet of valley and hill

as we look out
to buildings huddled together
a fountain pluming in the mist
an incline zippering up its track

remember the immigrant
who came here
his chisel and his mallet
to build these stairs
with concrete fists

remember him
on a steep hill
standing on an edge
the width of his feet
the width of misstep and fall

standing with his pick
picking away at a glacier of rock
dirt up his nose
dust in his eyes
grit between his teeth

and down his neck
a foreman who brushes his topcoat
adjusts his bowler hat
glances at his pocket watch
to time lunch

each step we take is
a step in the past
our ancestors
their uncertain futures
we on steady ground

each step, a step in the future
new immigrants
on the way up
and for every step we take
they take three
one forward, one backward, one waiting

■ ■ ■

Family Reunions

MARK SABA

It's the sixty-second year
family reunion, progeny of twelve siblings
over a hundred in attendance
on a beautiful day in Pittsburgh
the smoky sky now clear
lots of *kiełbasa* on the grill
a softball game, well-attended keg,
water balloon toss.

On the banner: steamship tickets
from Bremen, 1903, a Croatian town of origin,
marriage certificate, naturalization papers.

The party goes well into evening,
beer keg tapping dry, obligatory shots
of *šljivovica,* mandolin music holding steady

while all over the country
stand candlelight vigils
for those entering by another door,
the southern gate, where no statue
raises her arm in welcome
and all are quarantined,

children in one cage,
parents in another—
family reunions lost in translation.

■ ■ ■

John Kane

MAURICIO KILWEIN GUEVARA

This is a true story about the immigrant Kane,
how a hundred years ago in Pittsburgh he painted boxcars
black in the filthy car yards of the Baltimore & Ohio,
one after another until lunchtime. On his break
he'd mix up brighter colors; one side of the next
boxcar would be his wide, steel canvas. In the plain style,
high as he could reach with the green brush,
he'd make hills grow up, dreaming always of Scotland.
Up a stepladder he'd climb to have the sky
a field of pure blue and clouds
floating away, above the highland.
Down on earth he'd put two small girls beside a river,
a red maple, and the words *John Kane*
just as the whistle blew.

At one o'clock he'd start to cover his work with black paint.

Cinderman

ANDRENA ZAWINSKI

Those Saturdays when he'd pull an extra shift,
I'd trail the buckled sidewalk to the shadowy
pedestrian tunnel. As he checked to see me backing
along fences, ducking into bushes, I watched him.

Long legs sure in stride marching off to make another
month's rent, black lunchbox swaying, latch ticking
in sync with his steps in clunky steel-toed boots,
he smoothed his work shirt, straightened his cap,

a young man, his worth tied to being of use,
laboring toward a whistle and a timecard
at the end of the stretch of an extra stint. Back home,
I would wait for his stories to spill through the flat:

His pal Pokey Pete screwing up on the line again,
bad joke Old Joe told that made him laugh anyway,
Foreman Mack crazy enough to get married
to the shop secretary in these times at his age.

Like any Cinderman, he'd scrub the dark from his face
and hands making a murky mess of the porcelain sink,
slump at the kitchen table with a shot of Smirnoff
where earlier he gulped down a brew of Maxwell House.

I lived in this world of a man whose muscles always ached,
who drank too much, who never could make ends meet,
lived for him to pull me onto his lap each night to nuzzle
under his arm, fall asleep in the musky scent of him,

until he'd heave me up with a grunt, trudge up the flight
of stairs, loose steps groaning under the weight
of my limp body leaden with sleep, arms and legs draped
about the curve of his hunched back. Sandman, in my eyes.

Nine Irenes

JOCELYN HEATH

Potato-thick Slovak names drop off your tongue:
Dankocic. Paholic. You tap your cigarette

to a cadence of nine, girls from days of jacks
and school books now an old woman's memory game

against herself. *Sabucha* with the long braids,
Irene the year's favored name, its meaning *peace*.

You chant on: *Talepka* whose father spat black dust
and struck her red behind her knees.

And the steel-choked city descends through smoke
as your eyes fix on a far-off street, The Hollow

where *Tanczak* and *Vodjak* swing a clothesline
you jump under. *Zahorsky* claps rosy hands

that reach for you at Sunday mass. *Peace be with you*
nine times over, murmured through incense.

Markovic, the twin you never matched, grabs your hand
and pulls you homeward, through the alley's stink

of fish and cabbage, to the mother who loved her better.
We notice that your night is falling,

and though you forgot *Gabovic*, we won't tell you.
A touch brings you back to present peace.

Next month, another will go missing—
soon, only the sidewalk slap of the empty rope, turning.

Requiem for the Living

JOSEPH BATHANTI

When I pray for Phil on my morning run,
as I always have, and register
a small detonation in my chest
that he is gone, I call his name

loudly enough that hoodlum crows,
of whom I'm so sentimentally fond, lift
from the towering pines, as they call back.
Dorothy Day believed prayers for the dead

help them while they were living on earth.
I don't understand this,
but Phil and Rose are together tonight.
Everything is ahead; and, if I'm quiet,

for just another moment,
I'll find my hand upon the secret panel
that swings open their world,
and there they'll be—on the balcony

of their Polish Hill walk-up
on Beethoven Street.
It's April, a week from Easter.
Spring has promised not only to stay,

but dazzle: green and yellow,
trees and flowers, a madhouse of birds,
so warm, Phil wears his purple shirt,
the sun in Pittsburgh a miracle.

My impulse is to barge in, interrogate them.
But this is taboo.

Absolved of the dark caprice of time,
like postulants, they plan the future.

Phil paints the Sycamores,
his famous triptych of enormous oils—
studies of a mythic tree in Highland Park,
that grows at the entrance of a black block tunnel.

Rose's mauve batik dries on a chair's ladder-back,
her hair the pert yellow of pears,
skin pale as frost.
Cigarette smoke swaddles

fetal angels at their heads.
The chartreuse Allegheny
rolls toward the Monongahela.
You can see it from their fire escape.

You can see the gardens
the old Italian people in Bloomfield
plant on their roofs.
You can see Liberty Avenue.

■ ■ ■

Good Friday, Schenley Park, Pittsburgh, 2020

JIM DANIELS

A man and a woman on the bridge
above me in this city of bridges—
every bridge a bridge of sighs today/
this week/month/year—hold hands
with two toddlers.
                    Alone beneath them
on the park trail, I hear laughter

and look up. They let loose
tiny plastic figures with parachutes
and the wind takes them.
                              I climb
up crooked steps to find them
at the end of the bridge—one child
now carried—we keep
our distance, given the times.
The other child runs eager
to descend and chase
their dreams.
                    The man waves
to me. No one else out to witness
the joy. If I could bloom out
of my black mask
I would.
            I wave back
and the held child waves to me
over his mother's shoulder.
Then, a sudden snow squall—
upward from the hollow
and over the bridge. Even the hawk
cruising the hollow's seam
seems to stutter in flight.
Hard horizontal pellets
knock petals
                    from blossoming trees.
The family disappears down
the steps to follow their plan
but I fear they've lost sight of it
as I've lost sight of mine.
I do not touch the railing.
I stutter myself into a sigh
on the bridge—around me,
white snow rising,
                        white petals falling.

Dioramas

KRISTIN KOVACIC

Carnegie Museum of Natural History, Pittsburgh

My son presses his hot palms, lips
against the glass. He is one, and lost
to me on the scrub of the African plain,
the precise teeth of marmot and lynx.
How to keep him from savagery, the tender
licks of animal tongues? We are killing
a long winter afternoon, as we stroll
the dark marble streets of life interrupted,
the elk locked in battle, the lion clinging
by her claws to the Arab courier's camel.
Every lit world draws him in, takes
ticking seconds of his spectacular childhood.
When we emerge into the faded rushing day
I know that it is gone like all the others
and what I will become for him some day.
A woman in a glass box, interrupted
at some ordinary business, some misery
or pleasure. No longer his mother, but a place
for him to visit, and almost touch,
winter afternoons, out of the elements.

Tuesday Morning

SHARON FAGAN MCDERMOTT

How prompt we are to satisfy the hunger and thirst of our bodies.
How slow to satisfy the hunger and thirst of our souls.
—HENRY DAVID THOREAU

Blue truck's driving too fast up Cromwell,
the brick road around the corner from my house.
6:20 AM and he's all reckless disarray, blows
through the stop sign. I'm glad the two little
backpack boys aren't up and walking to school yet.
It doesn't take much to set my teeth on edge anymore.
This world's a careless place, a place without care
more often than I'd like. But on the next block,
Yvonne who owns the florist shop is getting into
her flowered van and smiles. I say, *You're up early*.
Love my work, she shoots back, without
a trace of irony. So now my mind's turned back to all
the flowering—dogwoods, pink and cream, mixing
petals with the light rain. Much of this year,
I felt broken, sewn up, unsure of what holds
a soul together, unsure of what binds us to
grace or strength in order to move forward.
It's Tuesday morning in the rain. Each brick
on the brick houses I pass shimmers dawn.
My beautiful dog will need toweling
when we get home. On a neighbor's stoop
I'm surprised by the sight of two white cats.
I name one Chaos. I name one Serenity.

Then It Was Simple

CORTNEY DAVIS

You walked up Sylvandell Drive
on the coldest night. Soon, Father would be home,

easing the gray Plymouth into the one-car garage,
and Mother, who was always home,

would be cooking meatloaf with its two
sizzling strips of bacon. Snow stung your face,

snow crunched beneath your boots and the glow
from Pittsburgh's steel mills hung in the sky.

In such a place, in 1955, Mary could appear to you
casually, leaning out the neighbor's window,

a blue domestic angel with a movie star face,
round arms crossed on the sill, her brown hair

in a friendly page boy. She smiled, you smiled back,
your sled tugging behind you,

grounding you, and the frozen snow and the whirl of gravity
holding you, and Mary,

as if she were not from another world,
so happy to see you.

Homage to Sharon Stone

LYNN EMANUEL

It's early morning. This is the "before,"
the world hanging around in its wrapper,
blowsy, frumpy, doing nothing: my
neighbors, hitching themselves to the roles
of the unhappily married, trundle their three
mastiffs down the street. I am writing this
book of poems. My name is Lynn Emanuel.
I am wearing a bathrobe and curlers; from
my lips, a Marlboro drips ash on the text.
It is the third of September twenty°°
And as I am writing this in my trifocals
and slippers, across the street, Sharon Stone,
her head swollen with curlers, her mouth
red and narrow as a dancing slipper,
is rushed into a black limo. And because
these limos snake up and down my street,
this book will be full of sleek cars nosing
through the shadowy ocean of these words.
Every morning, Sharon Stone, her head
in a helmet of hairdo, wearing a visor
of sunglasses, is engulfed by a limo
the size of a Pullman, and whole fleets
of these wind their way up and down
the street, day after day, giving to the street
(Liberty Avenue in Pittsburgh, PA)
and the book I am writing, an aspect
that is both glamorous and funereal.
My name is Lynn Emanuel, and in this
book I play the part of someone writing
a book, and I take the role seriously,
just as Sharon Stone takes seriously
the role of the diva. I watch the dark

cars disappear her and in my poem
another Pontiac erupts like a big animal
at the cool trough of a shady curb. So,
when you see this black car, do not think
it is a Symbol For Something. It is just
Sharon Stone driving past the house
of Lynn Emanuel who is, at the time,
trying to write a book of poems.

Or you could think of the black car as
Lynn Emanuel, because, really, as an author,
I have always wanted to be a car, even
though most of the time I have to be
the "I," or the woman hanging wash;
I am a woman, one minute, then I am a man,
I am a carnival of Lynn Emanuels:
Lynn in the red dress; Lynn sulking
behind the big nose of my erection;
then I am the train pulling into the station
when what I would really love to be is
Gertrude Stein spying on Sharon Stone
at six in the morning. But enough about
that, back to the interior decorating:
On the page, the town looks bald
and dim so I turn up the amps on
the radioactive glances of bad boys.
In a kitchen, I stack pans sleek with
grease, and on a counter there is a roast
beef red as a face in a tantrum. Amid all
this bland strangeness is Sharon Stone,
who, like an engraved invitation, is asking
me, *Won't you, too, play a role?* I do not
choose the black limo rolling down the street
with the golden stare of my limo headlights
bringing with me the sun, the moon, and
Sharon Stone. It is nearly dawn; the sun

is a fox chewing her foot from the trap;
every bite is a wound and every wound
is a red window, a red door, a red road.
My name is Lynn Emanuel. I am the writer
trying to unwrite the world that is all around her.

The Great Beauty

TOI DERRICOTTE

In the movie, flamingos migrate over Rome and rest
overnight on the terrace of Jep Gambardella, so that,

in the rose light of dawn, he walks out to find his saintly
old guest, Sister Maria, meditating among a flamboyance—

a hundred stand on pink stilt-like legs with roseate plumes
and beaks sturdy as lobster crackers. Some rest on one leg

or sit with legs tucked under them; some halfheartedly peck
at stone—as if they might find bread crumbs from last night's party.

But all are quiet. "I know all their Christian names,"
she brags under her breath to no one, or perhaps to God.

I never received such tidings from the universe, but Saturday

on my walk, checking my Fitbit again (3000 for an old lady is good), I
heard wing beats and cooing, and then, almost under my arm, one flew up

nearly brushing my hand—as if intentional—then twenty, thirty coming
from behind, as if they were pouring out of my back. I couldn't tell how

many would arrive, a hundred resting on the branches of a tree, and some
flying up to a balustrade, sitting in a long row stolid as judges. Why can't I

take evidence seriously? I (who half believe in God) spoke playfully—
not even remembering I had watched Sister Maria's flamingos two nights

before—"What are *you* doing here?" as if they were old friends or a bunch
of my kids showing up out of nowhere. I watched for a while and when
     they

just sat there, turning their heads, I went on with my walk—another 1500
steps to go. By the time I was almost home, I had persuaded myself: it was

only pigeons; perhaps hungry. But then they came back, from all around,
as if they were rising up out of the ground, as if they were being made

right before me, all the sounding wings, air whipping and breaking,
their gray-and-pink presences as if convincing me.

Doppelgänger

JUDITH VOLLMER

Old Peoples Savings Bank on Pittsburgh's "Wall Street"

Tower of verdigris and terracotta rosettes,
temple of vaults and glass walls
trembling, fractured,
you've stitched yourself

onto me, second spine
or mind, shadow and
conductor, my walk interrupted
by your twenty-seven

convex windows moon-silvered

so I'm spangled, tilted.
Lounging genius, once
you threaded the war money
of the city fathers

up your spiral stair
counting, hiding
sons of the rich
from The Ardennes to Kandahar.
Now your bronze doors

won't open
while you fashion,
tongue new money
through your neo-

Romanesque arches
damp with blankets and piss.

■　■　■

Ink

YONA HARVEY

Ink marks the spot you need
to remember lest you be lost
in that foliated forest
of a mind in which you go
round & round & round
in silence rather than
the "tumult & the shouting"
because, anyway, your voice
would get drowned out

if you went on like that, the echo
"flung up to heaven" & swallowed
in one airy gulp, the clouds
& absence, of rain hovering overhead,
no matter, you're not really in a forest,
that was just an option, an escape
you scribbled with your pen filled with black
shine & black smear from your fingers black
slick black shadow black direction
not shady or fearsome the black
of which you're made went to press
in the *Pittsburgh Courier* or *Amsterdam News*
or in the notations of Ida B. Wells
before a lecture or rebuttal, the ink flowed
& could not be deleted like a tweet
but maybe burned like paper
or too many twisted limbs & fruits
or churches or houses or whole towns,
"I heard tell," someone said, or "ink it,"
someone said later, said, "Let's go to press,"
or "Mine eyes have seen them
that sit in darkness," or "I've been lost
in the midnight of your irises"—someone
toss you a drinking gourd,
there's so much you
want to say about August & thirst
& playwrights inking the voices
of neighborhoods in the Hill Districts
or the systematic somethings recalled
in the corner booths of diners capturing
the sounds of the familiar men
& later being called across state lines
to finish that work with unfamiliar alphabets
away from homegrown tyrannies
conjuring Pittsburgh
scenes in new landscapes

like the ones we traversed way back when
& even now, of course, against the shucking
& the jiving the sideways slander
the questionable scripts & screenplays,
ink in archive, in sermon, in travel passes
transcended, someone had a mind to ink
as in John Biggers's gaze or Elizabeth Catlett's
linocuts, someone had a mind to say,
"Cleanse your face of cork & ash,
this story is going to print." & this is the ink
we splash whether we are those who leave
or those who stay & fight
the splendid errors of this place.

■ ■ ■

At the Cathedral of Hope

JANETTE SCHAFER

In Pittsburgh, after a cold dark winter—
    after the sun was hiding somewhere further south—

In this chapel of urban sanctuary—
    in this diamond of perfect acoustics—

A singer with a mouth full of petals
    altered a season of silence,
        brought the crickets and poems of spring;

and neither angels or pearls,
    or couples running nude through a park,
        or the wet grass of meadow sticking to the legs,

could have spoken the wanton language
    of the season so well—
        (and I am still translating.)

A Minyan Plus One

PHILIP TERMAN

For the eleven victims of the Tree of Life Synagogue
shootings in Pittsburgh, PA, on October 27, 2018.

was taken from us on the Shabbat,
the most joyous of the holidays,
the only holy day even God Himself

celebrates, the emulation of Eden,
the day of completion. Before
they could perform the service, before

they could take their seats and begin
the prayers, before the ark opened
and the Torah revealed,

before they could rise and sway
and chant their portion, the book
opened like wings in their steady hands,

though they know the blessings by heart.
I didn't know them, but I knew them
in the way we know those raised,

no matter where we originated,
in the same beliefs our ancestors
inherited all the way back into

those mysterious origins,
those stories of creation and exile,
of miracles and complicated kings,

of commandments and wisdoms—
"welcome the stranger"—
spread across the millennium.

We suffer the same persecutions,
celebrate the same triumphs, chant,
in the same order, the blessings,

hour after hour, holiday after holiday,
generation after generation,
Torah portion after Torah portion.

Before that week's Torah portion,
a minyan plus one was taken.
When they would have once again

heard the story of when Abraham,
our first Patriarch of Chutzpah,
approached and argued with the Lord:

"Will you sweep away the righteous
with the wicked?" And He answered:
"For the sake of ten, I will not destroy it."

And so, as on other days, on that day—
He did. He allowed the wicked
To sweep away the righteous.

*And when the LORD had finished
speaking with Abraham, He left.*
And took a minyan plus one.

And Abraham returned home.

°Minyan—A quorum of ten Jewish adults over the age of thirteen required for traditional Jewish public worship.

Dear Mr. Rogers Revisited

SHIRLEY STEVENS

That time I found my goldfish floating
at the top of the tank, you told me Death happens
in this life. I didn't want to accept that fact, but you helped,
even said a prayer when I buried him under our rose bush.
You were there to comfort me when I feared
being sucked down the drain during my bath
or down the toilet when I flushed. You always knew
the right thing to say. In September when the plane
crashed and crashed and crashed
into The World Trade Center, you were there,
told me parents would keep me safe.
When I sat cross-legged on the carpet beside Brother,
you said there was a holy space between the TV and us,
and I believed you.

Each day you entered my living room smiling,
slipped into the cardigan your mother knitted for you,
zipped it up the front then half way down again.
When you changed from loafers into sneakers,
I wished that I could loop and tie my laces the way you do.
You smiled and said, "You can. Keep practicing."

Tonight I stand outside the synagogue in Oakland;
my candle wavers in the wind and rain.
The Tree of Life's inverted,
roots in heaven, branches here on Earth.
"Look to the helpers," you remind me.
I promise to join in nurturing the almond,
believe it will blossom once again in spring
in the neighborhood.

The Jailer's Wife's Epithalamium
KATE SOFFEL 1902

ERINN BATYKEFER

In the warden's quarters, a home
like another cell: concrete floor under carpets,
barred windows behind lace.
Friends called at first, charmed by the thrill
of being escorted through prison gates
for tea. They peered through the curtains
at murderers' row and shivered,
and they didn't come back, certainly not
after the Biddle boys moved in.
I ironed my husband's shirts each day,
so he could deal punishment
in neat cuffs as if it was a solemn privilege.
He never wavered from his mission,
no matter how consuming. I tried
to be consumed with him. I walked across
the mist-cloaked yard with scripture,
I ministered to those condemned to death.
It was meant as a mercy to them, a doorway
into another life, but then a story scraped at me,
a kinship: Ed Biddle's hands were those of a banker
or a clerk. Not a butcher. Not him.
I notched the dark stones with days
as if I were prisoner too, punished unjustly
for what I might, but did not, do.
When I had been walled-in so long
I no longer knew the sky unslashed by iron,
a candle flamed to life in his cell
across the lowering blue of the prison yard,
and I struck a match to answer it.
My skin burned beneath my shift
with the silent language that exists
between me and the most lethal of killers.
I touched the letters at brow, throat, heart,

and planned an escape like pulling on a coat
against the cold: a way to choose my fate,
to own it. Ed Biddle's face half-shadowed by bars
smiled into the dark as we talked, and I knew
there would be a night when no light appeared
across the yard, that he would be gone
before the claxon sounded, and without me.
I spelled out the fiction I chose instead—
that I was loved, and would not be trapped
forever without cause—and kept my faith.

■ ■ ■

Walking in Homewood Cemetery During the Pandemic
JUDITH SANDERS

Like dogs, we need
    to be walked.
Sidewalks get crowded,

but the cemetery's lanes
    curve empty under waving trees,
and the dead don't sneeze.

They maintain social distance,
    six feet under. We're safer here
than among the living.

Strange to be alive
    among the dead—
but we are always.

You'd expect stumps
    bare as skeletons,
the sky low and dark

as a coffin lid,
     leering vultures,
littered bones.

But it's Eden here,
     the fresh leaves
pretty as youth.

We pause and note,
     this one had a friend's name,
that one was young,

that one had my birth year,
     but the implications
don't stick.

Here, mourners plant pinwheels,
     carve nicknames,
praise, and rhymes,

there, set stones,
     as hard and enduring
as grief.

Most lie unremembered,
     even grandees
in Ozymandian tombs.

This gravel path
     leads to a weedy field
soon sown with coffins.

Plenty of room—
     unless the pandemic
spikes.

This cemetery could engulf
    the city, since the dead
outnumber the living.

While they decompose,
    prone under the grass,
we sniff lilacs they fertilize,

hum to birdsong
    like odes, not dirges,
joke and hold hands.

Because for now,
    we can leave.

The Lost Continents

GARY FINCKE

Except for Etna's last owners who stall the arrival
    of eminent domain,
Everyone has died or forgotten about this avenue
    of porches and chairs
Not packed, not all of them, by the old women who sit
    to shame the bulldozers.
And what can I say, accidental visitor, to three
    of them settled in front
Of sooty windows where the future's freeway will please
    commuters to Pittsburgh?
That *ruin* is always prelude to developers, *forgetting*
    the great synonym
For improvement? In the wrecker's nearest empty lot
    I scrape my shoes
And say nothing about the nostalgia of men who search

for countries sunk miles
Beneath the oceans, not settling for Atlantis,
    so serious about
Our storybook origins, someone, not far from this street,
    finances a search
For Lemuria, the lost continent of the Indian Ocean.
    I say nothing
About the men who want to set the winch of wishful thinking
    to the weight of Mu,
Raise that shipwrecked world from deep in the Pacific
    for possible treasure.
Rocking in their wicker chairs, Mrs. Bondula and her sister
    might listen to me,
The aging neighborhood boy, say those are two more sites
    for the Garden of Eden
And fossils fortunate to belief. That while they dry, while
    those new continents
Open to the migration of seeds and birds, our children
    are driving over
A thousand sites of lost things to arrive at the rented rooms
    of personal history,
Their children, in turn, repeating "What?" as they marvel
    and brush themselves
Like the lucky at crash sites, listening to the old tales
    of emigration when
The oceans, accordingly, rose, when the displaced seas
    sloshed up the coasts
With the perpetual dreams of bonding that suggest
    someone will surely
Translate a prophecy scrawled in the waterproof words
    of a mother tongue,
Someone verifying its age to refute the skeptics,
    someone funding
Search after search for a swath of definitive relics while
    the world moves inland
To begin the long wait for the resurrected landscape.

Just now, these widows
Named Florence and Pearl and Heloise are singing
    the ancient round
Of *What's Happened?* So let me listen to them saying
    "You'll see some day"
In the terse tongue of the experienced. Let me enter
    the shops posted
Everything Must Go to buy one of everything
    in a gesture
Of tiny, fruitless charity. Let me carry away
    a miscellany
Of hand-painted animals, a dozen antique beer cans
    for a basement shelf.
Let me sit for shoe repair, stumble on the sudden lift
    of unworn heels
Before my hair is trimmed and oiled by the barber
    who's been doing
Crossword puzzles all day. Let me climb the steep street
    to the overlook
Soon to be blasted. Let me balance on the guardrail
    that has borne my name
And the names of a thousand children who signed
    the low, public wall
Of romanticism. Let me step up to teeter over
    everything about
To be buried. And let me challenge my balance
    while I memorize
The landfill where our descendants will test that mud
    of possible heaven,
And, whether settled or not, excavate its shale for the bones
    of paradise,
Traveling, if they discover nothing, to the next
    long-buried town,
Carrying the cumulative fear of faith to dive for
    the lost world not yet named.

Garlic Mustard

SHEILA SQUILLANTE

Squirrel Hill

It's raining and I don't want to go
with her into the small, sparse woods next
to the garage. She calls it "the forest"
and I remember the circle of stones
my sister and I built in our own
suburban copse. I'm tired and it's raining,
but this was my idea—
to go with Josie and sit with nature, to look

for things we've overlooked and turn
them into lines. She wants us to write together,
and I want her to feel mind and body-calm.
But more, even, than that, I want her to trust
her mother's word. So, under umbrellas we go.
I follow her to the base of the hill where I stop
and complain about the mud, but she keeps climbing.

She always keeps climbing. I am wearing the wrong shoes,
the wrong attitude. *Say yes!* I say in my head.
*So you'll get dirty, so what? Your daughter
doesn't care.* But Josie comes down
to me—not capitulation but compromise
because she's spotted her subject: a crop
of bitter, young Garlic Mustard blooming, lush
and invasive, below a canopy of dried-out vines.

We squat together and stroke the soft green leaves,
which can belong anywhere if they insist.
She writes in her notebook, *soft leaves.* She writes,
white petals and *breeze.* I am trying to teach my daughter

how to pay attention. How to see. I write in my
notebook the words *scentless* and *grassy.* I write

pink umbrella, but it's stopped raining. I hear cars,
creak of the locust trees, our breathing, so many birds.

■ ■ ■

The Allegheny River

JEFF OAKS

To stand near a river and feel the great slippery weight
sliding past like one of those long trains from childhood
you watched go on forever, waiting in a car
with one parent or the other sighing, tapping fingers
on the outside of the car door. The enormous water which
begins as threads, a luminescent rustle among pine needles
against old granite, which wind themselves together, falling toward
the lowest places it can find. Your mother dead now.
Mine soon to follow. Then suddenly another friend's mother gone.
The first poet I read who wasn't dead is now dead.
And I'm standing by the river watching it move on.
The dog is fetching the sticks I throw into it. He's just
learned how to swim, and now he comes out of the fat water
and spins his skin first one way and then another,
flinging water the way I used to think porcupines could
spray their quills. To stand and just watch its tons
move, slide, press on, all the weight of water,
without choice, without a thought for what goes into it,
or where it goes or what comes out again. To throw
a stick back into it for the dog to rescue.

D++ Dek Hockey League Champions (2012)

MIKE GOOD

Penn Hills

Sunshine likes right wing better now anyways. They say
he's not as mad as he used to be. Stress-fractures. Swollen-patella.
When the ref drops the ball, pushing and shoving resumes.
He says, "I'm not saying I'm not trying to brag. I'm harder to move."

Knee-brace. Stress. Swelling. Fractured
nine years. Going up the boards, taking a hit when he couldn't
move. "I'm not saying I'm not trying to brag."
It's as if everyone in adult league failed at something.

After nine years of trying not to budge, not even an inch,
they tell the same stories every year. They shake hands through broken
    teeth:
they thought, everyone in adult league failed at something. When Sunshine
    was a kid,
he flipped the ball onto his parents' roof, and it trickled like rain into the
    lawn.

Drinking through broken mouths, sharing the same stories every year.
Things are easier to hit when they're still, but harder to hit in stride.
Sunshine bobbles into the zone, stick raised, hits a wormburner nowhere,
takes a swing at the defenseman's shins. The ref calls him off the dek.

Things are harder to hit in-stride but there's no time to stand still.
Here, in Penn Hills, they run, never skate. They say it's not real hockey.
The ref calls them off the dek.
The ball can be difficult to predict. They are here and they are not,

and they run now with toenails falling off. Another ACL pops.
They're still out there, playing, spinning and hitting backwall too often.

Outside, people can be hard to predict. On the dek people are mostly who
    they are.
Sunshine knows they're not like some of the guys who've haunted this
    place forever.

Too often, even now, falling, hitting outside the cage.
Sunshine used to be bad at this. He likes the right wing better now
anyways. He's not like some of the guys who've haunted this place forever.
Shoving and pushing resumes. The ref throws a ball.

■ ■ ■

Father Rodney

RICHARD PIERCE

In the ancient Greek, "liturgy" means "work done for the people."

Someone calls around 9:30,
as he's brushing his teeth for bed.

An Orthodox in a nursing home
has passed in McKeesport,
and the priest is out-of-town.

Up since five, he drives
the hour north from Carmichaels, prays
for the soul, anoints the body.

Earlier, after Matins and the First Hour
and taking a call from Bishop Mitrophan,

it was fifty minutes south
to his mission church in Fairmont
for the Hours, Confession, and Liturgy,

then back to St. George's
for Great Vespers at four.

Most days, he reads the Bible
an hour aloud onto cassettes,
gives away full sets as gifts.

He's read it cover-to-cover
thirty-five times.

He prays the Jesus Prayer
when he drives
or returns calls from parishioners
on his cell.

He always wears pit boots
with his cassock.

It's after midnight as he sits
to untie them.

Past the picture window,
the coal stacks of the power plant
flash white into the sky.

Down the hill in low fog,
the Monongahela.

The plant's been closed for years.

First Day of the Hunt

PAULA BOHINCE

Plum

The schools always close, knowing
we're so country
all our boys will skip anyway,

and the valley rises together before dawn—

daughters pulling wool caps
past fathers' ears, reciting the profound
and elemental list:

rifle, rounds, knife, rope,

only to send each heavy man to the woods
where he'll slump the day in drifts
of solitude and prayer

while most deer stay down, evading
the unlucky, the night spent

visiting cousins: stroking curves
of antler, lengths of blood-stiffened fur.

Every year it's the same
soft and deliberate snow prints,
the waiting—

as if mine could emerge from his last hiding
place and walk the evening,
empty-handed, to me.

River of Mantises

GERALDINE CONNOLLY

Irwin, Westmoreland County

I watched a jar once
erupt into a river of mantises.
A blowsy afternoon. Grade
school. Pennsylvania.

The sugar-spun egg case hung
inside a jar from a twig.
We stared at its blankness.

Then suddenly, there
in the middle of math class
asleep over multiplication,

we woke to a jitterbug
of foaming bodies
that bubbled up

from the hardened froth
into a pale volcano
of sticks with giant ivory eyes.

All those bodies poured
out of the jar
down the windowsill

scampering over books
and crayons onto the floor.
When someone opened the door,

we all streamed,
a tangle of jumping legs,
thin arms, into a field,

to watch the mantises
tumbling into the green.
We followed them,

the tiny soothsayers,
prophets of possibility.
We went to

follow their hunger
into the wild,
devouring world.

VII. NORTH BY NORTHWEST: THE LAND OF ELK, FORESTS, AND LAKE ERIE

Where Girls Still Ride the Beds of Pickup Trucks

KAREN J. WEYANT

Elk County

The wind is always warm here. Breezes snap
through their T-shirts, hot metal and sun burn

their arms and bare legs. They stand
near the cabs, kneel by the rattling tailgates.

It's here where they learn how to catch maple seeds
in their teeth, and how to spit them out.

Here, they learn how to dig pebbles
and bits of gravel from beneath their skin.

Some say that their bodies turn hollow,
that one can hear wind whistling through their collar bones

and shoulder blades. Others say they almost sprout wings.
But they never fly. They only learn how to balance.

Even now, you will know them, these girls
who survived quick trips to grocery stores,

wrong turns on narrow one-way streets,
even moving days, when they sat propped up,

steadying chipped coffee tables and worn couches.
Their ponytails are tangled with knots

that never unraveled from the way the wind
always combed through their long hair.

Sanctuary of Fog

BYRON HOOT

Elk County

Sometimes you stumble into a sanctuary
unaware and some old, ancient form
of divinity ghosts into your vision
and you're suddenly worshipping the moment
you're in because there's nothing else to do
but stand in slight awe when
God was an elk in the mist looking
out, into you before it steps slowly,
suddenly out of sight the way the divine
likes to leave you with the certainty
seen and no words adequate,
so you're silent to proclaim the sanctuary
you've just been in as the fog follows
the elk in disappearing
and you recognize the trail you're on.

Antlers

PATRICIA THRUSHART

Clarington

It makes your heart
suddenly lurch,
as if your mortal body
and its cage of ribs
encased in skin and sinew
cannot contain it.
It wants to leap out,

breathless,
be subsumed
at the sight of an elk
standing simply,
its massive body balanced
beautifully on four frail legs,
and its turned head,
on its thick neck,
tapered and molded
and impossibly small,
bearing velvet tines
branched in veiny symmetry
and soaring high above its back.

O to carry such weight,
such nobility,
that a mere turn of the head
must be preplanned;
where the ripple of presence
goes beyond the boundaries
of the body
and extends into the space beyond:
space displaced by beauty.

Bird Watching in Bradford

HELEN RUGGIERI

under the long reach
of the great lakes
the refinery clouds
the bright blue air

gulls rise and fall
like scraps of paper

swimming in this
invisible ocean

on the river
six gulls settle down
forgetting the distance
or the new direction

the oil of our lives
smooths or smothers
we too are lost

do we stand at the center
of everything
or is it nothing

Grove City Morning

ERIC POTTER

Damp chill by the Bessemer,
fog on the football field,
goldenrod smoldering
at the edge of the bike path.

Three workers pouring
a sidewalk along Pine Street,
their smoky voices catch my ear
as I pedal past.

A pair of joggers panting along,
four turkeys foraging in a field,
a six-point standing
as still as a lawn statue

beneath an apple tree.

I wonder if he recognizes
what's squeaking past.
I wonder if he senses
what's to come—
the rut and rifle season,
bone-thin months of snow.

Eyes alert, muscles flexed
for flight, he tests the air
for a known threat,
untouched by hope or regret.

Migration

DAVID SWERDLOW

New Wilmington

What do these red-winged blackbirds know
of the man who killed himself,

what do they know in their abundance
from here in Pennsylvania's cattails

of the Honduran migrant whose name we've not
been told, who was crowded into one of those

Texas family detention centers? I'm listening
to the female birds' scolding

chatter; I'm listening for the world's
rotation into grief. Experts say

this will not be the last death. At dusk,
the flock fills an anonymous tree.

■ ■ ■

With Latin Filling the Lake

GEORGE LOONEY

Picture a destitute monk chanting
psalms down by the lake

no one recognizes. The Latin
sounds Polynesian

to the old men fishing
from the shore as if they could

eat any fish they catch. The monk
wants to tell them the sturgeon

on the lake bottom talk
to one another in Latin, that

his psalms are meant
to bless these fish that can

grow large enough to swallow
any one of them and still

be hungry. As the monk
finishes a psalm, a fish

not a sturgeon
leaps out of the lake and lands

beside his bare left foot and flaps
once and is still. The monk

lifts it and cradles it
in the form of a hammock

he's made in his robe
and makes the sign of the cross

at the old men who don't believe
what they just witnessed

before he heads for the overpass
under which he'll build a fire

to cook his fish over
and, as he eats, think about

the sturgeon and the Latin
they fill the lake with,

believing it's a blessing
not even he could offer

despite all the accoutrements
of his faith. Picture

that monk mumbling
stray Latin in his sleep

as the occasional headlights
flicker shadows along the concrete

walls adorned with graffiti,
language a blessing everywhere.

O! Erie!

CHUCK JOY

Flat blue bay, white pennants flapping,
the waterfront, the library,
every book patiently waiting.

The brick district, downtown coffeeshops,
art museum, residential, the park,
margins currently under construction.

Tall buildings: our skyscrapers.
You can look up a little bit.
A few people, some pushing shopping carts.

Remember, we are in the poorest zip code
of the many, many zip codes, the poorest,
yet a brilliant entertainment district,

the Warner to the ballpark and the playhouse,
smiling breweries and restaurants.
O! Erie! I have heard you called *Erieay*,

the vowels pronounced in a European way
or as an echo of the Senecas.
It's Spring, and the news promises

contagious infectious disease, pandemic
catastrophe, like that other century when you
were a capital of railroads and commercial fishing.

Sometimes I Forget You Lived in This City

COREY ZELLER

Erie

We're only as good as what instruments we haven't destroyed. Trumpet of dizzying stars. Drum of passion. Harp of sleep. Still, the broken music we've buried behind us rises up to find us on Peninsula Drive. We hear it as one might press their palm to a window pane just to feel its coldness. We hear it as if fingering the neck of a snapped guitar. Today I am alone. The weather seems to be only dreaming of itself, not happening, which reminds me of you. I forget, quite often, you lived in this city. You woke inside the same body you were born with and walked the same streets I walk now in the body I was born inside. We are only what's left of us. And what's left of us moves in the same rhythm over years, over decades, over centuries. Like a composer's fugue. Notes above notes, just barely touching. A song in love with a song.

■ ■ ■

August: Erie

DEBORAH BURNHAM

I'd run three miles at noon, punishing
my lonely skin whose only sin was longing
for the pressure of your hands against
my scalp and ribs

flushed and grimy, angry at the heat,
the stubborn space between us—months
apart, an ecstatic week, then the blank
months again.

I lay sweating on the bare floor while the sky
cooled and glazed. The storm raced off the lake

up to the dry ridge, the shore of the ancient
lake now shrunken.

Erie's practiced gales shook the willow, soaked
the blue curtain, flowed across my stiff, filthy
skin. On the sill, a bowl of green pears, hard
red plums, the fruit

of the lakeshore's sand and loam, the plums
unripe, sour, waiting for you because you love
tough green fruit, so like the town that grows it—
ten or so feet

of snow each winter, the chill reluctant
blossoms on the peach, apple, pear trees—
unfolding their white stars just as the last
snow melts, its white stars soaking the orchard soil.

■ ■ ■

Rapture

BERWYN MOORE

Presque Isle, Erie

The way milkweed pods flurry
on the limbs until rain intervenes.

The way contrails linger like cirrus,
a sigh, a ribbon of breath. The way

a zeppelin floats or a skateboarder
kickflips above the rim. The way ants

crawled out of the banana, still unpeeled,
the *oh* and shine of your gasp—*sweet*

herbaceous miracle, you said, then flung
them over the balcony where they caught

in the current, a momentary failure
of gravity. That summer at the lake, you

stood on the shore puffing your pipe,
not quite oblivious, when your not-yet-three-

year-old girl vanished under the water,
inflatable ring drifting. Glasses affixed,

camera swinging from your neck, you plunged
into the murky silence, water-logged shoes

dragging you down, tobacco flakes rising.
When finally your fingers brushed her belly,

you grabbed her, cradled her to the surface,
hair matted with leaves, fingers clutching

your tie, her sweet mouth stealing the air.
The moment relinquished its grief

and glistened, the air a bright cacophony
of wings. The way, even now, as snow

eclipses the trees, you recall it—
and clutch the edge of doom like a wall

that will keep you upright, the *oh* and shine
of your gasp welling up, your lips quivering.

Wind on the Bay

LAURA RUTLAND

Presque Isle Bay, Erie

The wind stirred a sky full of clouds
Like a mug of hot milk.
It assaulted the wings of birds.
Some triumphed against it.
Others flapped desperately,
lassoed into shuddering,
staggering circles of flight.
Bushes on the shore
shook pink flowers at the wind.
Grasses danced with it.
Queen Anne's Lace twirled
in white circles of celebration.

At the Rib Fest in Erie, PA

SEAN THOMAS DOUGHERTY

My wife says let's find the most wrecked crew
    because wrecked people make the best ribs.
We passed the clean-cut boys with collared shirts
    and the black crew from Texas with their professional
Pig Roast tees until we found a crew from Columbus
    where the lead guy handing out sugared bacon
had no teeth, like my wife, who long ago lost them
    to disease and drinking. And so, we said sure,
and we ordered a rack from the fat white kid
    in a straw hat, and my autistic daughter
ate a piece of brown sugared bacon the crew lead

handed to her and then when we went to buy more bacon
the man refused to take our money. He was a small white man
    in jeans and a tee shirt. He had a southern Ohio accent
full of rolling r's like the kids I knew growing up
    who'd moved up from Marietta or West Virginia
so their fathers could work in the factories of glass
    and steel along the lake. He was sober
though the cooks looked bourbon bad.
    We paid for our full rack and my daughter
took the bacon slabs and we hustled away amazed
    at such good fortune. Maybe it was some kind
of Appalachian solidarity, maybe he could smell
    the poverty in our blood, the long nightshifts
I work so we can buy meat, the lines on our faces,
    "maybe because I'm so cute" my wife said,
maybe he recognized our daughter as disabled.
    Disabled can get you things, this guy Danny
with Down Syndrome I used to take care of said.
    In the smoke house
of the sky distant storm clouds billowed.
    Black and white people wiped the grease
from their jowls. Sauce-stained napkins blew
    like omens at our sneakers. A clown handed out
animal balloons. A few drops of rain fell,
    and my daughter started to shriek
because she claims she's blind
    when water gets on her glasses.
I put my baseball cap on her head.
    Her voice sharp and brittle as glass
she will smash against the wall
    during her worst episodes.
In the smoke house of the world
    we wander blind in so many directions,
even the smallest kindness
    like a few free pieces of sugared bacon is suspect.
Why did he give the bacon to us,

my daughter kept perseverating. She needed an answer.
What could I tell her? Something about hunger.
How hard it is these days to tell kindness
from guilt or shame. You look then look away.
What will kill us or save us in the end?
This I know she's learned already: we take what meat is given;
we swallow its tough fatty sweetness down fast
as if someone will snatch it from our hands.

■ ■ ■

The Catcher and the Sighs

CEE WILLIAMS

Erie SeaWolves, 2019

We were still in it
right up
—until the final pitch
and then
          —the all encompassing banality
set the watchers and casual passengers adrift—
          towards
   a sea of what-ifs
          and there's always next season

only—
next season has yet to arrive
and our catcher
—he died

cracked skull
          skateboard riding
above the bluffs at
          midnight

or sometime shortly

—after the loss
    and the old hometown

—went back to what it always was
            a couple stops short of the Majors
Snow Globe champs
Jim Crow Award
        yard birds
on hungry nights
            no pot hot enough
                to take away
    the big league chew

and now to fly so—
            far away from away
                —from such things as last place
only to consecrate the rise with memorialized
—newspaper butterflies
            exalting the night
                a .200 hitter caught a tired—
extra-inning heater right
in the sweet spot
and we forgot all about—

what it takes
    to catch a game
to be the one squatting behind the plate
squinting
            —all the better to see the glittering bay
    the strength it takes
to make the throw to second plate

to wait for next season
for something—

resembling a new wardrobe
     new uniforms
uniform enlightenment
and maybe
just maybe
a lighter load
     —at the end of the shovel.

▓ ▓ ▓

Saw Again the Infamous Owl

LISA M. DOUGHERTY

Erie

Swooped then, just as before. In the crossroad of what my teenager knew as Ghost Lane. A place we partied down the road, amongst the tombstones found in the abandoned creek. It was there it lent its careless glide so close I could see nothing but *It* in front of my side of the windshield. So close I heard its talons ask a pane of glass to become not something between us. And so it didn't. As the tires chirped a quick "Oh Shit," it paused its flight. Lifted itself backward and spanned its wings, as if I weren't already impressed. Then thrust their might forward, climbing backward up a downward escalator, it pothered neither forward nor backward. And then, maybe I was just too overcome, maybe from the glint of amber. Eyes too often not hesitated for. Or was I too overwhelmed? Could he see the sun's white glare off my tightened grip? Have we both seen the same difference?

October Echo

MARJORIE WONNER

McKean

Secluded in the woods, I walk among the stones
reading names, the same names I saw on mailboxes
the last two miles: Aylesworth, Perry, The Ludlows.
The same as those on the road crossings:
Nye Road, Propeck Lane, Stancliff Corners;
Clinton Farm painted on a barn door;
a bed and breakfast sign: The Hale House.

Simple names, solid as the rock they're set in.
George Bond; his consort, Rebecca, Richard Davis,
dead at 26; and Mary, Benjamin, and Katherine Jones.
John Blount, Civil War vet; his wife, Julia.
Their son, Thomas, age. 2 yrs 8 mos 3 da.
Matta Tremaine, "Waiting over there for Daniel."

Those staunch, old names still echo
in the autumn afternoon like the lonely, haunting call
of the pheasant in the corn field beyond the trees.

■ ■ ■

Amphibians

TAMMY ROBACKER

Meadville, Crawford County

The French Creek
salamanders surfaced black
and fast. Like a dark mood.

Like my mother's
impatience. My father's rage.
I terrorized too

and swung a young one
till he broke free of his tail
to be rid of me. How

does one escape
their fate? Regenerate
tissue, tail, retina

of eye or tongue?
This heart of newt
is brute and old.

It pumps cold
family blood.
But still I try

to swim back
to what was good—
from tadpole

to tiny egg.
To jellied unload.
To the wet dream

of my possibility
before those two toads
got hold of me.

Fog Off the Allegheny

RICHARD KROHN

Venango County
After a photo by poet Steve Myers

Has to be Franklin, where French Creek comes in, angling down
from Buffalo St., roofs of store-bought sheds and assembled carports,
gambrels nestled among treetops like battered hats in scrubby brush,
past the fog, memories of oil-money mansards and heyday Victorians,
their ridges, pitches and eaves, gutters with just enough cant
to feed downspouts out the Allegheny, Ohio and Mississippi.

One of the town's few roofers, my father-in-law talked soffit and fascia,
the chore of dormers, his trick with steeples, how close he'd get to the
    cross,
the burn of his Camel wagging like warning the times I tossed tear-off
into the truck, rode shotgun to the dump, lugged 40-lb. bundles and clung
onto rungs, his teases not to look down, slapping on shingles, the hammer
a part of his hand, a few deft blows, lapping the next batch over.

From there often river fog, like in the photo, above it a hill line and vast
hardscrabble of highlands dropping to villages and scattered factories,
towns that had hoped to be cities, the realm of his duct-taped Dodge,
its next breakdown, or worse, inspection, looming like death threat—
he without pick-up was only half a man, he'd say, his pre-dawn extensions
snaking from the kitchen, the wink of a lamp hooked under the hood

as he trudged in for coffee, mumbling *solenoid, starter*, a belt too loose
to re-charge the Delco, other mornings flat on his back, so far under
I'd only see boots, his truck a gut-shot horse that couldn't be moved.
But he was stuck with it, too shrewd and mulish for shifts at "The Joy,"
where union wages bought motorboats for Pymatuning. No bosses for him
or his sons: solo cowpokes, a family of hammers, tool belts holstered to
    hips.

And the girl? In their drafty farmhouse she'd read every book she could,
and then again, rarely leaving the dirt road, Goodwill clothes no matter
until a recruiter came to her school, cash luring her to an Ivy, returning
with me to write history, *them book things*, he kidded, the miracle
at Drake Well, the town of Pit-hole going from boom to ghost,
then Model T, Pennzoil and Quaker State, the lubing of America.

But none of it work, not the book, the Iron City or ham loaf, daily refrains
about bastards in *Warshington*, our daughter's viola called a fiddle,
cousins' mocking her fear of dirt bikes and woodstoves, they on a first-
name basis with staff at the ER. Not even the marriage, and I haven't
gone back except for the photo, my daughter now in her 30s, fingers
rebelling against performance, Fog off the Allegheny, lifting and settling.

■ ■ ■

Runoff
STEVE MYERS

Sugarcreek, Venango County
For my granddaughter

Be sure you're alone. Find a rough boulder you can claim for your own.
Best to look down on a braided stream rolling between pine-topped hills.

No ancient sea made your weathered stone; a glacier dropped it. Climb on.
If you're warm, you're home. Fire-born, the boulder bears fire inside it
    still.

Bring a book. Bring bread spread with honey. Bring the music in your
    head.
Come each day, each season. Brown-branch November, lightning-bug
    June.

You'll have teachers enough: bee, beech, fox. Heron stalking the stream
    bed.

Watch how water fills all hollows, then flows on. Owl at dusk, thrush at
 dawn.

Many ways open to the world beyond, as in gray March's dimming light,
a doe breasts water to the far shore, turns away, steps out of sight.

The Field Mice of Arneman Road

JOHN REPP

Crawford Township

The field mice of Arneman Road filled the walls not long ago.
The poison sealed in the green pellets thinned their capillary walls
close enough to nothing the mice drowned in their own blood.
Vacuum the twenty-three pellet-piles. Scrub the floors & counters.

Blessed silence, broken by the music just one human could play.

Now the scrabbling again, as if they (field mice or gray, voles,
chipmunks, or—so the county's rodent pamphlet claims—moles)
shove hangers along a wooden dowel then crowd around a typewriter,
jamming the keys into a clump, scratching the enamel letters.

They must be killed just as their forebears were killed: without mercy.

Long ago, hamsters had a home in the attic, snakes in the cellar.
Feral cats grew fat in that simpler time of casually fouled nests,
but the pea beans must be secured, the bins of hand-milled flour,
the bricks of lard, thick-lipped jars of pickles & beets, tins of mackerel.

Blessed silence, broken by the music of one human eating.

Eclogue (Winter)

CHRISTOPHER BAKKEN

Crawford County

Pacing the hill in snow, the shot I hear
is from another hill, this blood I trace
a staggered, lung-shot deer's come from below,
the chill of such things heaving in the dusk
where even the creek has soldered to its rock.
More follow: fierce crows unstationed
east by ricochet to roost at Woodcock Dam.
These last mornings beat as hard as wings
against our stone house; a lid of rusted tin
traps the town for weeks of desperation.
Ten below. And our neighbor with his gun.

Pay attention, today's the twenty-third
of the year, risen from its six-deep tundra
to ravage our parcel of sluggish tilth.
We dig in vain among the hard, heaped banks
for the shells he chucked, find only boot-prints
and the drooled-on shreds of black cigars.
Who wants to be the thing that he hunts next?
Cold land, your punishment is our frontier:
we skim the soup from its fat, we stalk
the house, crouch when another blast rattles
shadows off the iced limbs of the valley.

discussion questions and writing prompts

GREETINGS FROM THE KEYSTONE STATE

1. In what ways does Jay Parini's poem "A Pennsylvania Journal" help introduce *Keystone Poetry: Contemporary Poets on Pennsylvania*?
2. In your opinion, which phrases best describe what it means to be a writer? Why? In what ways is writing also about listening, observing, and discovering?
3. Have you ever kept a writing journal? Here's your chance. As you are reading through and discussing *Keystone Poetry*, jot down ideas in your own Pennsylvania Journal. This can be a simple notebook—any size will do—set aside to record your ideas, insights, brainstorming, and draft poems. If you prefer a fancy journal, that's fine, too. The choice is yours.
4. For even more Pennsylvania inspiration, turn to the writing prompts in "Let's Write About It."

LET'S TALK ABOUT IT: *KEYSTONE POETRY*
Beginnings: Philadelphia and Its Suburbs

1. On what levels and in what ways is this section about "beginnings"? Moreover, how do the poems in this section better help you understand Philadelphia and its suburbs? Are there specific poems, phrases, images, or insights that connect to your personal experiences? That differ from or enlarge upon your historical or cultural understanding of the region?
2. What details in Daniel Donaghy's "What Cement Is Made of" help you identify with the cement makers' jobs? Their need to unwind after work? Throughout the anthology, which other poems give insight into both work and play, employment and relaxation?
3. Although much of this section focuses on city life, where do you see urban and rural life overlapping? Community and isolation intersecting? Hope and fear mixing? Begin by discussing two of the following: Chris Bullard's "At Schuylkill Park," Ross Gay's "To the Fig Tree on 9th and Christian," Jacqueline Osherow's "Breezeway, circa 1964," Amy Small-McKinney's "Walking

Toward Cranes," Nicole Miyashiro's "Linvilla," or other poems of your choosing from this section or elsewhere.

Within a city setting, have you also experienced moments of connection/ isolation or situations where the urban and rural intersect? Share some examples.

4. Divide into groups, with each group focusing on two different sections of Robbi Nester's poem "The Frankford Elevated Train." What do you learn about each listed El stop? How does this connect with the Buckminster Fuller quotation in the epigraph? Do you agree or disagree with Fuller? By searching online, what else can you find out about your assigned sections? How does this new information add to your understanding of the poem? Be prepared to share your ideas with others.

5. Which additional poems focus on specific neighborhoods or streets and the people who live there? What details make each area believable and distinct? Begin by discussing poems by Pollack, Fox, Chelius, Hilbert, Wisher, *or* other works of your choosing. How might you compare these pieces to poems in other sections that focus on particular streets or highways? (Some examples include poems by Stern, Kennedy, Fanelli, H. Myers, McDermott, C. Davis, Bathanti, Emanuel, and Repp.)

If you were to write about your own street, what details, insights, and stories might you include? Consider adding these ideas to your Pennsylvania Journal.

6. In what ways is a poem a type of map?

Now compare your insights to Grant Clauser's "A Map of Valley Forge." How does this poem, and others throughout the anthology, serve as a map? Where do you begin and end on a physical, metaphorical, or emotional level? Choose two additional poems from the anthology to discuss as examples.

7. Quickly list what you already know about two of the following: Indigenous peoples of Pennsylvania, Penn's Landing, the Founding Fathers, Quaker delegate John Dickinson, the Pennsylvania School of Horticulture for Women, the Mütter Museum, or the Franklin Institute. Next, take ten minutes to find out as much additional information as you can. Compare what you learned from the poets' portrayals of these peoples and places. What other historical figures or landmarks have you noticed throughout the anthology? How do the poets' accounts compare with your own recollections or experiences? What insights do the speakers of the poems have about themselves, about their families, or about Philadelphia?

South Central: Farmlands, Battlefields, and the Capital Region

1. The subtitle for this section is "Farmlands, Battlefields, and the Capital Region." Make a column for each and write down words, phrases, and images—lifted from the poems—that describe each category. Which, to you, most effectively evoke the region? Which, from your experiences, seem the most accurate? Discuss.

2. In "All Day Long There'd Been Papers," Robert Fillman pays tribute to Berks County poet and Kutztown University professor emeritus Harry Humes. Look up Humes's poem "Reading Late by a Simple Light" from his book *Winter Weeds* (University of Missouri Press, 1983), on page 26. In what ways does Fillman's poem reflect Humes's?

   Now, carefully read Humes's poem "My Father's Hands" included in the "Circling East" section. Look also at the biographical information for Fillman and Humes at the back of this anthology. How might all these factors enlarge your experience of this poem?

   Repeat the above, this time for Matt Perakovich's poem "Letter to Wemple from Gettysburg," looking up one of Richard Hugo's poems from *31 Letters and 13 Dreams* and the biography of Jerry Wemple at the back of this anthology. Or choose Le Hinton's "Wintergreen" after locating Robert Hayden's "Those Winter Sundays" online. How does reading the poems together enhance meaning? What do we learn about the relationships in each poem? The way one poet may influence another?

   If you so choose, now would be a good time to flip to your Pennsylvania Journal and write your own tribute—or "after"—poem.

3. What is the difference between passing through and living in a town? What is a part of Pennsylvania that you've merely traveled through but never spent time in? Compare your experiences to those described in Sonia Sanchez's "On Passing thru Morgantown, Pa." Before beginning, look up images of Vincent van Gogh's paintings and of the hills near Morgantown. Compare Sanchez's images with what you discover.

   Now, consider similar poems throughout this anthology. You may want to discuss Mark Danowsky's "Passing Through Southeastern Pennsylvania Towns in Winter," Gerald Stern's "No Wind," Matt Hohner's "Toward Pittsburgh," Ed Ochester's "Two Women Watched by Geese," or another poem of your choice. What do you learn about the mentioned locations? About the speaker of the poem?

4. Discuss the title of Heather H. Thomas's poem on page 52. How might you interpret the word *Reading*? In turn, how might your interpretation influence your reading of the poem? For example, what insights does the poem provide about the act of reading (the verb)? What allusions to literary texts? What, also, do you learn about the town of Reading, Pennsylvania? Can you argue for one interpretation over another? Both interpretations? In addition, what might the way the poem looks on the page add to your understanding?

What importance do other poems in this anthology place on reading, writing, music, or art? You may want to begin with three of the following: Sheila Squillante's "Garlic Mustard," Steve Myers's "Runoff," Yona Harvey's "Ink," Mauricio Kilwein Guevara's "John Kane," J. C. Todd's "At the Polish-American Festival, Penn's Landing," Sandy Feinstein's "In Reading," Maria James-Thiaw's "White Shore, 1963," and Maggie Anderson's "Heart Fire." What other examples can you find? What additional insights or personal memories can you add to the discussion?

5. Have you ever visited Gettysburg, Harrisburg, or Amish country in south-central Pennsylvania? Or read about them in school? Write a paragraph about what sensory details you remember from one or all. Now, choose your favorite lines from poems in this section that describe these areas.

For Amish country, consider poems by Russell, Sussman, Stern, Willitts, and one other poem of your choosing. For the capital region, consider James-Thiaw, Hoover, Watts, Garrigan, and another poem of your choosing. For Gettysburg, consider works by Adair, Perakovich, Minor, Chandler, and one other poem of your choosing.

In a group, discuss the ways each author (including you) approaches the town(s) from different perspectives. What other differences do you see in form, theme, and images? What other ideas do you have for your own poem or paragraph?

6. Look up Robert Frost's well-known poem "Mending Wall" and compare/contrast its phrases with Catherine Chandler's poem "Harrowing." Where do you agree or disagree with each author's insights?

In addition, considering the history of Shanksville, Gettysburg, and Nickel Mines, how does Chandler's use of rhyming couplets contribute to overall themes?

Finally, discuss how both Chandler's poem and Jonson Miller's "Flight 93 National Memorial" in "The Allegheny Highlands" section address crossing physical boundaries as well as boundaries of time.

7. In what ways is Nicole Santalucia's poem "Keystone Ode with Jane Doe in It" an ode? In what ways is it not? Search online for background information on this hate crime. What did you find that adds to your understanding of the poem? How does the poet's use of repetition underscore a sense of urgency?

Compare this poem to Michael Garrigan's "Bully Pulpit." Consider theme, structure, point of view, historical references, and other poetic techniques. Discuss.

How do poets Virginia Watts, Maria James-Thiaw, Cynthia Hogue, and Alyse Bensel similarly weave newspaper or conversational excerpts into their narratives using epigraphs or italics? What impact does this have on theme and tone?

Now, jot down excerpts from an overheard conversation, a recently read newspaper article, or an act of injustice from this past year. Which words or phrases might you italicize? Why? How might your recollections become topics for a poem?

Circling East: Mines, Mountains, and Mills

1. In "The Invader Alters Everything," Ann E. Michael states, "[W]hat I know from both / experience and metaphor is: / the invader alters everything. / We must adapt to what we / resist; there is no going back." Do you agree or disagree? Why? What other poems in this section might support this position? What examples from your own life?

Moreover, where in this section do individuals accept, seek shelter, or attempt escape from difficult times? How does the use of dialogue, detail, humor, and/or point of view help bring such experiences to life? Consider poems by Dorazio, Weaver, Upton, or a poem of your choice. For example, although Lee Upton's poem "The Naming of Bars" begins humorously, it ends more ominously. Can you find other poems in this section that address difficult topics?

Now, compare these poems to those in other sections: Maggie Anderson's "Heart Fire," Mary Rohrer-Dann's "Before He Fell, or Jumped," Carole Bernstein's "Quaker Memorial Service for a Young Girl, Germantown," and/ or another poem of your choosing. How do the authors use location, point of view, form, and images to depict personal tragedy?

2. How is the season surrounding Christmas portrayed in David Staudt's "Packerton" and Christine Gelineau's "Christmas in Public Square"? How would you describe the tone in each? Given the generally positive connotations of

the season, what surprises you about each poem? Be prepared to share several examples from the poems and your own personal experiences.

Now, discuss the different ways poets Gelineau, Wemple, Hancock, and basta experience and describe Wilkes-Barre. Consider voice, perspective, focus, and format. How do such poetic choices affect the overall impact of each piece? Your interpretation of the city? You also may want to consider how various poets present diverse perspectives on Philadelphia, Centralia, State College, Pittsburgh, Erie, and/or other locations.

Can you think of at least two different perspectives someone could use to describe your hometown?

3. Choose three poems from this section that better help you understand working in the mines or mills—or growing up in a coal, mountain, or mill town. List sensory details—what you can see, hear, smell, taste, or touch—that make the descriptions believable. If you could talk to individuals from these towns, what would you ask? What else would you like to know? Why?

Now consider depictions from "The Allegheny Highlands" section: Noah Davis's "Skins," Emily Miller Mlčák's "Jacks Mountain," Dave Bonta's "Blast Area," Todd Davis's "Until Darkness Comes," Edward Hirsch's "Windber Field," Barbara Sabol's "I'm from a one-way bus ticket," Sandee Gertz's "Steeltown Girls," Ed Ochester's "Two Women Watched by Geese," or others. What similarities and differences do you notice between these two sections of the anthology?

4. Is it true, as Jack Chielli claims in his poem, that "spring delivers us"? What evidence does he give in his poem? How does his use of positive and negative connotations affect the poem's overall impact?

How do other poets in this section and elsewhere use positive and negative connotations of seasons and weather to portray location, relationships, struggles, or joy? Find at least one example in each section of this anthology.

Do you also harbor memories of Pennsylvania somehow linked to weather or seasons? Choose one and create three images to describe this memory—positively, negatively, or using a combination of the two.

5. Some poets approach love and loss head-on. Others allow them in through the back door of their poems. How do poets Jan Beatty, James Najarian, Marianne Peel, Lisa Toth Salinas, Paul Martin, Harry Humes, Amanda Hodes, Angela Alaimo O'Donnell, Ed Ochester, or others use different approaches and perspectives to address love or joy—or the loss of place, family, innocence, or self? Discuss at least three poems.

What poems can you add to this thematic list, both from this section and elsewhere? In your opinion, what excerpts from the poems best capture these sentiments?

North Central: The Susquehanna Valleys and the Upstate Region

1. In what ways do the excerpts from Shara McCallum's "Susquehanna" give us a geographical and historical overview of the region? What does the poem say about boundaries? About time? About change? About memory?

   If you were to write your own version of this narrative, what insights might you include? What details?

2. Now consider how the Susquehanna River and its tributaries are portrayed in poems by Lauren, Gilman, Fifer, Wheeler, Djanikian, Crooker, Bond, or another poet of your choice. Find examples of positive and negative connotations. How would you describe each poem's tone?

   What is each narrator's connection to water? In these poems, how is water linked to memory, heritage, struggle, contentment, or relationships?

   In her poem "Susquehanna River Bathers," Elaine Terranova writes, "You could make a moral of this, / like the dazzle spinning off / Prometheus' hand: that water / completes us, that without it, / an animal is dust." Do you agree or disagree?

   Compare your ideas to water poems elsewhere in the anthology, including but not limited to poems by two of the following: MJ Moss, David Chin, Thomas Kielty Blomain, David Staudt, Linda Pennisi, Rachel Roupp, Nathaniel Ricketts, Jeff Oaks, Geraldine Connolly, George Looney, Deborah Burnham, Berwyn Moore, Laura Rutland, and Richard Krohn. Which descriptions ring most true to your own experiences? Why? Find a quote from each of your chosen poems that supports your views.

3. Like earlier-mentioned poems, Rebecca Lauren's "Gedachtniss Tag: Remembrance Day" responds to another author, in this case to poet Julia Spicher Kasdorf, also included in this anthology. Do a little online searching. What is "Remembrance Day"? Apply what you learn both to the Kasdorf epigraph and to Lauren's poem. How are the poem, the day, and the Kasdorf quotation intertwined?

   Review the biographies of both Lauren and Kasdorf at the back of this anthology, read Kasdorf's poem "Waking Up with Jerry Sandusky" in this section, and look up information about Jerry Sandusky. How does such additional information help you better understand the connection between the poets? The themes of each poem? In what ways is the process of remembering important to each, but for different reasons? Explain.

What additional connections might you make to poems (in this section and elsewhere) that reference battles, both military and personal? To the reasons we set aside time to remember: to honor another's sacrifice or to avoid repeating tragedy? Discuss such ideas in connection to your chosen poems.

4. In what ways is Dawn Leas's poem about and not about "Independence"? Can you find examples of similar paradoxes in other poems?

5. Pick a poem from this section that places you in a small town. What details do you find most believable? Why? Where do you agree or disagree with the author's insights? Which convey or contradict your own experiences with or opinions about small towns?

6. Pick a poem from this section that places you in rural Pennsylvania. What most intrigues you? Why? What differences do you see in this section in the way small cities, small towns, and more rural areas are described? Which similes, metaphors, and narratives best capture the location? With which do you most identify?

7. The term "Pennsylvania Wilds" refers to counties in both this and other sections of the anthology, specifically Lycoming, Tioga, northern Clinton, Warren, McKean, Potter, Elk, Cameron, Forest, Clearfield, Clarion, and Jefferson. To you, what sensory details and poetic insights best portray both the place and philosophy behind "Pennsylvania Wilds"? Come up with four examples from at least two different anthology sections.

What additional poems identify threats both to these areas of Pennsylvania and to the environment in general? You may want to begin by discussing two of the following: Craig Czury's "Evening Sky Diesel Blue purple tinge," K. A. Hays's "Lines written in the Walmart Supercenter parking lot, Lewisburg, Pennsylvania," Lilace Mellin Guignard's "Lullaby in Fracktown," Jeanne Murray Walker's "Poem about the Environment," Robin Becker's "Elegy for the Science Teacher," or another poem of your choice. How do your chosen authors use form, perspective, sensory details, or other poetic techniques to convey their concerns?

8. What is an event, a landmark, or a person most associated with a Pennsylvania town/city you know well? How might you describe any of these to someone unacquainted with this location?

Now, look up any such references in Marjorie Maddox's "Throwing like a Girl," Micah James Bauman and David J. Bauman's "Alvira," Deirdre

O'Connor's "At the Site of the Laurelton Village for Feeble-minded Girls of Childbearing Age," and Michael Hardin's "Sodom School, Northumberland County, PA." Discuss what you learned. How does each poem give us glimpses into the history, personages, or preconceptions of the event or location? In what ways does each poet offer new ways of seeing or understanding?

What examples can you add from your own experiences about these or other places in Pennsylvania? About changing preconceptions? Find additional examples from poems elsewhere in this anthology.

The Allegheny Highlands

1. Ann Hostetler's poem "Settlers in the Valley" begins "The records tell us." How does the poet take us, through imagination, beyond factual accounts of the settlers? Give specific examples from the poem, and then add a probable but imagined description of your own.

   Is there an object that has been passed down in your family? What is the story of its origin?

2. How do Emily Miller Mlčák's "Jacks Mountain" and Jack Troy's "Migration at Jacks Narrows" present different perspectives of the locale? Consider also the structure of each poem, the narrator's relationship to the area, and connections made to time, history, or nature.

3. Are you a bird-watcher? How might your observations of birds lead to new insights? Discuss how observing birds affects the narrator in two of the following: Jack Troy's "Migration at Jacks Narrows," Ed Ochester's "Two Women Watched by Geese," Todd Davis's "Until Darkness Comes"—or, from other sections, David Swerdlow's "Migration," Laura Rutland's "Wind on the Bay," Helen Ruggieri's "Bird Watching in Bradford," Lisa M. Dougherty's "Saw Again the Infamous Owl," Vernita Hall's "Winter Melon Soup," Anne Dyer Stuart's "Still April and No Spring," Julie Swarstad Johnson's "Greener Than," or another poem of your choice.

4. Have you ever lived in or heard others talk about a "blast area"? Have you ridden an old roller coaster, visited a Dairy Queen in your winter coat, or used an old-style wall telephone? Compare your experiences to those portrayed by Bonta, Welsch, Vallone, and Clifton. What did you learn from reading their poems? What insights of your own can you add? How would you describe the tone of each poem?

5. Using quotations from several poems, compare life in the valley, in the mountains, on the farm, and in the suburbs within this section of the anthology? Give at least two examples for each category. Now add similarities and differences from your own life as well as from other sections of *Keystone Poetry*, such as the poem "Sunrise on a Back Porch in Pennsylvania" by Gloria Heffernan in the "North Central" section and "Why Grandfather Counted the Stars" by Martin Willitts Jr. in the "South Central" section.

6. Which poems incorporate research, and which folktale? Which present the gray area between the two? What questions do such poems pose or answer? How would you address these same queries? What questions of your own would you ask?

7. Read Edward Hirsch's poem "Windber Field" and compare it to Wilfred Owen's poem "Miners," which you can find online, on the colliery disaster of 1918. Why do you think Hirsch's students responded to the poem the way they did? Have you similarly been affected by a poem or story that portrays people or places in Pennsylvania?

    How would you compare this poem to others in the anthology that reference other poems or poets?

8. Have you ever visited the Flight 93 National Memorial or the Johnstown Flood Museum? Or discussed the surrounding area in a class? Write down what you already know about 9/11's United Airlines Flight 93, the closing of the ductile iron foundry in Somerset, and Johnstown's industry and its 1889 and 1936 floods. Next, spend ten minutes finding additional information online. Compare phrases from your notes with phrases by poets Hirsch, Sabol, Roupp, Gertz, Miller, or T. Davis. Discuss. What did you learn from the poems? From your additional brief research? What ideas do you have for your own poem, story, or essay?

Three Rivers and Old Mills

1. This section contains poems about driving toward Pittsburgh, about living in the city, and about moving away from Pittsburgh into the suburbs or more rural areas. Discuss in what ways one poem leads to the next. In addition, choose one poem that, to you, exemplifies each category. What do we learn about the narrators in your chosen poems? About the person's heritage? About Pittsburgh? Use specific quotations from the poems to support your insights.

2. In what ways is Pittsburgh defined by its people, rivers, bridges, hills, parks, industry, sports, museums, buildings, and neighborhoods? List phrases from any of the poems as answers. Which descriptions and insights most intrigue you? Which add to your understanding of the city's diversity? Why and how?

3. Nathaniel Ricketts's "Rivers" and Terrance Hayes's "Some Maps to Indicate Pittsburgh" are both "after" poems—inspired by another poem, poet, or artist. After considering Julie Swarstad Johnson's poem "Greener Than" in the "North Central" section, researching Michael Baldwin and Mel Ramsden, and reading Ricketts's, Johnson's, and Hayes's brief biographies at the end of this anthology, what connections do you see between the poets and those inspiring them? Between the shape of the poems and their themes? For reference, you may want to read Julie Swarstad Johnson's poem "Rivers of Arizona" from her collection *Pennsylvania Furnace*.

4. Consider the role of titles and subtitles for the poems in this section. Which underscore overall themes? Which are ironic or humorous? Which add helpful factual information? Which surprise you or make you laugh? Discuss your reactions with a partner, then come up with two possible titles for your own poems or brief essays about Pittsburgh or Pennsylvania.

5. What do we learn from this section's narratives of immigration? List specific passages as examples. Begin by considering work by Wesley, Corso, Saba, Guevara, Zawinski, Heath, or another poem of your choice.

   In what ways do these narratives overlap with or differ from those presented in other sections of this anthology? Discuss examples from at least two other sections.

   Consider interviewing one or more relatives about their immigration to Pennsylvania. Imagine yourself in their situation. How would you capture their voice and narrative?

6. How is identity influenced by one's chosen (or imposed) line of work? Choose two poems from this section and discuss how the poet re-creates a person or occupation. What can you see, smell, hear, taste, or touch? What do you now better understand about that worker's life and job? Next, choose and then discuss two poems from other sections that also address the relationship between work and identity.

7. Several poems in this section reference the COVID pandemic, the Tree of Life synagogue shooting, suicide, and other tragic situations. Discuss how each author uses various poetic techniques to approach such difficult topics. What insights do you gain? What observations can you add? What connections can you make to poems in other sections?

Now consider poems throughout the anthology that instead depict joy or meditate on the distant past. How do the poets approach these topics? In your opinion, which poems most powerfully depict happiness, grief, nostalgia, regret, unity, or another emotion? Discuss various perspectives, approaches, and insights throughout *Keystone Poetry*.

8. What do references to August [Wilson], John Biggers, Elizabeth Catlett, Ida B. Wells, the Hill District, *Pittsburgh Courier*, and *Amsterdam News* add to your understanding of Yona Harvey's "Ink"? Why is it important to remember, as the first lines say, that "[i]nk marks the spot"? That the last lines acknowledge "this is the ink / we splash whether we are those who leave / or those who stay & fight / the splendid errors of this place"?

What does this poem tell us about artistic expression, voice, and identity? About staying in or leaving Pittsburgh? What other poems in this and other sections address similar themes?

9. What is the meaning of the word *sanctuary*? In Janette Schafer's poem "At the Cathedral of Hope," in what ways is the chapel an "urban sanctuary"? Discuss this poem's sharp contrast to Philip Terman's "A Minyan Plus One." Find two other poem pairings throughout the collection that present similar contrasts.

In addition, in what ways might individuals be considered sanctuaries, as longtime Pittsburgh resident Mr. Rogers is in Shirley Stevens's poem?

Finally, looking ahead to the next section, discuss how Byron Hoot's "Sanctuary of Fog"—alongside poems by Laura Rutland and Steve Myers— presents nature as a refuge. Now, referring to earlier sections, in what ways do Crooker, Willitts, Heffernan, and Szybist discover respite?

North by Northwest: The Land of Elk, Forests, and Lake Erie

1. In what ways does Karen J. Weyant's poem "Where Girls Still Ride the Beds of Pickup Trucks" help introduce this section?

2. Where would you consider nature to be the protagonist in these poems? The antagonist? The predator or the prey? Be prepared to defend your position with examples. Consider also what roles elk, birds, salamanders, field mice, and/or humans play in these poems.

3. Discuss Deborah Burnham's poem "August: Erie." How does she allow the reader both to feel the heat and to experience the city? In what ways would this poem be different if it were about walking through the city in spring, biking through Erie in autumn, or riding the bus in winter? Discuss how the

season, mode of transportation, point of view, and use of details also help us understand the relationship. Compare this to at least two other poems in the anthology that detail modes of transportation—how we get from point A to point B and what we experience in the process.

4. How does the body of Berwyn Moore's poem define its title, "Rapture"? Can you find other examples throughout the anthology where the body of the poem responds to, comments on, or defines the title? Consider Julie Standig's "New Hope," Michael Quinn's "Home," Catherine Chandler's "Harrowing," Cynthia Hogue's "Election," Dawn Leas's "Independence," Julie L. Moore's "Nurse in Need," Jan Beatty's "Dreaming Door," Judith Vollmer's "Doppelgänger," Gary Fincke's "The Lost Continents," Christopher Bakken's "Eclogue (Winter)," or other poems of your choosing.

5. Sean Thomas Dougherty's poem "At the Rib Fest in Erie, PA" ends with these lines: "we take what meat is given; / we swallow its tough fatty sweetness down fast / as if someone will snatch it from our hands." How does the poem build to this revelation? Discuss.

6. How would you describe the tone and point of view in Cee Williams's "The Catcher and the Sighs"? How does his title employ literary allusion, and why? In addition, how does the poem portray both hope and lack of hope on and off the field? Discuss the ending in terms of the rest of the poem. Where do you see similar themes throughout the anthology?

7. What does Tammy Robacker's poem "Amphibians" also tell us about family relationships? Use quotations from the poem to support your ideas.

8. Richard Krohn's "Fog Off the Allegheny" is an ekphrastic poem, that is, it responds to another work of art, in this case a photo by the poet Steve Myers. Working with a partner, try to reconstruct the photograph by what you learn in the poem.

   Next, discuss in what ways the poem takes us beyond the photo. What else do we learn and experience?

   Finally, what connections can you make to the poem that follows Krohn's ("Runoff," by Steve Myers)? If you were going to create a photograph from "Runoff," what details would you include?

LET'S WRITE ABOUT IT: *KEYSTONE POETRY*
Your Pennsylvania Journal: Writing Prompts

1. Using the "Let's Talk About It" questions as a starting point, draft poems based on any three of your discussion responses.

2. Focusing on a specific season, describe your hometown, as Eileen Daly Moeller does in "Philadelphia: Early Summer," through a series of comparisons, one extended metaphor per stanza.

3. Write a poem entitled "Home" (as Michael Quinn does), "Kitchen Table" (as Hayden Saunier does), "The Ritual" (as James Brasfield does), "Sunrise on a Back Porch in Pennsylvania" (as Gloria Heffernan does), "The Dairy Queen in [your town] Opens for Spring" (as Antonio Vallone does), "Towards [your town]" (as Matt Hohner does), "I'm from a one-way bus ticket" (as Barbara Sabol does), "Arriving in [your town]" (as Matthew Ussia does), "Life on the Farm: Things to Count On" (as JoAnne Growney does), "First Day of the [Fill in an event]" (as Paula Bohince does), or "Where Girls [or fill in the blank] Still [fill in the blank]" (as Karen J. Weyant does). Include as many sensory details as you can to thoroughly describe the place and memories associated with a Pennsylvania location.

4. Write a tribute—or "after" poem—in response to an author's work that has impacted your life. For inspiration, re-read the following: Robert Fillman's "All Day Long There'd Been Papers," Matt Perakovich's "Letter to Wemple from Gettysburg," Le Hinton's "Wintergreen," Rebecca Lauren's "Gedachtniss Tag: Remembrance Day," or Nathaniel Ricketts's "Rivers."

5. Many poems in this anthology reference historical and recreational or cultural events. Which ones have you lived through, participated in, or visited? For example, the pandemic, a flood, a cultural festival, a sporting event, a museum, a national memorial, a protest march, a bar or bat mitzvah, a family camping trip, a blast area, an amusement park, a holiday celebration, a superstition, a presidential election? In what ways are your memories similar or different from what's recorded in the anthology poem? Now, choose the same or a corresponding event. Write about it from your point of view. What details will you include? How will you claim the narrative as your own?

6. A number of poems retell experiences further back in history. It's your turn to tell the tale. Spend at least twenty minutes researching the historical person, event, or place. Use what you learned to draft a new poem.

   Before beginning, think about who might narrate the experience? A building, a soldier, a senator, the perpetrator, an artist, a grandparent, the town itself, you? For inspiration, see poems by Freeman, Cohen, Garrigan, Watts, Hostetler, Guevara, Levin, Batykefer, Terman, Willitts, Weaver, or another poet of your choice. If writing a persona poem (using the voice of someone other than yourself), carefully consider diction, tone, pacing, and perspective. Who will you become? Where will you begin? How will you retell this part of Pennsylvania's history?

7. Son and father Micah James Bauman and David J. Bauman researched and composed "Alvira" together. Collaborating with another poet, research and compose a poem about a specific Pennsylvania event or location. Afterward, describe your collaborative process. In what ways did it differ from writing the poem individually?

8. Write about what happened on a specific date in Pennsylvania. This could be significant on a personal level or on a national scale. You choose. For ideas, see Steve Pollack's "December 26, 1960."

9. Museums connect us to the past, future, and, often, ourselves. After reviewing poems in the anthology that reference such sites, record your initial responses. In your Pennsylvania Journal, list something you learned about the museum but also about the narrator, the reader, or the world. Now, write your own poem located in or inspired by a visit to one of Pennsylvania's many museums. If you like, you may visit a new-to-you museum virtually.

10. In his poem "The Quaker Delegate from Pennsylvania," Joshua P. Cohen portrays John Dickinson's fear of public speaking. In Jerry Wemple's "Wilkes-Barre" and Maria James-Thiaw's "White Shore, 1963," the authors portray housing discrimination. Joseph Dorazio in "The Ruins of Bethlehem Steel" and Todd Davis in "Until Darkness Comes" depict large-scale unemployment. Finally, in "One day," Valerie Fox records struggles to "find your true compass." Using these or different poems for inspiration, write your own experience of a similar situation.

11. Write an ode (a poem of praise) to something or someone you associate with Pennsylvania. It could be your hometown, a sports team, a museum, a season, a beloved, or an activity like hanging laundry, hunting, fishing, hiking, swimming, running, or sledding. For ideas, review work by Joy, Szybist, Sornberger, Vallone, Fifer, Djanikian, Maddox, Chelius, Anderson, Kress, Murphy, Hilbert, Pollack, C. Davis, Fanelli, Beatty, Bakken, or another poem of your choice.

   As another option, list which food and drinks are specific to certain parts of Pennsylvania. Plinkies? Cheesesteaks? Winter melon soup? Halupkis? Boilo? Birch beer? Cabbage? Ribs? Moon pies? Kielbasa? Others? After locating examples in the anthology, write your own ode to or complaint about Pennsylvania fare.

12. Expanding on the above, consider anthology poems that capture the struggles, lessons, and joys of hard work and hard play. Using specific sensory details, help us understand a job you've loved or hated, a sport you've excelled or failed at, a pastime or passion you've followed wherever it leads you (dancing, fishing, hunting, cooking, taxidermy, hiking, bird-watching,

cycling, swimming, and the like). Now, re-create this experience in a poem. As an added challenge, incorporate powerful verbs and at least three of the following: simile, metaphor, alliteration, assonance, consonance, and onomatopoeia.

13. Often ordinary events or objects serve as catalysts for poems. Write about something ordinary that we might take for granted. Consider as models Jayne Relaford Brown's "Dirt," Hayden Saunier's "Kitchen Table," Katy Giebenhain's "Taxidermy in South Central Pennsylvania," Erin Hoover's "Retail Requiem," and Linda Pennisi's "The Viaduct."

14. Consider how we define language or language defines us. Compose a piece that defines specific words in the context of the poem. For ideas, review work by Pennisi, M. J. Bauman and D. J. Bauman, Heath, Looney, Fincke, Johnson, and Moore. Don't be afraid to start with a dictionary or thesaurus. Consider also how context often shapes interpretation.

    As another option, write a poem that defines an abstract word as Amanda Hodes does for "memory" in her poem "When they say to leave, she says:"; use at least three similes or metaphors.

15. Alexander Pope famously argued about poetry, "The sound must seem an echo of the sense." Architect Louis H. Sullivan coined the phrase "Form follows function." Considering how poets in this anthology use form and sound to underscore theme, write your own fixed form, concrete or "shaped," or prose poem where the work's form enhances the poem's meaning. Before beginning, refer to online guides to specific poetic forms.

    For additional inspiration, review Angela Alaimo O'Donnell's sonnet variation "Immigrant Song"; Mike Good's pantoum "D++ Dek Hockey League Champions (2012)"; Catherine Chandler's rhyming couplets in "Harrowing"; Lynn Levin's ballad ("Sleepless Johnston"); villanelles by Mary Rohrer-Dann ("Before He Fell, or Jumped") and Lilace Mellin Guignard ("Lullaby in Fracktown"); Jay Parini's "A Pennsylvania Journal," concrete/shaped poems by Ricketts, Corso, and Hayes; and prose poems by Weaver, Wemple, Hays, Leas, Perakovich, and Zeller.

    As another option, fill a poem with sound! Using alliteration, assonance, consonance, and/or onomatopoeia, re-create a scene set in Pennsylvania. Nathalie F. Anderson's "Sweat," Nicole Miyashiro's "Linvilla," Judith A. Kennedy's "Longfellow Pine," Erin Hoover's "Retail Requiem," Harry Humes's "My Father's Hands," and Deborah Burnham's "August: Erie" are just a few examples from the anthology.

16. Write a poem in which you use your name or the names of those in your neighborhood, as modelled by Marjorie Wonner in "October Echo" and

Lynn Emanuel in "Homage to Sharon Stone." Alternatively, write a poem about the name of a place. Take into consideration poems by Upton, Miller Mlčák, Crooker, and the Baumans. Research the origin of the name.

Or, if you prefer, draft a poem in which you respond to or interact with a celebrity—real, imaginary, or literary. You may again consider Lynn Emanuel's poem as well as Marjorie Maddox's "Throwing Like a Girl," Shirley Samuel's "Dear Mr. Rogers Revisited," or Eileen Daly Moeller's "Philadelphia: Early Summer."

17. Draft a poem that includes at least two questions prompted by an experience or location in Pennsylvania. For ideas, review several of the following: Jan Freeman's "At the Crest of the Meadow," Chloe Martinez's "Giant Heart," Jacqueline Osherow's "Breezeway, circa 1964," Michael Quinn's "Home," Cynthia Hogue's "Election," Virginia Watts's Pennsylvania's Governor Advises Voluntary Evacuation," Susan Weaver's "In the Allentown Shelter Kitchen," Deirdre O'Connor's "At the Site of the Laurelton Village for Feeble-minded Girls of Childbearing Age," K. A. Hays's "Lines written in the Walmart Supercenter parking lot, Lewisburg, Pennsylvania," Charles Clifton's "Somewhere in Pennsylvania," Ed Ochester's "Two Women Watched by Geese," Lisa M. Dougherty's "Saw Again the Infamous Owl," or another poem of your choice.

18. After re-reading David Livewell's "Our Fathers in Philadelphia," write a parody of a famous text. Set the poem in Pennsylvania.

19. Compose a poem that repeats the phrase "if you are . . ." as Anne Dyer Stuart does in her poem "Still April and No Spring" or the phrase "So she . . ." as Nicole Santalucia does in "Keystone Ode with Jane Doe in It." As another option, try varying repetition as Mary Rohrer-Dann does when she alternates "Before he fell, or jumped" and "Before he jumped, or fell" or as Noah Davis does in his poem "Skins." Consider the impact on theme and pacing. Place the poem in Pennsylvania.

20. Write a poem in which one experience reminds you of another. For an example, see Toi Derricotte's "The Great Beauty," Gerald Stern's "No Wind," Robin Becker's "Elegy for the Science Teacher," Gary Fincke's "The Lost Continents," or another poem of your choosing.

21. Model a poem after Corey Zeller's piece "Sometimes I Forget You Lived in This City." Include geographical details from a Pennsylvania town in which you've lived.

22. After interviewing a family member for additional information, draft a poem about or in the voice of a relative or friend. For this exercise, Julie L. Moore's "Nurse in Need," Vernita Hall's "Winter Melon Soup," Martin

Willitts Jr.'s "Why Grandfather Counted the Stars," Harry Humes's "My Father Hands," Paul Martin's "Turning Over," or David Chin's "American Water" excerpts may serve as muse. Be sure to complete enough research to ensure accuracy or believability. Locate the poem in a specific Pennsylvania location and feel free to incorporate positive and/or negative memories.

You may find further inspiration in Marianne Peel's "Huckleberries and Homebrewed Boilo," Le Hinton's "Wintergreen," Cortney Davis's "Then It Was Simple," Matthew Ussia's "Arriving in Westmont," JoAnne Growney's "Life on the Farm: Things to Count On," and Jonson Miller's "Flight 93 National Memorial."

23. An elegy is written for someone who has died or is dying (physically or emotionally). It could also be about a place that you miss, even a department store, or the victims of a tragedy. Write an elegy to a person or a place somehow connected in your mind to Pennsylvania. In addition to some of the poems in the previous prompt, the following works may serve as aids: Robin Becker's "Elegy for the Science Teacher," Lisa Toth Salinas's "Litany of Dyings," Maggie Anderson's "Heart Fire," Michael Quinn's "Home," Barbara Crooker's "Worlds End," Julie Swarstad Johnson's "Greener Than," nicole v basta's "the next field over," Shara McCallum's "Susquehanna" excerpts, Micah James Bauman's and David J. Bauman's "Alvira," Alison Carb Sussman's "Lost Brother, 2019," Erin Hoover's "Retail Requiem," Julia Spicher Kasdorf's "Waking Up with Jerry Sandusky," Virginia Watts's "Pennsylvania's Governor Advises Voluntary Evacuation," Mary Rohrer-Dann's "Before He Fell, or Jumped," Carole Bernstein's "Quaker Memorial Service for a Young Girl, Germantown," and others.

Alternatively, visit a cemetery. After reviewing Emily Miller Mlčák's "Jacks Mountain," Judith Sanders's "Walking in Homewood Cemetery During the Pandemic," and Melanie Simms's "At the Riverview Cemetery, Northumberland, PA," draft a poem based on your observations. In doing so, try to connect the past with the present.

24. Imagine returning to a town in Pennsylvania fifty years from now. In what ways will it have changed? Or will it be the same? Using James Najarian's poem "Kempton, PA: After My Death" as an example, write about your town and what it might look like fifty years from now—or even a century later.

looking back, looking forward: intersections with *common wealth*

To view or order the anthology that inspired *Keystone Poetry*, please go to *Common Wealth: Contemporary Poets on Pennsylvania* (University Park: Penn State University Press, 2005), https://www.psupress.org/books/titles /0-271-02721-5.html.

LET'S TALK ABOUT IT: *COMMON WEALTH*

1. Choose three of the "Let's Talk About It: *Keystone Poetry*" discussion questions. Apply these to *Common Wealth: Contemporary Poets on Pennsylvania* (hereafter abbreviated as *CW*). What did you discover?

2. Many, though not all, of the poets in *Keystone Poetry* (hereafter *KP*) also appeared in *CW*. In each anthology, locate poems by the same authors. What similarities and differences do you notice in theme and poetic techniques? What most surprised you? Would you recognize any of the poets just by style or tone? Now, search online for additional pieces by the same poets. How does this expand your understanding of each writer's range or voice?

3. Identify similar themes woven throughout both *CW* and *KP*. How do perspective and location affect each?

   Which topics in *CW* do *not* appear in *KP*? Likewise, are there narratives you would like to see included that did not appear in either anthology? A poem on the Grange Fair or Knoebels Amusement Park? A reflection on skateboarding? A response to a political protest in Pittsburgh? A festival in your hometown? If you were to write one of these, what details might you include? Where would you place it within the anthology? Why?

4. Although *KP* includes only one poem per poet, it does incorporate a larger number of poets. Pick five poets in *KP* who did not appear in *CW*. What do these authors' perspectives add to your understanding of the state? What additional insights or experiences of your own could you add to either anthology?

5. Pick one poem that you feel best represents each section of *CW* and one poem that you feel best represents each section of *KP*. Be prepared to explain your reasoning. What similarities of style, focus, form, and theme do you notice among your chosen poems? What differences?

   Now discuss your selections with others in your group. Did anyone choose the same poems? How much did familiarity with Pennsylvania locations, interest in historical events, or preferences in style influence each group member's choices?

   If you were to put together a poetry anthology on any subject, what subject might you choose? Dance? Video games? Basketball? Your hometown? Art? Hip-hop? Hunting? Nursing? Family? Once you've chosen a topic, how would you organize the poems into separate sections? Share your ideas.

6. Choose any two poems from a section assigned by your instructor. Brainstorm about what most intrigues you. The points of view? The settings? The tension? The relationships? The images? Connections to history and traditions? Connections to your own life experiences?

   Take twenty minutes to briefly research the location, author, and any unfamiliar terms, phrases, or ideas mentioned in the two poems. For example, if you've never heard of a palimpsest, of borscht, of Worlds End State Park—or if you need a refresher on Catherine the Great or the Molly Maguires—conduct a quick online search.

   You can find out more about the authors by looking at the short biographies in the back of the book and, because a lot has happened since the anthology was published in 2005, at this helpful site: https://pabook.libraries.psu.edu/literary-cultural-heritage-maps-pa/about-literary-and-cultural-heritage-maps-pennsylvania.

   How does a little bit of digging expand your own understanding of the two poems *and* the section of the anthology? What can you share with others from your brief research *and* from your own experiences that might help them better understand the poems? For instance, maybe you've attended the Bloomsburg Fair, have studied Gettysburg, have lived in Erie, or are a Pittsburgh Pirates fan. Maybe you have a grandparent who worked in the mines or steel mills. Whatever your experience or expertise, be prepared to share your insights. If you like, you may repeat the same process for *KP*.

7. What do you see as the connections between place and the self? Between the outer landscape of a particular town, city, or region and the inner landscape (thoughts, feelings, identities, perspectives) of the people who live

there? Give examples from *CW*. In addition, how has place influenced you? How has it influenced your worldview or your writing? You may also want to use poems from *KP* as examples.

8. Consider the significance of the anthology title *Common Wealth* (two words) as opposed to *commonwealth* (one word). What is the historical association of the word *commonwealth* (one word) to Pennsylvania? In what ways do the poems in this collection also highlight a type of wealth common to many living in the state? How is the book's title thus a pun or "play on words"?

How would you define the "common wealth" included in the anthology? List examples from three poems that support your response.

Next, look up the definition of *keystone*. What variations in meaning might this word convey? How might these apply to the poems in *KP* and to the history and nickname of Pennsylvania? Choose three poems that you think connect particularly well to such meanings. Be prepared to explain your reasoning.

9. A title is the reader's first impression of a poem. It may entice us to read more, may clarify a situation, may locate us in a particular place, may highlight themes, may underscore irony, may introduce the speaker of the poem, or may serve some other purpose. As a group, choose four poems from *CW*. Discuss what you see as the significance and purpose of each title. What does each add to your understanding of the poem? For more ideas, see question #4 under "Three Rivers and Old Mills."

If you were to choose a title for a poem about your hometown, what might it be?

10. Consider how various poets in *CW* use line breaks, stanza breaks, section markers, and concrete/shaped poems to emphasize words, phrases, themes, or shifts in focus or time. Discuss with your group two examples that catch your attention. Why might the authors have made these choices? How do they emphasize the overall themes of the poem?

Next, discuss the above, this time choosing two poems from *KP*.

Finally, focus on one of the poems that you've reviewed. It can be from either of the anthologies. Retaining the same words, give the poem a different "shape." This may mean creating alternate line or stanza breaks, merging sections, or reformatting a poem to look like a particular object—the Liberty Bell, a road, or a mountain, for instance.

Be prepared to share your restructuring choices—and their overall effect—with the class.

11. Discuss the covers of *CW* and *KP*. In your opinion, what does each add to the anthology or to individual poems?

LET'S WRITE ABOUT IT: *COMMON WEALTH*

1. Pick three prompts from Let's Write About It: *Keystone Poetry*. This time, read the exercises with *CW* in mind. Do the same prompts, coupled with works from *CW*, inspire different poems? Try it and see.

2. Gabriel Welsch's "Pennsylvania" introduces us to *CW* through a panoramic view of the state. Similarly, in his poem "Philly Things," David Livewell presents a sweeping overview of Philadelphia's landmarks and traits, while in "Mennonites," Julia Spicher Kasdorf portrays an entire community of people.

   It's your turn. Define, through a poem or paragraph, the state of Pennsylvania, one of its cities, or a community of its people.

3. After reading the poems "The Map," "Route 81," "Crazy Mary Rides the El," "Bells," "Route 222: Reading to Kutztown," "Bus Stop at West 12th Street," "Driving in Someone Else's Light," or another poem of your choice, write about driving across or accessing public transportation in Pennsylvania. Use strong verbs to capture a sense of motion as well as detailed images to portray location. You may want to compare your ideas to what you discovered in question #3 of the "North by Northwest" section above.

   Now, revisit the poem "The Map." As a class, read the poem aloud with half of the class loudly chiming in on the pronouns *my, I, me, we*, and the other half forcefully stating—as the pronouns appear in the poem—*you, your, our, us*. How does the author's use of pronouns emphasize differing views on driving, on relationships, and on life? What other descriptions in the poem support this? How might the final stanza change or affect your interpretation?

   Write a poem using pronouns and images to contrast points of view. As an added challenge, try surprising the reader in your final stanza.

4. In her persona prose poem, "If You Are Reading This," Lynn Levin uses personal ads in old newspapers to present relationships across Philadelphia's distinct neighborhoods. Using Levin's poem and style as a model, create your own personal ad. You may want to research additional examples online. Be sure to include a post office box number at the end.

5. Barbara Crooker's poem "Christ Comes to Centralia" depicts an unusual visitor to the abandoned mining town of Centralia. Create a vivid scene, presented as true, in which a famous character appears in a specific Pennsylvania town.

6. Using Harry Humes's "Showing a Friend My Town" as an example, compose a poem with the same title. Focus on your town. What landmarks, linked with memories, will you include?

7. Did you grow up in a town where you wanted to live forever? Or one that you couldn't wait to leave? Using Jason Moser's "We Never Leave," Sandra Kohler's "Renovo," Gregory Djanikian's "Going Back," Kristin Kovacic's "Leaving Pittsburgh," or Patricia Jabbeh Wesley's "This Hill Will Get You There," locate us in that place. Employing detail and simile/metaphor, put us in your shoes walking those same streets.

8. Jeanne Murray Walker's "Colors," JoAnne Growney's "Apollo Is a Pink Town," and Maggie Anderson's "Gray" use color to portray place. Focusing on color and hue, describe a specific location in Pennsylvania.

9. "Listening to Jimmy Garrison (Pittsburgh, Pa.)," "The Dancing," "Me 'n Bruce Springsteen Take My Baby Off to College," "Polka Dancing to Eddie Blazonczyk and His Versatones in Coaldale, Pennsylvania" all reference music or musicians—but in very different contexts. After reading these pieces, write a poem to or about your favorite musician. Don't be afraid to learn a bit more through research before beginning your draft. You may want to compare your insights to what you noted for question #4 of "South Central."

   As another option, complete a draft where music underscores the central tensions of the poem.

10. With a partner, find out more about the Three Mile Island nuclear disaster; about the Johnstown Flood and other Pennsylvania floods; about United Airlines Flight 93; about racial discord, immigration, unemployment rates, or coal mining and railroad disasters in Pennsylvania; about the Battle of Gettysburg; or about another topic of your choice. For example, see "Three Mile Island Siren," "Imagining the Johnstown Flood," "Home Town," "The Agnes Mark," "Altoona," "Twelve Facts about the Immigrants: A Prose Poem," "Acoustic Shadows," "Pennsylvania September: The Witnesses," "In Her Mind, She's Already Quit," "Laid Off in July," "Integration (Kennywood Park, June 1963)," "Cousin, Will You Take My Hand," and "So the Coal Was Gone" for ideas. In addition, you also could review what you learned for question #7 of "South Central" or #8 of "The Allegheny Highlands."

   After brainstorming ideas, draft a poem about a recent conflict, injustice, or natural disaster set in Pennsylvania.

11. Consider the poems "Gettysburg" and "The Battlefield Museum Guide Speaks." How do the poems present different views on the ways some tourists perceive or understand battlefields?

   Write a poem from the perspective of a tourist visiting a location in Pennsylvania.

12. Do you disagree with the way any of the *CW* poets have portrayed a particular location or experience? If so, respond to what they've written. Use examples and details in your poem that emphasize how your interpretation differs.

13. Jeffrey Oaks's "My Father Likes Pittsburgh," Marjorie Maddox's "Buggy Ride at Sixteen," Len Roberts's "Climbing the Three Hills in Search of the Best Christmas Tree," and Robin Becker's "The Poconos" all give us the perspective of one family member. Rewrite one of these poems (or another of your choice) but from a different family member's perspective. For example, you may choose the point of view of the father in Oaks's or Maddox's poem, the son in Roberts's poem, or the mother in Becker's poem. Tentatively title the poem something like "The Father Responds to Jeffrey Oaks's Poem 'My Father Likes Pittsburgh.'" You may adjust the title later.

14. Have you lived in a town that has changed drastically over time? Using Ann E. Michael's poem "Sprawl," Sandra Kohler's "Renovo," and/or a *KP* poem as inspiration, write about the ways your town has changed—for better or worse. Be sure to include what you can see, hear, smell, taste, and touch, along with several similes and metaphors.

15. Heather H. Thomas weaves a house prayer into her poem "Wallace Stevens House Prayer," Leonard Kress adapts the meditations of Saint Ignatius in "Spiritual Exercise, Kensington, Philadelphia," and Sandra Kohler references well-known insights from the philosopher Heraclitus in "Naming Heraclitus." Briefly research the house prayer, Wallace Stevens, Saint Ignatius's spiritual exercises, and the teachings of Heraclitus. How does what you learn add to your understanding of the poem?

    Write your own response to a religious or philosophical teaching that intrigues you.

16. Have you ever participated in sports, either as a child or as a young adult? Perhaps you are a die-hard fan of one or more Pennsylvania teams. If so, what memories do you have of these experiences?

    Re-read the poems "Rowers on the Schuylkill," "Our Lady of the Cabbages," "The Little League World Series: First Play," "Class A, Salem, the Rookie League," "Steelers! Steelers! Steelers!," or another poem of your choice. You also may want to consider poems about sports included in *KP.*

    Now write a poem about your own athletic endeavors or achievements. As another option, draft a poem directly addressing your favorite Pennsylvania sports team. Let the cheering begin!

17. John Updike, author of the poem "Shillington," also was an acclaimed novelist, short story writer, essayist, literary and art critic, and two-time winner of the Pulitzer Prize, among other honors. Looking through the biographies in *CW* and *KP*, find other Pennsylvania authors who write in more than one genre.

Do you see yourself as primarily a fiction writer, essayist, poet, or dramatist? Or do you, as Updike did, write in several genres? What do you see as the overlap between these genres? Share your responses.

Reread the poem "Shillington." In the final lines, Updike explains, "We have one home, the first, and leave that one. / The having and leaving go on together." In what ways is this true? Draft a poem that answers this question, using examples from your own hometown. For more inspiration, review questions # 7 and #8 from the "North Central" section above.

Now go the extra mile! Answer the question using a different genre, in a short story, say, or an essay.

18. Write about the physical or emotional process of writing. See "In Cursive" as one example. You also may want to refer to "A Pennsylvania Journal" in *KP*.

As another option, write an "ars poetica" (a meditation on the art of poetry). Include a reference to Pennsylvania or to a Pennsylvania poet.

19. *CW* ends with Sharon F. McDermott's poem "The History of Summer." Draft a poem titled "The History of Autumn," "The History of Winter," or "The History of Spring." Divide your poem into four or five sections, with each section conveying specific memories through vivid descriptions. In what ways have such memories shaped your view of Pennsylvania?

For additional information on each author, please visit Pennsylvania Center for the Book's Literary and Cultural Heritage Maps of PA: https://pabook.librar ies.psu.edu/literary-cultural-heritage-maps-pa.

acknowledgments

We would like to thank Commonwealth University–Lock Haven for an alternative workload leave that provided time to complete this project. In addition, we are grateful to Commonwealth University–Bloomsburg for partial permissions funding; to Russ Gleeson for his foundational work on podcasts promoting poems in this anthology; and Rick Landesberg for the evocative cover.

This anthology would not have been possible without the many Pennsylvania poets who submitted their work and/or generously recommended other poets connected to the Keystone state. Nor would work on this twentieth anniversary edition have begun without the support of our families and loved ones and the strong encouragement of *Common Wealth* and *Keystone Poetry* contributors Steve Myers and Sean Thomas Dougherty.

We acknowledge and honor the Native Peoples whose homelands we write about.

Finally, many thanks to Penn State University Press for accepting the anthology and, specifically, to Kathryn Yahner, Maddie Caso, Laura Reed-Morrisson, Regina Starace, Brian Beer, Cayla Caruso, and Kendra Boileau for working alongside us to bring our vision into classrooms and homes.

Many of the poems in this anthology have been previously published. We are thankful to the people and institutions, listed below, who generously granted us permission to reprint. All other poems are previously unpublished and appear courtesy of the poet.

Allison Adair: "Gettysburg" from *Shenandoah* 65, no. 2 (2016). © 2025 Allison Adair.

Maggie Anderson: "Heart Fire" from *Cold Comfort*, by Maggie Anderson, 1986. © 2025 Maggie Anderson. Reprinted with permission of the University of Pittsburgh Press.

Nathalie F. Anderson: "Sweat" from *Crawlers*, The Ashland Poetry Press, 2006. © 2025 Nathalie Anderson. Reprinted with permission of the publisher.

Christopher Bakken: "Eclogue (Winter)" from *Goat Funeral*, Sheep Meadow Press, 2007. © 2025 Christopher Bakken. Reprinted with permission of the author.

nicole v basta: "the next field over" from *the next field over*, Tolsun Books, 2022. © 2025 nicole v basta.

Erinn Batykefer: "The Jailer's Wife's Epithalamium" from *Bluestem*, January 2020. © 2025 Erinn Batykefer.

Joseph Bathanti: "Requiem for the Living" from *Presence: A Journal of Catholic Poetry*, 2022. Used with permission.

Jan Beatty: "Dreaming Door" from *Jackknife*, by Jan Beatty, © 2017. Reprinted with permission of the University of Pittsburgh Press.

Robin Becker: "Elegy for the Science Teacher" from *The Black Bear Inside Me*, by Robin Becker, © 2018. Reprinted with permission of the University of Pittsburgh Press.

Paula Bohince: "First Day of the Hunt" from *Slate*, May 15, 2007. © 2025 Paula Bohince. Reprinted with permission of PARS International.

Bruce Bond: "North: 1991." Used with permission of the author.

James Brasfield: "The Ritual" from *Cove*, Louisiana State University Press, 2023. © 2025 James Brasfield. Reprinted with permission of the publisher.

Chris Bullard: "At Schuylkill Park" from *Rainclouds of y*, Moonstone Press, 2024. © Chris Bullard.

Catherine Chandler: "Harrowing" from *Lines of Flight*, © Catherine Chandler, 2011. Used by permission of Able Muse Press. © 2025 Catherine Chandler.

Joseph Chelius: "Halfball" from *The Art of Acquiescence*, Word Poetry, 2014. Reprinted with permission of the publisher.

David Chin: "American Water (Excerpts)" from *Word Fountain: The Literary Magazine of the Osterhout Free Library*, Spring/Summer 2017, 39–43. © 2025 David Chin.

Grant Clauser: "A Map of Valley Forge" from *Muddy Dragon on the Road to Heaven*, Codhill Press. © Grant Clauser. Reprinted with permission of the publisher.

Geraldine Connolly: "River of Mantises" from *Aileron*, Terrapin Books, 2018. © 2025 Geraldine Connolly. Reprinted with permission of the publisher.

Paola Corso: "On the Way Up: Pittsburgh StepTrek" from *Vertical Bridges: Poems and Photographs of City Steps*, Six Gallery Press, 2020. © 2025 Paola Corso. Reprinted with permission of the publisher.

Barbara Crooker: "Worlds End" from *Gold*, Cascade Books, 2013. © 2025 Barbara Crooker.

Craig Czury: "Evening Sky Diesel Blue purple tinge" from *Thumb Notes Almanac*, FootHills Publishing, 2016. © 2025 Craig Czury.

Mark Danowsky: "Passing Through Southeastern Pennsylvania Towns in Winter" from *Grey Sparrow Journal*, no. 44 (July 31, 2024). © Mark Danowsky.

Cortney Davis: "Then It Was Simple" from *Leopold's Maneuvers*, University of Nebraska Press, 2004. © 2025 Cortney Davis.

Noah Davis: "Skins" from *Of This River*, Wheelbarrow Books, Michigan State University Press, 2020. © 2025 Noah Davis. Reprinted with permission of the publisher.

Todd Davis: "Until Darkness Comes" from *Coffin Honey*, Michigan State University Press, 2022. © 2025 Todd Davis. Reprinted with permission of the publisher.

Toi Derricotte: "The Great Beauty" from the *New Yorker*, October 26, 2020. © 2025 Toi Derricotte.

Gregory Djanikian: "Stepping Stones" from *SALT #3, a journal of poetry*. © 2025 Gregory Djanikian.

Daniel Donaghy: "What Cement Is Made of" first appeared in the *Notre Dame Review*, no. 37 (Winter/Spring 2014).

Joseph Dorazio: "The Ruins of Bethlehem Steel" from *Philadelphia Poets* 12, no. 2 (2006). © 2025 Joseph Dorazio.

Sean Thomas Dougherty: "At the Rib Fest in Erie, PA" from *The Dead Are Everywhere Telling Us Things*, Jacar Press, 2022. © 2025 Sean Thomas Dougherty. Reprinted with the permission of the author.

Lynn Emanuel: "Homage to Sharon Stone" from *Then, Suddenly*, University of Pittsburgh Press, 1999. © 2025 Lynn Emanuel. Reprinted with permission of the author.

Sharon Fagan McDermott: "Tuesday Morning" from *Gyroscope Review*. © 2025 Sharon Fagan McDermott. Reprinted with permission of the author.

Ken Fifer: "Shiners" from *Caravaggio's Kimono*, Longleaf Press, 2024. © 2025 Ken Fifer.

Robert Fillman: "All Day Long There'd Been Papers" from *House Bird*. Copyright © 2022 by Robert Fillman. Reprinted by permission of Terrapin Books.

Gary Fincke: "The Lost Continents" from *The Literary Review*, Spring 1998. Reprinted in *Blood Ties: Working Class Poems*, Time Being Books, 2002. © 2025 Gary Fincke. Reprinted with permission of the author.

Valerie Fox: "One Day" from *Hanging Loose* 99 (2011). © Valerie Fox.

Robbie Gamble: "Tioga County, PA" from *Muddy River Poetry Review*. © 2025 Robbie Gamble.

Michael Garrigan: "Bully Pulpit" from *River, Amen*, Wayfarer Books, 2023. © 2025 Michael Garrigan. Reprinted with permission of the publisher.

Ross Gay: "To the Fig Tree on 9th and Christian" from *Catalog of Unabashed Gratitude*, by Ross Gay, © 2015. © 2025 Ross Gay. Reprinted with permission of the University of Pittsburgh Press.

Christine Gelineau: "Christmas in Public Square" from *North American Review* 301, no. 2 (2016): 41. © 2025 Christine Gelineau.

Sandee Gertz: "Steeltown Girls" from *The Pattern Maker's Daughter*, Bottom Dog Press, 2012. © 2025 Sandee Gertz.

Katy Giebenhain: "Taxidermy in South Central Pennsylvania" from *Sharps Cabaret*, by Katy Giebenhain, is reprinted by permission of Mercer University Press, © 2017.

JoAnne Growney: "Life on the Farm: Things to Count On" first appeared as "Things to Count On" from *Red Has No Reason*, Plain View Press, 2010. © 2025 JoAnne Growney. Used with permission of the author.

Mauricio Kilwein Guevara: "John Kane" from *Postmortem*, University of Georgia Press, © 1994. Reprinted with permission of the author.

Lilace Mellin Guignard: "Lullaby in Fracktown" from *Poetry*, January 2016. © 2025 Lilace Guignard.

Vernita Hall: "Winter Melon Soup" from *American Poetry Review* 49, no. 5 (2020). © 2025 Vernita Hall.

Terrance Hayes: "Some Maps to Indicate Pittsburgh" from HOW TO BE DRAWN, Penguin Publishing Group, 2015. © 2025 Terrance Hayes. Used by permission of Penguin Books, an imprint of Penguin Publishing Group, a division of Penguin Random House LLC. All rights reserved.

K. A. Hays: "Lines written in the Walmart Supercenter parking lot, Lewisburg, Pennsylvania" from *Anthropocene Lullaby*, Carnegie Mellon University Press, 2022. © 2025 K. A. Hays.

Jocelyn Heath: "Nine Irenes" from *Foundry*, December 2017. © 2025 Jocelyn Heath. Reprinted with permission of the author.

Ernest Hilbert: "Center City" from *Barrow Street*, Fall/Winter 2010. Reprinted in *Last One Out*, Measure Press, 2019. © Ernest Hilbert.

Edward Hirsch: "Windber Field" form *Stranger by Night*, Knopf, 2020. © 2025 Edward Hirsch.

Matt Hohner: "Toward Pittsburgh" from *Thresholds and Other Poems*, Apprentice House, 2018. © 2025 Matt Hohner.

Byron Hoot: "Sanctuary of Fog" from *Piercing the Veil: Appalachian Visions*, 2020. © 2025 Byron Hoot. Reprinted with permission of the author.

Erin Hoover: "Retail Requiem" from *No Spare People*, Black Lawrence Press, 2023. © 2025 Erin Hoover. Reprinted with permission of the publisher.

Harry Humes: "My Father's Hands" from *Poetry Northwest*. © 2025 Harry Humes. Reprinted with permission from the author's estate.

Julie Swarstad Johnson: "Greener Than" from *Pennsylvania Furnace*, Unicorn Press, 2019. © 2025 Julie Swarstad Johnson.

Julia Spicher Kasdorf: "Waking Up with Jerry Sandusky" from *As Is*, by Julia Spicher Kasdorf, © 2023. Reprinted with permission of the University of Pittsburgh Press.

Judith A. Kennedy: "Longfellow Pine" from *Salted Wakings*, Finishing Line Press, 2019. © 2025 Judith Kennedy. Reprinted with permission of The Permissions Company, LLC on behalf of Finishing Line Press.

Kristin Kovacic: "Dioramas" from the *Pittsburgh Post-Gazette*, November 27, 1994. Subsequently reprinted in *House of the Women*, Finishing Line Press, 2016. © 2025 Kristin Kovacic. Reprinted with permission of The Permissions Company LLC on behalf of Finishing Line Press.

Leonard Kress: "Bridesburg" from *Walk Like Bo Diddley*, Black Swamp Poetry Press, 2019. © 2025 Leonard Kress.

Rebecca Lauren: "Gedachtniss Tag" from *The Schwenkfelders*, Seven Kitchens Press, 2010. © 2025 Rebecca Lauren.

Dawn Leas: "Independence" from *The Sin of Being Okay*, Kinsman Avenue Publishing, 2025. © 2025 Dawn Leas.

Lynn Levin: "Sleepless Johnston" from *Lyrical Ballads*, reprinted in *The Minor Virtues*, Ragged Sky Press, 2020. Used with permission of Ragged Sky Press and the author.

David Livewell: "Our Fathers in Philadelphia," reprinted by permission from *The Hudson Review* 66, no. 1 (Autumn 2016). Copyright © 2025 by David Livewell.

Marjorie Maddox: "Throwing Like a Girl" from *African American Review* 52, no. 4 (2019). © 2025 Marjorie Maddox. Reprinted with permission of the author.

Paul Martin: "Turning Over" from *Mourning Dove*, Comstock Review, 2017. Reprinted in *The Backwaters Press Anthology* and *American Life in Poetry*. © 2025 Paul Martin.

Shara McCallum: "Susquehanna (Excepts)" from *The Face of Water: New and Selected Poems*, Peepal Tree Press, 2011. © 2025 Shara McCallum. Reprinted with permission of the publisher.

Abby Minor: "Gettysburg Poem #3" from *Emulate*, Spring 2020. © 2025 Abby Minor.

Berwyn Moore: "Rapture" from *Ruminate Journal*, no. 33 (Winter 14/15). Reprinted in *Sweet Herbaceous Miracle*, BkMk Press, 2018. © 2025 Berwyn Moore. Reprinted with permission of the author.

Erin Murphy: "Central Pennsylvania" from *Assisted Living*, Brick Road Poetry Press, 2018. © 2025 Erin Murphy.

James Najarian: "Kempton, PA: After My Death" from *Sulphur River Literary Review*. © 2025 James Najarian.

Robbi Nester: "The Frankford Elevated Train" from *A Likely Story*, Moon Tide, 2014. © 2025 Robbi Nester.

Jeff Oaks: "The Allegheny River" from *The Fourth River*, no. 10 (2013). © 2025 Estate of Jeff Oaks.

Deirdre O'Connor: "At the Site of the Laurelton Village of Feeble-Minded Girls of Childbearing Age" from *The Cupped Field*, Able Muse Press, 2020. © 2025 Deidre O'Connor. Reprinted with permission of the publisher.

Angela Alaimo O'Donnell: "Immigrant Song" from *Holy Land*, Paraclete Press, 2022. © 2025 Paraclete Press.

Jacqueline Osherow: "Breezeway, Circa 1964" from *With a Moon in Transit*, Grove Atlantic, 1996. © 2025 Jacqueline Osherow. Reprinted with permission of the publisher.

Marianne Peel: "Huckleberries and Homebrewed Boilo" from *Apricity Magazine*, January 24, 2017. © 2025 Marianne Peel. Reprinted with permission of the author.

Linda Pennisi: "The Viaduct" from *The Burning Boat*, Nine Mile Press, 2022. © 2025 Linda Pennisi.

Richard Pierce: "Father Rodney" from *Image*, no. 90. © 2025 Richard Pierce. Reprinted with permission of the author.

Steve Pollack: "December 26, 1960" from *From Generation to Generation*, Finishing Line Press, 2020. © 2025 by Steve Pollack. Reprinted with permission of The Permissions Company LLC on behalf of Finishing Line Press.

Michael Quinn: "Home" from *Carve Magazine*, Spring 2021. © 2025 Michael Quinn.

John Repp: "The Field Mice of Arneman Road" from *The Furious Gazelle*, April 25, 2017. © 2025 John Repp. Reprinted with permission of the author.

Tammy Robacker: "Amphibians" from *Villain Songs*, MoonPath Press, 2018. © 2025 Tammy Robacker. Reprinted with permission of the publisher.

Sarah Russell: "In Amish Country" from *Today and Other Seasons*, Kelsay Books, 2020. © 2025 Sarah Russell.

Barbara Sabol: "I'm from a one-way bus ticket" from *Imagine a Town*, Sheila-Na-Gig Editions, 2020. © 2025 Barbara Sabol.

Sonia Sanchez: "On Passing Thru Morgantown, Pa" from *Shake Loose My Skin: New and Selected Poems*, Beacon Press, 1999. © Sonia Sanchez. Reprinted with permission of the author.

Judith Sanders: "Walking in Homewood Cemetery During the Pandemic" from *Gyroscope Review*. © 2025 Judith Sanders. Reprinted with permission of the author.

Nicole Santalucia: "Keystone Ode with Jane Doe in It" from *The Book of Dirt*,

New York Quarterly Books, 2020. © 2025 Nicole Santalucia. Reprinted with permission of the publisher.

Hayden Saunier: "Kitchen Table" from *A Cartography of Home*. Copyright © 2021 by Hayden Saunier. Reprinted by permission of Terrapin Books.

Janette Schafer: "At the Cathedral of Hope" from *Peacock Journal*. © 2025 Janette Schafer. Reprinted with permission of the author.

Amy Small-McKinney: "Walking Toward Cranes" from *Walking Toward Cranes*, Glass Lyre Press, 2017. © Amy Small-McKinney. Reprinted with permission of the publisher.

Judith Sornberger: "Prayer Flags" from *Encore: More Poems by Parallel Press Poets*, 2006. © 2025 Judith Sornberger.

Sheila Squillante: "Garlic Mustard" from the *Pittsburgh Post-Gazette*, November 10, 2017. Reprinted with permission of the author.

Julie Standig: "New Hope" from *The Forsaken Little Black Book*, Kelsay Books, 2022. © 2025 Julie Standig.

David Staudt: "Packerton" from *The Gifts and Thefts*, Backwaters Press, 2001. © 2025 David Staudt.

Gerald Stern: "No Wind" from *The Red Coal*, Houghton Mifflin, 1981. © 2025 Gerald Stern. Reprinted with the permission of the author's estate.

Anne Dyer Stuart: "Still April and No Spring" from *What Girls Learn*, Finishing Line Press, 2021. © 2025 Anne Dyer Stuart.

David Swerdlow: "Migration" from *Nightstand*, Broadstone Books, 2023, used by permission.

Mary Szybist: "Here, there are Blueberries" from *Incarnadine*, Graywolf Press, 2012. © 2025 Mary Szybist. Reprinted with the permission of The Permissions Company, LLC on behalf of the Graywolf Press, Minneapolis, Minnesota, graywolfpress.org.

Philip Terman: "A Minyan Plus One" from *This Crazy Devotion*, Broadstone Books, 2020, used by permission. © 2025 Philip Terman.

Elaine Terranova: "Susquehanna River Bathers" from *Damages*, Copper Canyon Press, 1995. © 2025 Elaine Terranova.

Heather H. Thomas: "A Girl, Reading" from *Vortex Street*, FutureCycle Press, 2018. © 2025 Heather H. Thomas.

Patricia Thrushart: "Antlers" from the *Brookville Mirror*, August 1, 2018. © 2025 Patricia Thrushart. Reprinted with permission of the author.

J. C. Todd: "At the Polish American Festival, Penn's Landing" from *Crab Orchard Review* 6, no. 2 (2001). © 2025 J. C. Todd.

Lee Upton: "The Naming of Bars" from *Of Burgers & Barrooms, Main Street Rag*, 2018. © 2025 Lee Upton.

Judith Vollmer: "Doppelgänger" from *The Sound Boat: New and Selected Poems*, University of Wisconsin Press, 2022. Reprinted with permission of the University of Wisconsin Press. © 2025 the Board of Regents of the University of Wisconsin System. All rights reserved.

G. C. Waldrep: "Mütter Museum with Owl" from *The Earliest Witnesses*. Copyright © 2021 by G. C. Waldrep. Reprinted with the permission of The Permissions Company, LLC on behalf of Tupelo Press, tupelopress.org.

Gabriel Welsch: "The Oldest Roller Coaster in the World" from *Tar River Poetry*, Spring 2009. © 2025 Gabriel Welsch.

Jerry Wemple: "Wilkes-Barre" from *We Always Wondered What Became of You*, Broadstone Books, 2024. © 2025 Jerry Wemple. Used with permission.

Patricia Jabbeh Wesley: "Pittsburgh" from *Vox Populi*, December 9, 2020. © 2025 Patricia Jabbeh Wesley. Reprinted with permission of the author.

Karen J. Weyant: "Where Girls Still Ride the Beds of Pickup Trucks" from *Rattle*, December 13, 2017. © 2025 Karen J. Weyant. Reprinted with permission of the author.

Yolanda Wisher: "5 South, 43rd Street, Floor 2" from *Monk Eats an Afro*, Hanging Loose Press, 2014. Reprinted with permission from the publisher.

Andrena Zawinski: "Cinderman" from *Overthrowing Capitalism 6*, Revolutionary Poets Brigade, San Francisco, 2019. Reprinted with permission of the author.

the poets

ALLISON ADAIR is the author of *The Clearing* (Milkweed, 2020), winner of the Max Ritvo Poetry Prize. Her poems appear in *Best American Poetry*, *Threepenny Review*, *Kenyon Review*, and *ZYZZYVA* and have received the Pushcart Prize, the *Florida Review* Editors' Award, and the Orlando Prize. Originally from central Pennsylvania, Allison teaches at Boston College. Visit her at allisonadair.com.

MAGGIE ANDERSON is the author of five books of poetry, including *Dear All*, *Windfall: New and Selected Poems*, *A Space Filled with Moving*, *Cold Comfort*, and *Years That Answer*. She has edited several thematic anthologies, including *A Gathering of Poets*, a collection of poems read at the twentieth-anniversary commemoration of the shootings at Kent State University in 1970. Her awards include two fellowships for the National Endowment for the Arts; fellowships from the Ohio, West Virginia, and Pennsylvania Councils on the Arts; and the Ohioana Library Award for contributions to the literary arts of Ohio. The founding director of the Wick Poetry Center and of the Wick Poetry Series of the Kent State University Press, Anderson is professor emerita at Kent State University and lives in Asheville, North Carolina. maggieandersonpoet.com

NATHALIE F. ANDERSON'S books of poetry include *Following Fred Astaire*, *Crawlers*, *Quiver*, *Stain*, *ROUGH*, and the chapbook *Held and Firmly Bound*. Her poems have appeared in *Atlanta Review*, *DoubleTake*, *Natural Bridge*, the *New Yorker*, *Nimrod*, *Plume*, and elsewhere; she collaborated in 2021 with artist Susan Hagen and poet Lisa Sewell on *Birds of North America*. Anderson has authored libretti for five operas in collaboration with Philadelphia composer Thomas Whitman. She recently retired from Swarthmore College, where she served as the Cummins Professor of English Literature and directed the program in creative writing.

CHRISTOPHER BAKKEN is the author of the culinary memoir *Honey, Olives, Octopus: Adventures at the Greek Table* and three books of poetry: *Eternity & Oranges*, *Goat Funeral*, and *After Greece*. His poetry, nonfiction, reviews, and translations have appeared in the *Paris Review*, *Ploughshares*, *Southern Review*, *Wall Street Journal*, *New England Review*, *Hudson Review*, *Parnassus: Poetry in Review*, *Iowa Review*, and elsewhere. Please see christopherbakken.com.

JOSEPH BATHANTI is the former North Carolina poet laureate (2012–14) and recipient of the North Carolina Award in Literature. He is the author of twenty-two books, including *Light at the Seam*, from LSU Press. *Light at the Seam* won the 2022 Roanoke Chowan Prize, awarded annually by the North Carolina Literary and Historical Association for the best book of poetry in a given year, and the 2023 Brockman-Campbell Award, given annually by the North Carolina Poetry Society, for the best book of poetry published by a North Carolina poet in the previous year. Bathanti is McFarlane Family Distinguished Professor of Interdisciplinary Education at Appalachian State University. He served as the 2016 Charles George VA Medical Center Writer-in-Residence in Asheville, North Carolina, and is the cofounder of the Medical Center's creative writing program. He was inducted into the North Carolina Literary Hall of Fame in 2024. Please see https://english .appstate.edu/faculty-staff/directory/joseph-bathanti.

ERINN BATYKEFER earned her MFA from the University of Wisconsin–Madison and is the author of *Allegheny, Monongahela* (Red Hen Press, 2009), *The Artist's Library* (Coffee House Press, 2014), and *Epithalamia*, winner of the 2019 Autumn House Press Chapbook Prize. She lives with her family in Pittsburgh.

GRACE BAUER has published six books of poems—most recently *Unholy Heart: New and Selected Poems* (Backwaters Press / University of Nebraska, 2021). Previous books include *MEAN/TIME, Nowhere All at Once, Retreats & Recognitions, Beholding Eye*, and *The Women at the Well*, as well as several chapbooks. She also coedited the anthology *Nasty Women Poets: An Unapologetic Anthology of Subversive Verse* (Lost Horse Press, 2017). Her poems, essays, stories, and reviews have appeared in numerous journals and anthologies. She has received a Nebraska Book Award, a Book of the Year Award from the Society of Midwest Authors, the Idaho Poetry Prize, Individual Artist Grants from the Nebraska Arts Council and the Virginia Commission for the Arts, and residencies at the Kimmel Harding Nelson Center and VCCA. After living and teaching in Lincoln, Nebraska, for more than twenty-five years, she has recently returned to her native Pennsylvania. She lives in Philadelphia. gracebauerpoet.com/index.php /about

In addition to coauthoring *Mapping the Valley: Hospital Poems*, DAVID J. BAUMAN has written two other poetry chapbooks: *Angels & Adultery* (Seven Kitchens Press, 2018) and *Moons, Roads, and Rivers* (Finishing Line Press, 2017). David has work published in journals and anthologies, including *New Ohio Review, Valparaiso Poetry Review, Crab Creek Review, Blood Orange Review*, and *The MacGuffin*. davidjbauman.com

MICAH JAMES BAUMAN's poems have been published in *South 85 Journal*, *Whale Road Review*, *Anti-Heroin Chic*, and *sage cigarettes*. He was a Best of the Net nominee in 2020. His chapbook *Mapping the Valley: Hospital Poems* (Seven Kitchens Press, 2021) is a collaboration with his father, David J. Bauman.

JAN BEATTY's eighth book, *Dragstripping*, was published by the University of Pittsburgh Press (2024). Her memoir, *American Bastard*, won the Red Hen Nonfiction Award. Recent books include *The Body Wars* and a chapbook, *Skydog* (Lefty Blondie Press, 2022). Beatty has worked as a waitress, abortion counselor, and in maximum security prisons. janbeatty.com

ROBIN BECKER has published eight collections of poetry, most recently *The Black Bear Inside Me* (2018) in the Pitt Poetry Series. Her poems and book reviews have appeared in the *American Poetry Review*, *Poetry*, the *New Yorker*, the *New York Times*, and elsewhere. A Liberal Arts Research Professor Emeritus (Penn State University), Becker divides her time between central Pennsylvania and rural New Hampshire.

ALYSE BENSEL is the author of *Spoil* (Stephen F. Austin State University Press, 2024) and *Rare Wondrous Things* (Green Writers Press, 2020), as well as three chapbooks, including *Lies to Tell the Body* (Seven Kitchens Press, 2018). Born and raised in York, Pennsylvania, she now lives in the North Carolina mountains, where she is an associate professor of English at Brevard College and directs the Looking Glass Rock Writers' Conference. Find her online at alysebensel.com.

CAROLE BERNSTEIN is the author of two poetry collections from Hanging Loose Press, *Buried Alive: A To-Do List* and *Familiar*, as well as a chapbook, *And Stepped Away from the Circle* (Sow's Ear Press). Her poems have appeared in *Antioch Review*, *Apiary*, *Bridges*, *Chelsea*, *Hanging Loose*, *Paterson Literary Review*, *Poetry*, *Rat's Ass Review*, *Shenandoah*, and *Yale Review* and in anthologies such as *American Poetry: The Next Generation*, *The Weight of Motherhood*, and *Unsettling America*. She holds an MA from the Johns Hopkins Writing Seminars. A happily transplanted New Yorker, Bernstein has lived in Philadelphia's Fairmount neighborhood for twenty-five years. carolebernstein.com/creative-works

Scranton poet THOMAS KIELTY BLOMAIN is the author of *Gray Area* (Nightshade Press / Keystone College Books), *Blues from Paradise* (Foothills Publishing), and *Yellow Trophies* (New York Quarterly Books); coeditor of *Down the Dog Hole*; and editor of *5 Poets* (Nightshade Press). His poetry appears in several anthologies, including *Coalseam*, *Palpable Clock*, *Pennsylvania Seasons* (University of Scranton Press, 2008), and *Common Wealth* (Penn State University Press, 2005). A graduate of Keystone Junior College and Dickinson College, he also writes songs and stories; he lives in the city's Hill Section with his wife, Jessica.

PAULA BOHINCE is the author of three poetry collections from Sarabande, most recently *Swallows and Waves* (2016). paulabohince.com

BRUCE BOND is the author of more than thirty-five books, including *Patmos* (Juniper Prize, University of Massachusetts, 2021), *Behemoth* (New Criterion Prize, 2021), *Liberation of Dissonance* (Schaffner Award for Literature in Music, Schaffner, 2022), *Choreomania* (MadHat, 2023), *Invention of the Wilderness* (LSU Press, 2023), *Therapon* (with Dan Beachy-Quick, Tupelo, 2023), and *Vault* (Richard Snyder Award, Ashland, 2023). Among his forthcoming books are *Lunette* (Wishing Jewel Prize Editor's Selection, Green Linden), *The Silent Conversation* (Vern Rutsala Prize Editor's Selection, Cloudbank), and *The Dove of the Morning News* (Test Site Poetry Award, University of Nevada). Other honors include the Crab Orchard Open Competition Book Prize, the Elixir Press Poetry Award, the *Tampa Review* Book Prize, the Lynda Hull Memorial Poetry Award, the James Dickey Prize, the Meringoff Prize, two TIL Best Book of Poetry Prizes, fellowships from the NEA and the Texas Institute for the Arts, and seven appearances in *Best American Poetry*. His website is brucebond.com.

DAVE BONTA (davebonta.com) lives and writes in the Little Juniata watershed near Tyrone, where he grew up.

JAMES BRASFIELD lived for many years in State College, Pennsylvania, where he retired from teaching at Penn State. He has published three books of poems and a book of translations. Twice a Senior Fulbright Fellow to Ukraine, he has received fellowships in poetry from the Pennsylvania Council on the Arts and the National Endowment for the Arts. He is a recipient of the American Association for Ukrainian Studies Prize in Translation and the PEN Award for Poetry in Translation. He currently resides in Belfast, Maine.

JAYNE RELAFORD BROWN is the author of *My First Real Tree*, a book of poems from Foothills Press, and was the eighth poet laureate of Berks County, Pennsylvania. Her poems have recently appeared in *CALYX*, *Gyroscope Review*, and *Persimmon Tree*. She lives and gardens in Berks County with her partner of forty years.

A native of Jacksonville, Florida, CHRIS BULLARD is a retired judge who lives in Philadelphia. In 2022, Main Street Rag published his chapbook *Florida Man* and Moonstone Press published his chapbook *The Rainclouds of y*. Finishing Line

Press published his chapbook *Lungs* in 2024. He was also nominated in 2024 for the Pushcart Prize.

DEBORAH BURNHAM is the author of two published books: *Anna and the Steel Mill* and *Tart Honey*. She has won the Seven Kitchens' Keystone Chapbook series prize twice, for *Still* and *Among Our Other Dead*. She recently moved from Philadelphia to a small town—a lovely place, but she misses trains, busses, and sidewalks. For several decades, she worked at the University of Pennsylvania, advising and teaching students. While she doesn't miss grading papers, she does miss working with students and talking about poetry.

CATHERINE CHANDLER, who was raised in Wilkes-Barre, Pennsylvania, is the author of *The Frangible Hour*, recipient of the Richard Wilbur Award; *Lines of Flight*, shortlisted for the Poets' Prize; *Glad and Sorry Seasons*; *This Sweet Order*; *Pointing Home*; and *Annals of the Dear Unknown*, a historical verse-tale based on the settlement of Wyoming Valley, Pennsylvania, in the 1770s. She is a winner of the Howard Nemerov Sonnet Award, the Leslie Mellichamp Prize, and the *Lyric Quarterly* Prize. Catherine's detailed bio, podcasts, SoundCloud audio recordings, reviews, and other information are available on her poetry blog, *The Wonderful Boat*, at cathychandler.blogspot.ca.

JOSEPH A. CHELIUS is the author of two collections of poetry: *The Art of Acquiescence* (2014) and *Crossing State Lines* (2020), both published by WordTech Communications. He is a former Bucks County poet laureate (2000) and worked for many years as a senior editor and editorial director in the healthcare communications industry. Joe grew up in southwest Philadelphia and in the Delaware County suburbs. He received a BA from LaSalle University and an MA in creative writing from Temple University. His work has appeared in such journals as *Commonweal, Poetry East, Poet Lore, Rattle, Schuylkill Valley Journal*, and *THINK.*

JACK CHIELLI grew up in a family that loved poetry. Summer evenings at the family's beach cottage would often be spent with his mother and older siblings taking turns reading their favorite poets. His poems have appeared in a number of literary journals. He is vice president of enrollment management, marketing, and communications for Mount St. Mary's University. Jack's career has included work as a newspaper journalist, magazine editor, and political communications director. He lives in Frederick, Maryland, and has an MA in poetry from Wilkes University and a BA in writing from Roger Williams University.

DAVID CHIN'S poems have appeared in various journals and anthologies. He has published two books of poetry, *Chalked in Orange* and *The China Cupboard and the Coal Furnace*. Chin has lived in northeastern Pennsylvania for over twenty-five years. He teaches at Penn State Wilkes-Barre, where he is the program coordinator of English.

GRANT CLAUSER is the author of several books, including *Muddy Dragon on the Road to Heaven* (Codhill Press, 2020). His poems have appeared in the *American Poetry Review*, *Greensboro Review*, *Kenyon Review*, and other journals. He was the 2010 Montgomery County poet laureate. He camps, hikes, and gardens in Pennsylvania and teaches at Rosemont College. grantclauser.com

CHARLES CLIFTON is a Pitt-Johnstown professor emeritus and member of the NAACP Executive Committee, Johnstown District. He writes for the *Tribune-Democrat*.

JOSHUA P. COHEN is a librarian at Elizabethtown College in Pennsylvania. In addition to poetry, he writes plays and songs. His poems have been nominated for the Pushcart Prize and the Best of the Net and were most recently published in the *Westchester Review* and the *Hawaii Pacific Review*. His plays have been performed in Lancaster and the central Pennsylvania region.

GERALDINE CONNOLLY was born in western Pennsylvania. She has published four poetry collections, including *Province of Fire* (Iris Press, 1998) and *Aileron* (Terrapin Books, 2018). She has taught at the Writers Center in Bethesda, Maryland, the Chautauqua Institution, and the University of Arizona Poetry Center. She has received fellowships from the National Endowment for the Arts, the Maryland Arts Council, and Bread Loaf Writers Conference. Her work appears in many anthologies, including *Poetry 180: A Poem a Day for American High School Students*, *A Constellation of Kisses*, and *The Sonoran Desert: A Field Guide*. She lives in Tucson, Arizona. Her website is geraldineconnolly.com.

PAOLA CORSO is the author of seven books of poetry and fiction set in her native Pittsburgh area, where her southern Italian immigrant family members were steelworkers. Her latest are *Vertical Bridges: Poems and Photographs of City Steps*; *The Laundress Catches Her Breath*, winner of the Tillie Olsen Award for Creative Writing; and *Catina's Haircut: A Novel in Stories*. As a member of the Park Slope Windsor Terrace Artists collective, Corso's photographs have been exhibited in galleries, libraries, and open houses. She cofounded Steppin Stanzas, a grassroots performing arts project to celebrate city steps. She also cofounded The Ferlinghetti Girls to celebrate Lawrence Ferlinghetti's vision of free speech and poetry for the people. She divides her time between New York's grid and Pittsburgh's grade. Visit her at www.paolajocorso.com.

BARBARA CROOKER is the author of twelve chapbooks and ten full-length books of poetry, including *Some Glad Morning* (Pitt Poetry Series, University of Pittsburgh Press, 2019), which was longlisted for the Julie Suk award from Jacar Press; *The Book of Kells*, which won the Best Poetry Book of 2019 Award from Poetry by the Sea; and *Slow Wreckage* (Grayson Books, 2024). Her other awards include Grammy Awards Finalist, the WB Yeats Society of New York Award, the Thomas Merton Poetry of the Sacred Award, and three Pennsylvania Council fellowships in literature. Her work appears in literary journals and anthologies, including *The Bedford Introduction to Literature*. barbaracrooker.com

CRAIG CZURY is from the Wilkes-Barre area of Pennsylvania and the author of *Postcards & Ancient Texts* (a forty-year collection of napkin poems), *Fifteen Stones* (prose poems from Italy, Chile, Lithuania, and the spaces between), and *Thumb Notes Almanac: Hitchhiking the Marcellus Shale* (docu-poems from his observations and interviews while hitchhiking rural roads in the heart of northeastern Pennsylvania's "fracking" region). A 2022 Fulbright Scholar to Chile, he is currently living in Scranton (Dunmore), where he continues his weekly online Life-Writing from Cyberia workshops and community writing projects. craigczury.com

JIM DANIELS has authored thirty collections of poetry, seven collections of fiction, and four produced screenplays. His most recent books include *The Luck of the Fall* (fiction; Michigan State University Press) and *The Human Engine at Dawn* (Wolfson Press) and *Comment Card* (Carnegie Mellon University Press), both poetry. His first collection of nonfiction, *An Ignorance of Trees*, is forthcoming from Cornerstone Press. He has also edited or coedited six anthologies. He is a recipient of two fellowships from the National Endowment for the Arts and two from the Pennsylvania Council on the Arts. His work has been published in the *Best American Poetry* and *Pushcart Prize* volumes. He lives in Pittsburgh and teaches in the Alma College low-residency MFA Program.

MARK DANOWSKY is editor-in-chief of *ONE ART: a journal of poetry*. His poetry collections include *Meatless* (Plan B Press), *Violet Flame* (tiny wren lit), *JAWN* (Moonstone Press), and *As Falls Trees* (NightBallet Press). His latest, *Take Care*, is forthcoming from Moon Tide Press.

CORTNEY DAVIS, a nurse practitioner, is the author of five poetry collections, most recently *I Hear Their Voices Singing: Poems New & Selected* and *Daughter*. She is also the author of three memoirs and coeditor of three anthologies of creative writing by nurses. Honors include an NEA Poetry Fellowship, three Connecticut Commission on Tourism and the Arts Poetry Grants, the *Prairie Schooner* Poetry Prize, the Wheelbarrow Poetry Prize, a Benjamin Franklin Gold Medal in Non-Fiction Award, a Tillie Olsen Creative Writing Award, and two Connecticut Center for the Book Awards. Her poems have appeared in *Last Stanza, inScribe, Poetry, Hanging Loose, Bellevue Literary Review, Nostos, Hamilton Stone Review, CALYX, Intima,* and other journals and anthologies.

NOAH DAVIS grew up in Tipton, Pennsylvania, and writes about the Allegheny Front. His forthcoming poetry collection, *The Last Beast We Revel In,* will be published by CavanKerry Press. Davis's first collection, *Of This River,* won the Wheelbarrow Emerging Poet Book Prize from Michigan State University's Center for Poetry, and his poems and prose have appeared in *The Sun, Southern Humanities Review, Best New Poets, Orion, Year's Best Sports Writing, North American Review,* and elsewhere. His work has been awarded a Katharine Bakeless Nason Fellowship at the Bread Loaf Writers' Conference and the Jean Ritchie Appalachian Literature Fellowship. Davis earned an MFA from Indiana University and currently lives with his wife, Nikea, in Massachusetts. noahdaviswriter.word press.com

TODD DAVIS is the author of eight books of poetry, most recently *Ditch Memory: New & Selected Poems* (2024) and *Coffin Honey* (2022), both published by Michigan State University Press. His writing has won the Foreword INDIES Book of the Year Bronze and Silver Awards, the Midwest Book Award, the Gwendolyn Brooks Poetry Prize, the Chautauqua Editor's Prize, and the Bloomsburg University Book Prize. He is an emeritus fellow of the Black Earth Institute and teaches environmental studies at Penn State University's Altoona College. He is coeditor, with Noah Davis, of *A Literary Field Guide to Northern Appalachia* from University of Georgia Press (2024). todddavispoet.com

TOI DERRICOTTE's sixth collection of poetry, *I: New and Selected Poems,* was shortlisted for the 2019 National Book Award. She won the Pegasus Award from the Poetry Foundation in 2023, the Wallace Stevens Award from the Academy of American Poets in 2021, and the Frost Medal from the Poetry Society of America in 2020. With Cornelius Eady, she cofounded Cave Canem, a home for the many voices of African American poetry, in 1996. toiderricotte.com

GREGORY DJANIKIAN has published seven collections of poetry with Carnegie Mellon, the latest of which is *Sojourners of the In-Between* (2020). His poems have appeared in many journals, most recently in *Bennington Review, Crazyhorse, New Ohio Review, Poet Lore, Poetry International,* and *Raleigh Review,* and in

279

many anthologies, including *Good Poems, American Places* (Viking), *Killer Verse: Poems of Murder and Mayhem* (Knopf), *Becoming Americans: Four Centuries of Immigrant Writing* (Library of America), *Language for a New Century: Contemporary Poetry from the Middle East, Asia & Beyond* (Norton), and *180 More: Extraordinary Poems for Every Day* (Random House). gregorydjanikian.com

DANIEL DONAGHY is the author of five poetry collections, including *Somerset*, co-winner of the Paterson Poetry Prize; *Start with the Trouble*, winner of the University of Arkansas Press Poetry Prize; and *Streetfighting*, a Paterson Poetry Prize Finalist. He received *Southern Humanities Review*'s Auburn Witness Poetry Prize for his poem "Tulsa Triptych." Originally from Philadelphia, he is now a professor of English at Eastern Connecticut State University. danieldonaghy.com

JOSEPH DORAZIO'S poems have appeared in over sixty-five literary venues, including the *Southampton Review, Worcester Review, Atlanta Review, Hong Kong Review, Hampden-Sydney Review, Maynard, Pamplemousse, Schuylkill Valley Journal, West Texas Literary Review, Fourth River*, and elsewhere. The author of five chapbooks of poetry, Dorazio's poems have been anthologized and set to music. He lives in Wayne, Pennsylvania.

LISA M. DOUGHERTY is the author of *Somewhere on the Ledge of Fallen Things*, forthcoming from Propel Books's disability poetry series in conjunction with Syracuse University Press. She is the coauthor of *The Answer Is Not Here* (Night Ballet Press, 2019) and the chapbook *Small as Hope in the Helicopter Rain* (Cervena Barva Press).

SEAN THOMAS DOUGHERTY'S twenty books include *Death Prefers the Minor Keys* (BOA Editions, 2023) and *The Dead Are Everywhere Telling Us Things*, winner of the 2021 Jacar Press Full Length book contest. He works as a medical technician and caregiver for folks with traumatic brain injuries. His website is seanthomas doughertypoet.com.

FAITH ELLINGTON is a poet and a PhD candidate at Louisiana State University. She received her undergraduate degree from the University of Iowa in English and creative writing. Her writing explores place, the body, and violence. *Fortuna Redux*, her first full collection of poetry, will be available in spring 2025 through Gnashing Teeth Publishing. Her creative works can be found at faithellington.com.

LYNN EMANUEL is the author of *Noose and Hook*; *Hotel Fiesta*; *The Dig*; *Then, Suddenly—*; *The Nerve of It: New and Selected Poems*, which received the Lenore Marshall Award from the Academy of American Poets; and most recently, *Transcript of the Disappearance, Exact and Diminishing*. Her work has been collected numerous times in *Best American Poetry* and included in *The Oxford Book of American Poetry*. She has been published and reviewed in the *New York Times Book Review*, *New York Review of Books*, *LA Review of Books*, *BOMB Magazine*, *Poetry*, and *Publisher's Weekly*. She has been a judge for the National Book Awards and has taught at many venues, including the Warren Wilson Program and the Bread Loaf Writers' Conference.

SHARON FAGAN MCDERMOTT is a poet, essayist, and a teacher of literature at Winchester Thurston School in Pittsburgh. She has four collections of poetry published—the chapbooks *Voluptuous, Alley Scatting* (Parallel Press), and *Bitter Acoustic* (winner of the 2011 Jacar Press chapbook competition) and her full manuscript, *Life Without Furniture*, published by Jacar Press in 2018. Recently, Fagan McDermott's first collection of essays, *Millions of Suns: On Writing and Life*, was coauthored by M. C. Benner Dixon through the University of Michigan Press. It is part of their Writers on Writing series and was named one of the "Best Books for Writers" by *Poets & Writers* magazine. sharonfaganmcdermott.com

BRIAN FANELLI is the author of *Waiting for the Dead to Speak* (NYQ Books, 2016), winner of the Devil's Kitchen Poetry Prize. He is also coeditor of the recent anthology *Currents in the Electric City: A Scranton Anthology* (Belt Publishing). Brian's creative writing and essays on film have been published in the *LA Times*, *Paterson Literary Review*, *Main Street Rag*, *Pedestal*, *Schuylkill Valley Journal*, *Bright Lights Film Journal*, *Signal Horizon Magazine*, and elsewhere. Brian has an MFA from Wilkes University and a PhD from Binghamton University (SUNY). He is an associate professor of English at Lackawanna College. brianfanelli.com

SANDY FEINSTEIN'S poetry appeared most recently in *Willows Wept* (2024) and in 2023 in *Pivot*, the *Humanities Review*, and *Seems*. Her chapbook, *Swimming to Syria*, published by Penumbra Press, was released in 2021.

KEN FIFER is the author of five poetry collections, most recently *Caravaggio's Kimono* (Longleaf Press, 2024). His poems have appeared in such journals as *Barrow Street*, *California Quarterly*, *Epoch*, *New Letters*, *Literary Review*, *Missouri Review*, and *Ploughshares*. He has taught and read at conferences, poetry festivals, and universities from Ankara to Paris. A professor emeritus at Penn State University, he lives and works in Center Valley, Pennsylvania, with his wife and extended family, six dogs, two cats, and a parrot.

ROBERT FILLMAN is the author of *House Bird* (Terrapin, 2022) and *November Weather Spell* (Main Street Rag, 2019). Individual poems have appeared in such venues as the *Hollins Critic*, *Poetry East*, *Salamander*, *Spoon River Poetry Review*,

Tar River Poetry, and *Verse Daily*. His criticism has been published in *ISLE: Interdisciplinary Studies in Literature and the Environment*, *CLAJ: The College Language Association Journal*, and elsewhere. He holds a PhD in English from Lehigh University and teaches at Kutztown University in eastern Pennsylvania. robertfillman.com

GARY FINCKE has published fifteen poetry collections, including ones that won prizes from Ohio State, Michigan State, Arkansas, Jacar, and Stephen F. Austin. His newest collection is *For Now, We Have Been Spared* (Slant Books, 2024).

VALERIE FOX is a poet and fiction writer. Her poetry books include *The Rorschach Factory*, *The Glass Book*, and *Insomniatic*. Her stories have appeared in the Best Small Fictions and Best Microfiction series as well as *The Group of Seven Reimagined: Contemporary Stories Inspired by Historic Canadian Paintings*. With visual artist Jacklynn Niemiec, Valerie created *The Real Sky*, a collaborative artists book in an edition of twenty-six handmade copies. She coauthored, with Lynn Levin, *Poems for the Writing: Prompts for Poets*. She's taught writing at Drexel University (in Philadelphia), including with Writers Room, and at Sophia University (in Tokyo). Her I handle is @valeriefoxpftw.

JAN FREEMAN is the author of three books of poetry, most recently *Blue Structure* (Calypso Editions). Her fourth collection, *The Odyssey of Yes and No*, was completed during a recent fellowship at MacDowell. Her poems have appeared in *American Poetry Review*, *Barrow Street*, *Brooklyn Rail*, *North American Review*, *Painted Bride Quarterly*, *Plume*, *Poetry*, *Salamander*, and many other publications. She is the founder and former director of Paris Press (now part of Wesleyan University Press) and teaches ekphrastic poetry workshops and the MASS MoCA Writing Through Art Poetry Retreats. janfreeman.net

ROBBIE GAMBLE was born in Philadelphia. He is the author of *A Can of Pinto Beans* (Lily Poetry Review Press, 2022). His poems have appeared in *Poet Lore*, *Post Road*, *Salamander*, and *The Sun*. He is the poetry editor of *Solstice: A Magazine of Diverse Voices*, and he now divides his time between Boston and Vermont.

MICHAEL GARRIGAN writes and teaches along the Susquehanna River in Pennsylvania. He loves exploring the riverlands and believes that every watershed should have a poet laureate. He is the author of two poetry collections—*River, Amen*, and *Robbing the Pillars*. His writing has appeared in *Orion*, *River Teeth*, *Flyfish Journal*, and *North American Review*. He was the 2021 artist in residence for the Bob Marshall Wilderness Area, and you can read more of his work at mgarrigan.com.

ROSS GAY grew up in the Philadelphia suburbs, playing football and basketball, and he later attended Lafayette College, where he played football and discovered his love of poetry. He's the author of four books of poetry: *Against Which*; *Bringing the Shovel Down*; *Be Holding*, winner of the PEN American Literary Jean Stein Award; and *Catalog of Unabashed Gratitude*, winner of the 2015 National Book Critics Circle Award and the 2016 Kingsley Tufts Poetry Award. He has also published three essay collections: *The Book of Delights, Inciting Joy*, and *The Book of (More) Delights*. rossgay.net/about

CHRISTINE GELINEAU is the author of three full-length books of poetry: *Crave* from NYQ Books; the book-length sequence *Appetite for the Divine*, published as the Editor's Choice for the Robert McGovern Prize from Ashland Poetry Press; and *Remorseless Loyalty*, winner of the Richard Snyder Memorial Prize, also from Ashland Poetry Press. Gelineau's poetry and essays have been widely published in journals and online in venues such as *Verse Daily* and *Rattle*. A recipient of the Pushcart Prize, she teaches in the Maslow Family Graduate Program in Creative Writing at Wilkes University, having retired from Binghamton University, where she taught for twenty-six years and served as associate director of the creative writing program. Gelineau lives on a farm in the Susquehanna River Valley, just north of the state line but within sight of Pennsylvania. christinegelineau.com

SANDEE GERTZ is a native of western Pennsylvania and the author of *The Pattern Maker's Daughter*, a poetry collection published by Bottom Dog Press in 2012. She has published her poetry, essays, and memoir pieces in literary journals for over twenty-five years, including *Green Mountains Review, Gargoyle, Poet Lore, Northern Appalachia Review, Wild Roof Journal, Cathexis Northwest Press, Café Review*, and more. She was recognized as one of sixteen working-class poets in *World Literature Today* and is a Sandburg-Livesay Poetry Award winner. More recently, she won the Mary Jean Irion Prize in Poetry from the Friends of the Chautauqua Writers' Center, judged by Mary Biddinger. She is currently working to complete a novel and teaches English and creative writing at Cumberland University as an associate professor. Her MFA is from Wilkes University. Her website can be found at sandeegertz.com.

Based in Adams County, KATY GIEBENHAIN is the author of *Sharps Cabaret* (Mercer University Press, 2021). Her poems and prose have appeared in *New Welsh Review, Arkansas Review, Examined Life Journal, Poetry X Hunger, Pittsburgh Quarterly, BMJ Medical Humanities* blog, and elsewhere. She occasionally blogs at *Big Pharma and the Barkeep*. Her creative writing MPhil is from University of South Wales (Glamorgan). Giebenhain co-hosts a poetry series at The

Ragged Edge Coffeehouse in Gettysburg with Alan Bogage and Marty Malone. katygiebenhain.com

S. E. GILMAN has worked in social services, publishing, bookstores, kitchens, and academia. She has taught writing and literacy tutoring in a variety of contexts—in universities, community settings, at a correctional institution, and on reservations. Native to Galveston, Texas, she has lived in Austin, Texas; various towns in New Hampshire; Davis, California; and now in central Pennsylvania. Her publications include essays in the anthologies *Letters to Our Children: Lesbian and Gay Adults Speak to the New Generation* and *Where We Find Ourselves: Jewish Women Around the World Write About Home.* Her short fiction has appeared in *Common Bonds: Stories By and About Modern Texas Women,* and in the magazines *Permafrost, Hawaiian Review, Stone Drum, Oxford Magazine, modern words,* and others. Gilman's poetry has appeared more recently in *Meat for Tea* and *Word Fountain.*

MIKE GOOD lives in Pittsburgh and is the managing editor of Autumn House Press. Some of his recent poetry and book reviews can be found in *Bennington Review, Colorado Review, Five Points, Greensboro Review, Missouri Review, Ploughshares, Prolit, Puerto del Sol, Sugar House Review, Terrain.org, Waxwing, ZYZZYVA,* and elsewhere. He has received scholarships from *The Sun* and the Sewanee Writers' Conference. Find more at mikegoodwrites.wordpress.com.

JOANNE GROWNEY grew up on a farm near Indiana, Pennsylvania, and started loving poetry while very young—initiated by R. L. Stevenson's *A Child's Garden of Verses.* However, her college education was funded by a science scholarship, which led to a career in mathematics. She taught math courses for many years at Pennsylvania's Bloomsburg University. Now, in retirement, she continues to enjoy reading and writing in both these fields—and is perhaps best known for her blog, *Intersections—Poetry with Mathematics,* which can be found at poetrywithmathematics.blogspot.com. A sampling of her non-mathy work can be found at joannegrowney.com.

MAURICIO KILWEIN GUEVARA was born in Boyacá, Colombia, and raised in Pittsburgh. He has published four collections of poetry and a book of translations in Spain. His play, *The Last Bridge / El último puente,* received a fully staged reading Off-Broadway. A selection of his poetry will be included in *Latino Poetry: The Library of America Anthology,* edited by Rigoberto González. He taught creative writing and literature for many years in the English department at the University of Wisconsin–Milwaukee. Learn more about the author at kilweinguevara.com.

LILACE MELLIN GUIGNARD lives with her husband and two children in rural north-central Pennsylvania, where she enjoys playing outdoors and is associate editor and publisher of *Mountain Home* magazine. She has taught creative writing, outdoor recreation leadership, and women's studies at Mansfield University. Her poetry has appeared in *CALYX*, *Ecotone*, and *Poetry*. She is the author of the chapbook *Young at the Time of Letting* Go (Evening Street Press, 2016) and the adventure memoir *When Everything Beyond the Walls Is Wild: Being a Woman Outdoors in America* (Texas A&M University Press, 2019). For more information, see tentofonesown.com.

VERNITA HALL is the author of *Where William Walked: Poems About Philadelphia and Its People of Color*, winner of the Willow Books Grand Prize and the Robert Creeley Prize (Marsh Hawk Press, 2019), and *The Hitchhiking Robot Learns About Philadelphians*, winner of the Moonstone Press Chapbook Contest. Her poems have appeared in *Poetry*, *American Poetry Review*, *African American Review*, *Barrow Street*, *The Common*, *River Styx*, *Solstice*, *Hopkins Review*, *Arts & Letters*, and elsewhere. She holds an MFA in creative writing from Rosemont College and serves on the poetry review board of *Philadelphia Stories*. vernitahall.com

STANTON HANCOCK is a writer, musician, and educator currently living in Pennsylvania's Lehigh Valley with his wife, daughter, and several cats. When he isn't writing or performing his poetry, you can find him at the local record store or composing and performing music. He has an MFA in creative writing from Wilkes University and is currently working on a novel.

Originally from Los Angeles, MICHAEL HARDIN has lived in Danville, Pennsylvania, since 1999 with his wife and two children. He is the author of a chapbook, *Born Again*, from Moonstone Press (2019); has had poems and flash creative nonfiction published in *Seneca Review*, *Wisconsin Review*, *North American Review*, *Quarterly West*, and elsewhere; and has been nominated for a Pushcart Prize.

YONA HARVEY is the author of *You Don't Have to Go to Mars for Love* (2020), winner of *The Believer* Book Award in Poetry, and *Hemming the Water* (2013), winner of the Kate Tufts Discovery Award. Her writing has appeared in numerous publications and earned a Guggenheim Fellowship and Japan Creative Artists Fellowship. She lived in Pittsburgh for several years before moving to Northampton, Massachusetts, where she is the Tammis Day Professor of Poetry at Smith College. Her website is yonaharvey.com.

TERRANCE HAYES is the author of six prizewinning collections of poetry and has received numerous accolades for his work, including a MacArthur Foundation Fellowship and a National Book Award. His most recent books are *So to Speak* (Penguin Poets, 2023), *Watch Your Language: Visual and Literary Reflections on a Century of American Poetry* (Penguin Books, 2023), and *American Sonnets for My Past and Future Assassin* (Penguin Poets, 2018). Hayes has had a long connection to the city of Pittsburgh, studying poetry there as a graduate student and then returning to teach at Carnegie Mellon University and the University of Pittsburgh.

K. A. HAYS is the author of *Anthropocene Lullaby* (Carnegie Mellon, 2022) and three prior full-length collections of poetry. Hays teaches in the creative writing program at Bucknell University and lives with her family in Lewisburg, Pennsylvania. kahays.com

JOCELYN HEATH is an associate professor of English at Norfolk State University. Her debut poetry collection, *In the Cosmic Fugue*, was published in 2022. Her writing has appeared in *The Atlantic, Crab Orchard Review, Poet Lore, Sinister Wisdom, Fourth River*, and elsewhere. jocelynheath.wordpress.com/bio

GLORIA HEFFERNAN'S *Exploring Poetry of Presence* (Back Porch Productions) won the 2021 CNY Book Award for Nonfiction. She received the 2022 *Naugatuck River Review* Narrative Poetry Prize. Gloria is the author of the collections *Peregrinatio: Poems for Antarctica* (Kelsay Books) and *What the Gratitude List Said to the Bucket List* (New York Quarterly Books). Her forthcoming chapbook, *Animal Grace*, was selected for the Keystone Chapbook Series prize. Her work has appeared in more than one hundred publications, including *Poetry of Presence: A Companion Guide for Readers, Writers, and Workshop Facilitators* . To learn more, visit gloriaheffernan.wordpress.com.

ERNEST HILBERT is the author of the poetry collections *Sixty Sonnets, All of You on the Good Earth, Caligulan*—selected as winner of the 2017 Poets' Prize—and *Last One Out* (Measure Press, 2019). His fifth book, *Storm Swimmer*, was selected by Rowan Ricardo Phillips as the winner of the 2022 Vassar Miller Prize. Visit him at ernesthilbert.com.

LE HINTON is the author of seven poetry collections, including *Elegies for an Empire* (2023) and *Sing Silence* (2018). His work has been widely published and can be found in *Best American Poetry 2014, Baltimore Review, Progressive Magazine, Pleiades, Summerset Review*, and elsewhere. His poems have received multiple nominations for the Pushcart Prize. His poem "Epidemic" won the *Baltimore Review*'s 2013 Winter Writers Contest. In 2014 it was honored by the

Pennsylvania Center for the Book, and in 2021 it was featured on the WPSU program *Poetry Moment*. His poem "Our Ballpark" can be found outside Clipper Magazine Stadium in Lancaster, Pennsylvania, incorporated into Derek Parker's sculpture *Common Thread*. More information can be found at LeHinton.com.

EDWARD HIRSCH, a MacArthur Fellow, has published ten books of poems and six books about poetry, including *How to Read a Poem and Fall in Love with Poetry* (1999), a national bestseller; *The Living Fire: New and Selected Poems* (2010), which brings together thirty-five years of his work; *100 Poems to Break Your Heart* (2023); and *Gabriel: A Poem* (2014), a book-length elegy for his son that the *New Yorker* called "a masterpiece of sorrow." He is the president of the John Simon Guggenheim Memorial Foundation.

AMANDA HODES is a writer and news media artist. She is currently lecturer of poetry in creative writing at Oberlin College and Conservatory. Her poetry has been published in *Black Warrior Review, Prairie Schooner, Pleiades, AMBIT, Denver Quarterly, PANK, West Branch, Quarterly West, Interim Poetics*, and elsewhere. She also has an MFA in creative writing from Virginia Tech and an MA in creative writing from the University of East Anglia. As an artist, she is interested in sound installation as a route to a somatic, spatial poetics. Such work has been exhibited in venues such as the Crisp-Ellert Art Museum, Torpedo Factory, Abington Arts Center, Hirshhorn Sound Scene Festival, Ammerman Center for Arts and Technology, AUDIRE, and Dartington International Music Festival. amandakhodes .wixsite.com/home

CYNTHIA HOGUE's tenth poetry collection is *instead, it is dark* (Red Hen Press, 2023). Her ekphrastic COVID-19 chapbook is entitled *Contain* (Tram Editions, 2022), and her third collaborative translation from the French of Nicole Brossard is *Distantly* (Omnidawn, 2022). She served as the second director of the Stadler Center for Poetry at Bucknell University from 1995 to 2003. There, she trained in conflict resolution with the Mennonites, earning her certificate in conflict mediation. Among her honors are a Fulbright Fellowship to Iceland, two NEA Fellowships, and the Harold Morton Landon Translation Award from the Academy of American Poets. She served as guest editor for *Poem-a-Day*, sponsored by the Academy of American Poets, for September 2022. Hogue was the inaugural Maxine and Jonathan Marshall Chair in Modern and Contemporary Poetry at Arizona State University. She lives in Tucson. Her website is cynthiahogue.com.

An editor with *Loch Raven Review*, MATT HOHNER (MFA, Naropa University) has published two collections: *At the Edge of a Thousand Years*, winner of the 2023

Jacar Press Full-Length Book Prize, and *Thresholds and Other Poems* (Apprentice House, 2018). He has held two residencies at the Virginia Center for the Creative Arts, with one forthcoming at Anam Cara in Ireland. His publications include work in *Prairie Fire, Rattle: Poets Respond, takahē, New Contrast, Narrative Magazine, Poetry Ireland, Prairie Schooner, Baltimore Review*, and elsewhere. matthohner .wordpress.com

BYRON HOOT was born and raised in Appalachia. He left, then returned, and now lives in the wilds of Pennsylvania. He is retired and a nemophilist: one who is fond of forests or forest scenery. He also is a haunter of the woods and regularly spends time in a particular place. To him, this is not escapism but in the tradition of Thoreau, Leopold, Berry, and others who see our humanness in our response to the land, which, in turn, is a reflection of how we treat ourselves and others. Hoot writes of what he knows in hope of a "new heaven and earth" where we can be the brothers and sisters we are. For more information, see hootnhowlpoetry.com.

Born in Harrisburg, Pennsylvania, and raised in Perry and Cumberland Counties, ERIN HOOVER is the author of two poetry collections, *Barnburner* (Elixir, 2018) and *No Spare People* (Black Lawrence, 2023). She currently lives in Tennessee and teaches creative writing as an assistant professor of English at Tennessee Tech University. More poems and professional updates are available at her website, erinhooverpoet.com.

ANN HOSTETLER is the author of two collections of poetry, *Safehold* (2018) and *Empty Room with Light* (2002), and the editor of *A Cappella: Mennonite Voices in Poetry* (2003). She is professor emerita at Goshen College in Goshen, Indiana, where she taught literature and creative writing for twenty-two years. She edits the *Journal of Mennonite Writing* (www.mennonitewriting.org) and is the publisher of Painted Glass Press (www.paintedglasspress.com). Her poems and essays have appeared in *American Scholar* and numerous other journals and anthologies, including *Common Wealth: Contemporary Poets on Pennsylvania*. annhostetler.com

HARRY HUMES was born in Girardville, Pennsylvania, in Schuylkill County. The geography of that place permeates his work with stories of his parents and siblings trying to scratch out a hardscrabble life. Humes spent his career teaching at Kutztown University and now lives in the countryside with his wife. He's the author of fourteen books of poetry, among them *August Evening with Trumpet, Ridge Music*, and *Butterfly Effect*, which was selected by Pattiann Rogers as a winner of the National Poetry Series. His poetry has won many awards, including the Devins Award, the Theodore Roethke Poetry Prize, and a National Endowment for the Arts Poetry Fellowship.

MARIA JAMES-THIAW is a poet, playwright, professor, and busy mom of two. A graduate of Goddard College, she is the author of four books and two choreopoems for the stage. A dynamic spoken-word artist, she writes about social justice topics and the oral histories she collects as part of her American Griot Project. In 2018 her choreopoem, *Reclaiming My Time: An American Griot Project*, won the Art of Protest Poetry Prize from the Center for American Literary Studies at Penn State University. In 2023 she joined the movement to end hair texture bias with her choreopoem *HairStory: Reclaiming Our Crown*. When she isn't writing, performing, and teaching, Maria can be found relaxing with an adult coloring book and her favorite Zora Neale Hurston mug full of coffee. mariathepoet.com

JULIE SWARSTAD JOHNSON is the author of the poetry collection *Pennsylvania Furnace* (Unicorn Press, 2019) and coeditor of the anthology *Beyond Earth's Edge: The Poetry of Spaceflight* (University of Arizona Press, 2020). She has served as poet in residence at Lowell Observatory in Flagstaff, Arizona, and at Gettysburg National Military Park, which led to the chapbook *Orchard Light* (Seven Kitchens Press, 2020). She lives in Tucson and works as an archivist and librarian at the University of Arizona Poetry Center. julieswarstadjohnson.com

CHUCK JOY is a poet born in Cleveland and residing in Erie. He has a BA from Fordham University (1973) and an MD from the University of Pittsburgh School of Medicine (1978). He is a child psychiatrist whose poems have appeared in many magazines, including *Tempus*, *Tobeco*, *Lilliput Review*, *Great Lakes Review*, *JAMA*, and *Main Street Rag*. His books include *Vinyl* (What Why Aesthetics), *Percussive* (Turning Point), and *Said the Growling Dog* (Nirala Publications). Joy hosted weekly poetry events for years in Erie at Erie Book Store and then at Calamari's. He was poet laureate for Erie County, Pennsylvania, from 2018 to 2021. To find out more, see chuckjoy.com.

JULIA SPICHER KASDORF has published five collections of poetry, most recently *As Is* (Pitt Poetry Series, University of Pittsburgh Press, 2023). In collaboration with photographer Steven Rubin, she published *Shale Play: Poems and Photographs from the Fracking Fields* (Keystone Books, 2018). Other poetry collections include *Poetry in America* (2011), *Eve's Striptease* (1998), and *Sleeping Preacher* (1992), all from the Pitt Poetry Series. A professor of English, Kasdorf directs the creative writing program at Penn State University. juliakasdorf.com

JUDITH A. KENNEDY lives along the Susquehanna River in Lancaster County, Pennsylvania. She has two books of poetry, *To See in the Night* and *Salted Wakings*. She is working on a third book, *Variances of Light*. "In the Center of the Fire" was set to music for choir by composer Bruce Pennycook of the Butler School of

Music at the University of Texas at Austin. She participates in spoken-word performances with Write Face, a support group for veterans, with poems inspired by her great-grandfather's Civil War memoir. She currently serves on borough council and chairs the Marietta Tree Commission, which has partnered with Keystone Ten Million Tree Project and the Chesapeake Bay Foundation.

KRISTIN KOVACIC'S essays have won the Pushcart Prize, the Pennsylvania Council on the Arts Fellowship, and the Orison Books Prize for Best Spiritual Writing, among other awards. Her work has appeared recently in *Slate, Belt, Coachella Review, Chautauqua, Table Magazine*, and other publications. She is the author of the essay collection *History of My Breath* and the poetry chapbook *House of Women*, and, with Lynne Barrett, she coedited *Birth: A Literary Companion*. She has taught nonfiction writing at every level, including at Winchester Thurston School, the Pittsburgh High School for the Creative and Performing Arts, and in the graduate programs of Carlow University and Chatham University. She lives and works in a deconsecrated Catholic church on the South Side of Pittsburgh.

LEONARD KRESS grew up in and around Philadelphia. He studied religion at Temple University, creative writing at Columbia University, and Polish at the Jagiellonian University in Krakow, Poland. He has published poetry, fiction, nonfiction, and translations in literary journals like *Massachusetts Review, Iowa Review, American Poetry Review*, and *Harvard Review* as well as seven poetry collections, including *Living in the Candy Store, Walk Like Bo Diddley*, and *The Orpheus Complex*. His most recent collections are *Craniotomy Sestinas* and *Poppy Seeds*. He has also published a translation of the nineteenth-century Polish romantic epic *Pan Tadeusz* by Adam Mickiewicz. He has been awarded two Individual Artist Fellowships from the Ohio Arts Council and three fellowships in poetry and playwriting from the Pennsylvania Council on the Arts. leonardkress.com

RICHARD KROHN has spent much of his life in Pennsylvania, mostly in the Lehigh Valley but also for several years in Venango County. His car travel and bicycling have taken him to every corner of the state. He currently teaches economics and medical Spanish at Moravian University in Bethlehem. In addition to some history writing about Moravian schools and about Allentown, he has published work in *Tar River, Poet Lore, Journal of NJ Poets, Rio Grande*, and elsewhere. Always eager to talk about Pennsylvania and about poetry, he can be reached at krohn.richard@gmail.com.

PETER KROK is the editor of *Schuylkill Valley Journal* and serves as the humanities and poetry director at the Manayunk-Roxborough Art Center. His poems have appeared in *American Poetry, America, Midwest Quarterly, Poet Lore, Potomac Review, Fulcrum, THINK*, and more. His book *Looking for an Eye* was published in 2008.

REBECCA LAUREN grew up in Pennsylvania's Susquehanna Valley and currently lives in Philadelphia, where she serves as assistant provost for academic operations at Eastern University and as managing editor of Saturnalia Books. Her writing has been published in *Mid-American Review, Prairie Schooner, Southeast Review, Ruminate*, Salon.com, *Journal of Feminist Studies in Religion, Cincinnati Review*, and elsewhere. Her chapbook, *The Schwenkfelders*, won the Keystone Chapbook Prize and was published by Seven Kitchens Press. She is the recipient of an Academy of American Poets award.

DAWN LEAS is the author of *A Person Worth Knowing* (Foothills Publishing), *Take Something When You Go* (Winter Goose Publishing), *The Sin of Being Okay* (Kinsman Avenue Publishing), and *I Know When to Keep Quiet* (Finishing Line Press). Her poetry has appeared in *Verse-Virtual, Redheaded Stepchild, New York Quarterly*, the *Paterson Literary Review, Literary Mama, Pedestal Magazine, SWWIM*, and elsewhere. She's a writer, writing coach, teaching artist with Arts in Education NEPA and Pennsylvania Arts in Education Program (PAEP)—partner organizations of the Pennsylvania Council on the Arts—and the program coordinator for the Maslow Family Graduate Program in Creative Writing at Wilkes University. She's also a proud back-of-the-pack runner, hiker, salt-water lover, and mom of two grown sons. Visit thehammockwriter.com.

LYNN LEVIN is the author of nine books, most recently the short story collection *House Parties* (Spuyten Duyvil, 2023) and the poetry collection *The Minor Virtues* (Ragged Sky, 2020). Her poems, essays, and stories have appeared in *Scientific American, Boulevard, Artful Dodge, Michigan Quarterly Review, Superstition Review*, the *Saturday Evening Post*, and other places. She teaches English and creative writing at Drexel University and, for many years, taught at the University of Pennsylvania. A Bucks County poet laureate, she lives in Southampton, Pennsylvania. Her website is lynnlevinpoet.com.

DAVID LIVEWELL won the T. S. Eliot Poetry Prize for *Shackamaxon* (Truman State University Press, 2012). His poems have appeared in *Poetry, Threepenny Review, Hudson Review*, and other journals. He lives with his family just outside his hometown of Philadelphia; his next collection is forthcoming from Able Muse Press.

GEORGE LOONEY'S recent books include *The Visibility of Things Long Submerged*, which won the BOA Editions Short Fiction Award, and *The Acrobatic*

Company of the Invisible, which won The Cider Press Review Editors' Poetry Prize. He founded the BFA in Creative Writing program at Penn State Behrend, serves as editor of the international literary journal *Lake Effect* and translation editor of *Mid-American Review*, and was cofounder of the original Chautauqua Writers' Festival. georgelooney.org/about

RACHAEL LYON is a poet, essayist, and translator. Her chapbook, *The Normal Heart and How It Works* (2011), is a love letter to her defective heart. She received a Fulbright grant to Vienna, Austria, to translate poetry from German. Her most recent translation, *a tree full of pearl-gray doves* (2018), is a collection of poetry by Irmgard Löschner. Lyon's work has appeared in *Southern Review*, *Hopkins Review*, and elsewhere. Read more at rachlyon.com.

Professor emerita of English and creative writing at the Lock Haven campus of Commonwealth University, MARJORIE MADDOX has published seventeen collections of poetry, most recently *In the Museum of My Daughter's Mind* (Shanti Arts, 2023), a collaboration with her artist daughter Anna Lee Hafer; *Small Earthly Space* (Shanti Arts, 2024), a collaboration with artist Karen Elias; *Seeing Things* (Wildhouse, 2025); and the forthcoming *Hover Here* (Broadstone, 2025). Additional books include the prose collection *What She Was Saying* (Fomite, 2017) and four children's and YA books. With Jerry Wemple, she is coeditor of *Common Wealth: Contemporary Poets on Pennsylvania* (Penn State University Press, 2005). Assistant editor of *Presence: A Journal of Catholic Poetry*, she also hosts *Poetry Moment* at WPSU-FM. For more information, please see marjoriemaddox.com.

PAUL MARTIN'S "Turning Over" previously appeared in *The Backwaters Press Anthology*; the prizewinning chapbook *Mourning Dove* (*Comstock Review*); and Ted Kooser's *American Life in Poetry*. His book *Closing Distances* was published by Backwaters Press. He has published six chapbooks, three of them prize winners.

CHLOE MARTINEZ is a poet, a translator, and a scholar of South Asian religions. She is the author of the collection *Ten Thousand Selves* (The Word Works, 2021) and the chapbook *Corner Shrine*. Her work has appeared in *Ploughshares*, *Poetry*, *Prairie Schooner*, *AGNI*, *Beloit Poetry Journal*, and elsewhere. Her translations have won the Robert Fitzgerald Prize and the Anne Frydman Prize. She is an editorial board member for *Beloit Poetry Journal* and the poetry editor for the *Journal of Feminist Studies in Religion*. She works at Claremont McKenna College. chloeavmartinez.com

From Jamaica, and born to a Jamaican father and a Venezuelan mother, SHARA MCCALLUM has published six books in the United States and United Kingdom, most recently *No Ruined Stone*, winner of the 2022 Hurston/Wright Legacy Award for Poetry. An anthology of her poems in Spanish, *La historia es un cuarto*, was published in 2021 in Mexico. Awards for her work include a Musgrave Medal, NEA Fellowship, Guggenheim Fellowship, and others. McCallum is an Edwin Erle Sparks Professor of English at Penn State University and faculty in the Pacific University low-residency MFA. For a longer bio and more information, visit her website: sharamccallum.com.

ANN E. MICHAEL lives in eastern Pennsylvania, where she ran the writing center at DeSales University for many years. Her most recent collection is *Abundance/Diminishment*. Her book *The Red Queen Hypothesis* won the 2022 Prairie State Poetry Prize; she's the author of *Water-Rites* (2012) and six chapbooks. She maintains a long-running blog at annemichael.blog.

JONSON MILLER grew up in Johnstown, Pennsylvania, and now lives in Bucks County with his partner. He's a historian by profession. His poetry and fiction have appeared in *Blue Collar Review*, *Ninnau*, and *Schuylkill Valley Journal*. "Flight 93 National Memorial" and other poems are largely about either his family's two-hundred-and-fifty-year history in southwestern Pennsylvania or his experiences growing up in a working-class family in a deindustrializing steel town.

ABBY MINOR lives in the ridges and valleys of central Pennsylvania, where she works on poems, essays, gardens, and projects exploring regional and reproductive politics. Her first book, *As I Said: A Dissent* (Ricochet Editions, 2022), is a collection of long documentary poems concerning abortion, justice, and citizenship in US history. Granddaughter of Appalachian tinkerers and Yiddish-speaking New Yorkers, she teaches poetry in her region's low-income nursing homes, volunteers with the internationally active group Abortion Conversation Projects, and co-directs an arts education nonprofit called Ridgelines Language Arts.

NICOLE MIYASHIRO was born in Pennsylvania and spent her teens in Media, where she often strolled to the historic Linvilla Orchards—a place that was nearly destroyed by a 2002 barn fire yet perseveres. She holds an MFA from Rosemont College and has received support from the Pennsylvania Center for the Book—Penn State University Libraries, the Can Serrat International Art Residency, and Vermont Studio Center. Her work appears in *Bi Women Quarterly*, *CALYX*, *Hudson Review*, *Nasty Women Poets* (Lost Horse Press), and elsewhere.

EMILY MILLER MLČÁK'S family has deep roots in Pennsylvania. She was born in New England but returned to Pennsylvania for college. A poet and essayist, Emily also writes and delivers the occasional sermon as well as performing as a singer. She is currently the co-director of the Young Writers Workshop at Bard College and an ADHD coach at Thresholds Coaching. She thinks a lot about what it means to be human. She finds joy in open-water swimming, painting, and weight lifting.

EILEEN DALY MOELLER lives in southern New Jersey with her husband, Charlie. Born in 1950 and raised in Paterson, New Jersey, she has an MA in creative writing from Syracuse University. Her poems have appeared in numerous literary journals and anthologies. She has four books: *Firefly, Brightly Burning* (Grayson Books, 2015), *The Girls in Their Iron Shoes* (Finishing Line Press, 2017), *Silk City Sparrow* (Read Furiously Inc., 2020), and *Waterlings* (WordTech Communications, 2023). Her blog is *And So I Sing: Poems and Iconography* at eileenmoeller.blogspot.com.

BERWYN MOORE'S poetry awards include the *Five Points Journal* James Dickey Prize, the *Bellevue Literary Review* Magliocco Prize, and the John Ciardi Poetry Book Prize for her collection, *Sweet Herbaceous Miracle* (BkMk Press, 2018). Moore served as the first poet laureate of Erie County, Pennsylvania, in 2010. She is professor emerita at Gannon University, where she was named Distinguished Faculty in 2012. She and her husband live in Erie.

A Best of the Net and eight-time Pushcart Prize nominee, JULIE L. MOORE is the author of four poetry collections, including, most recently, *Full Worm Moon*, which won a 2018 Woodrow Hall Top Shelf Award and received honorable mention for the Conference on Christianity and Literature's 2018 Book of the Year Award. Recent poetry has appeared in *African American Review, Image, One, Quartet, SWWIM, Thimble*, and *Verse Daily*. Learn more about her work at julielmoore.com.

MJ MOSS is an old hippie living along the Susquehanna River in northeast central Pennsylvania. She has lived other places, done many things, and always keeps a kite in the trunk.

ERIN MURPHY is the author or editor of thirteen books, including *Human Resources* (forthcoming from Salmon Poetry); *Fluent in Blue* (Grayson Books); and *Bodies of Truth: Personal Narratives on Illness, Disability, and Medicine* (University of Nebraska Press), winner of the Foreword INDIES Book of the Year Award. She is a professor of English at Penn State Altoona and poetry editor of the *Summerset Review*. She serves as the inaugural poet laureate of Blair County, Pennsylvania, where she is an inductee in the Blair County Arts Hall of Fame. erin -murphy.com

HEATHER MYERS is from Altoona, Pennsylvania. She has an MFA in creative writing from West Virginia University. She is a PhD candidate in creative writing at the University of North Texas. She was a 2018 AWP Intros Award Winner. Her work can be found in *Door=Jar, The Journal, Palette Poetry, Puerto del Sol,* and elsewhere. heathervmyers.com

STEVE MYERS is a professor of English and assistant director of the creative writing MFA at DeSales University. He is the author of the poetry collection *Memory's Dog* as well as the chapbooks *Work Site* and *Last Look at Joburg*. He lives in Center Valley, Pennsylvania.

JAMES NAJARIAN grew up on a goat farm in Berks County, Pennsylvania. He teaches nineteenth-century British literature at Boston College, where he edits the journal *Religion and the Arts*. He is the author of *The Goat Songs*, which won the Vassar Miller prize.

ROBBI NESTER is a retired college educator and author of four books of poetry. She currently hosts and curates two monthly poetry reading series. Learn more at her website, robbinester.net.

JEFF OAKS was the author of two books of poetry, *Little What* and *The Things*, both published by Lily Poetry Review Books. A recipient of three Pennsylvania Council on the Arts fellowships, he published poems in a number of literary magazines, most recently in *Georgia Review, Missouri Review, Superstition Review, Tupelo Quarterly*, and elsewhere. He taught writing at the University of Pittsburgh. Known as a brilliant writer and teacher, he died on December 20, 2023.

The influential editor of the Pitt Poetry Series from 1978 to 2021, ED OCHESTER helped foster the careers of Sharon Olds, Toi Derricotte, Billy Collins, Etheridge Knight, and numerous others, many of whom went on to earn prestigious honors, including the National Book Award. The author of fourteen books of poems, Ochester's own work as a poet was highly regarded. Ochester was the recipient of grants from the National Endowment for the Arts and the Pennsylvania Council on the Arts, among others, and served as president of the Associated Writing Programs. He passed away in 2023.

DEIRDRE O'CONNOR is the author of two books of poems, most recently *The Cupped Field*, which received the 2018 Able Muse Book Award. Her work has appeared in *Poetry, Cave Wall, Fourth River, Rust + Moth*, and other journals. A native of Pittsburgh, she lives in central Pennsylvania and directs the writing center at Bucknell University. For more information, see her website, deirdre-oconnor.com.

ANGELA ALAIMO O'DONNELL, PHD, is a professor, poet, scholar, and writer at Fordham University in New York City and serves as associate director of Fordham's Curran Center for American Catholic Studies. Her publications include two chapbooks and nine full-length collections of poems, including *Dear Dante* (Paraclete, 2024) and *Holy Land* (2022), which won the Paraclete Press Poetry Prize. In addition, O'Donnell has published a memoir about caring for her dying mother, *Mortal Blessings: A Sacramental Farewell*; a book of hours based on the practical theology of Flannery O'Connor, *The Province of Joy*; and a biography, *Flannery O'Connor: Fiction Fired by Faith*. The latter won the Catholic Press Association Prize for best biography in 2015. Her groundbreaking critical book on Flannery O'Connor, *Radical Ambivalence: Race in Flannery O'Connor*, was published by Fordham University Press in 2020. angelaalaimoodonnell.com

JACQUELINE OSHEROW'S ninth collection of poems, *Divine Ratios: Poems*, was published by LSU Press in 2023. She's received grants from the John Simon Guggenheim and Ingram Merrill Foundations and the NEA as well as the Witter Bynner Prize. Her poems have appeared in the *New Yorker*, *Paris Review*, *American Poetry Review*, *Best American Poetry*, *Jewish American Literature: A Norton Anthology*, *Penguin Book of the Sonnet*, and many other anthologies and journals. She's Distinguished Professor of English at the University of Utah.

JAY PARINI, a poet, novelist, and biographer, teaches at Middlebury College in Vermont. His nine novels include *The Last Station* and *Benjamin's Crossing*. His memoir *Borges and Me: An Encounter* is being made into a film. His biographical subjects include Steinbeck, Frost, and Faulkner. He has written many other works of nonfiction, including *Promised Land: Thirteen Books that Changed America*. His *New and Collected Poems: 1975–2015* appeared in 2016.

MARIANNE PEEL is a poet, musician, and retired English teacher. She received a Fulbright-Hays Program award to further her research in Nepal and Turkey. Her poetry has appeared in numerous print and online journals. *No Distance Between Us* is her debut book.

LINDA PENNISI is the writer-in-residence at Le Moyne College. She is the author of *Seamless*, winner of the 2003 Perugia Press Prize; *Suddenly, Fruit* (Carolina Wren Press, 2006); and *The Burning Boat* (Nine Mile Press, 2022), as well as the chapbook *Miniscule Boxes in the Bird's Bright Throat*.

MATT PERAKOVICH is a writer, artist, and editor living in Bloomsburg, Pennsylvania.

RICHARD PIERCE is a professor of English at Waynesburg University. His poems have appeared in *Ninth Letter*, *Poet Lore*, *Birmingham Poetry Review*, *Image*, and other journals. His chapbook, *The Book of Mankey*, was published by Cooper Dillon Books. He lives in Waynesburg with his wife, Blenda.

STEVE POLLACK hit half-balls with broomsticks, rode the Frankford El to Drexel University, and crossed the equator on the USS *Enterprise*. He advised governments, directed an affordable housing co-op, and built hospitals, science labs, and public schools. Poetry found him later. His work has appeared in *Poetica Magazine, Schuylkill Valley Journal, Copperfield Review*, and other journals. His chapbook, *L'dor Vador—From Generation to Generation*, was published by Finishing Line Press. On the first Saturday of each month, he circles with Forgotten Voices Poetry Group at the Indian Valley Public Library in Telford, Pennsylvania.

ERIC POTTER, a resident of Grove City, Pennsylvania, is a professor of English at Grove City College, where he teaches courses in poetry and American literature. His poems have appeared in such journals as *32 Poems, Molecule, Spiritus, Presence*, and *Midwest Quarterly Review*. He has published two chapbooks and a full-length collection, *Things Not Seen* (2015).

MICHAEL QUINN is a writer born in Philadelphia. His poetry has appeared in the *Chiron Review, Carve*, and *Rust + Moth*. He is the author of the plays *Get It Together, Fishtown*, and *The River East*. He is a graduate of Boston College and lives in Villanova, Pennsylvania. mpquinn.net

JOHN REPP is a poet, fiction writer, folk photographer, and digital collagist living in Erie, Pennsylvania. His most recent of many collections of poetry is *The Soul of Rock & Roll: Poems Acoustic, Electric & Remixed, 1980–2020*, published by Broadstone Books. His obsessively updated website is johnreppwriter.com.

NATHANIEL RICKETTS is a writer from Pittsburgh. His poems can be found in *Tampa Review* and *Peace, Land, & Bread*. He is currently based in West Virginia.

TAMMY ROBACKER grew up in Meadville, Pennsylvania, and spent many childhood summers escaping a turbulent home life—preferring to get lost in the local woods with neighborhood friends or to find magical adventures down at the "crick." Tammy graduated from the Rainier Writing Workshop MFA program in creative writing, poetry, at Pacific Lutheran University (2016). She won the 2015 Keystone Chapbook Prize for her manuscript *R*. Her second poetry book, *Villain Songs*, was published with MoonPath Press (2018). Tammy served as poet laureate of Tacoma during 2009–10 and is a Hedgebrook writer-in-residence. She published her first collection of poetry, *The Vicissitudes*, in 2009 (Pearle Publications) with a generous TAIP grant award. Tammy's poetry has appeared in *Harpur Palate, Tinderbox, Chiron Review, Duende, So to Speak, Crab Creek Review, WomenArts*, and many more. She lives in Washington state and works in education technology.

MARY ROHRER-DANN grew up in Philly, and while its cadences still shape her work, she has long lived in State College, Pennsylvania, where she was a teaching professor at Penn State University. She is the author of *Accidents of Being: Poems from a Philadelphia Neighborhood*, *Taking the Long Way Home*, and *La Scaffetta: Poems from the Foundling Drawer*. Both *Accidents* and *La Scaffetta* were adapted to the stage and produced by Tempest Productions. Her work also appears in *Clackamas Review*, *Flash Boulevard*, *Literary Mama*, *Slant*, *Five South*, *Orca*, *Indiana Review*, and elsewhere. When not writing, she paints, hikes, bikes, sometimes gardens, and volunteers with various local nonprofits. Find her at maryrohrerdann.com.

RACHEL ROUPP is a poet from the mountains of Pennsylvania. She proudly graduated from Mansfield University of Pennsylvania and went on to earn an MFA. Her poetry has appeared in *Crab Fat Magazine*, *Persephone's Daughters*, *Honey & Lime*, *Rust + Moth*, and elsewhere. By day she serves over three hundred children and seventy colleagues as the community relations associate at an independent grade school in Pittsburgh. Her work can be found at rachelroupp.com. She lives every day to make Dolly Parton proud of her.

HELEN RUGGIERI has published close to two hundred poems in magazines, academic journals, and anthologies. She is the author of *The Poetess* and two chapbooks, *Concrete Madonna* and *The Rock City Hill Exercises*. Later books include *Glimmer Girls*, *Butterflies Under a Japanese Moon*, *The Kingdom Where Everybody Sings Off Key*, *The Kingdom Where No One Keeps Time*, *The Sapphires*, and *Blue Elegies*. helenruggieri.com

SARAH RUSSELL'S poetry and fiction have been published in *Rattle*, *Misfit Magazine*, *Third Wednesday*, *Poetry Breakfast*, and many other journals and anthologies. She is a Pushcart Prize and Best of the Net nominee. She has two poetry collections published by Kelsay Books, *I lost summer somewhere* and *Today and Other Seasons*. Her novella *The Ballerina Swan Lake Mobile Homes Country Club Motel* was published by Running Wild Press. She blogs at SarahRussellPoetry.net.

LAURA RUTLAND, a transplant from Georgia to Erie, Pennsylvania, recently retired from teaching English at Gannon University, where she continues to teach part-time. Her poetry has appeared in *Autumn Sky Poetry Daily*, *Gallery and Studio Arts Journal*, *Anglican Theological Review*, and elsewhere. In the Erie region, her work has been included in collections edited by Erie poet laureates Berwyn Moore and Marisa Moks-Unger. She was recently the featured poet for the inaugural edition of *Poets Hall: The Periodical*, edited by Cee Williams and Greg Brown, and she is excited about the recent release of her chapbook of fantasy poetry, *A Dragon Woman's Journey*.

MARK SABA is a native of Pittsburgh. He is the author of poetry books *Flowers in the Dark* and *Calling the Names* as well as *Ghost Tracks: Stories of Pittsburgh Past* and the novellas *A Luke of All Ages / Fire and Ice*. His work has appeared widely in literary magazines around the United States and abroad. A graduate of Wesleyan University (BA) and Hollins College (MA), he is also a painter, and he recently retired from Yale University as a medical illustrator and graphic designer. Please see marksabawriter.com.

BARBARA SABOL's third full-length collection is *WATERMARK: Poems of the Johnstown Flood of 1889* (Alternating Current Press, 2023). She is the associate editor of *Sheila-Na-Gig online* and edited the anthology *Sharing This Delicate Bread: Selections from Sheila-Na-Gig online*. Her honors include an Individual Excellence Award from the Ohio Arts Council and Ohio Poet of the Year. Barbara conducts poetry workshops through Literary Cleveland. She is a retired speech pathologist who lives in Akron, Ohio, with her husband and wonder dog. barbarasabol.com

LISA TOTH SALINAS is a genealogist, poet, and author of *Smallest Leaf*, awarded the Eakin Manuscript Prize by the Poetry Society of Texas. Although she calls Texas home, her family's roots in the Pennsylvania coal region date back to the mid-nineteenth century, and her ancestors frequently appear within her written work. Lisa's poems have appeared in various anthologies and journals, such as *Encore, Presence, St. Austin Review*, and more; she has been twice featured within the poetry/visual art exhibit *Color:Story*.

SONIA SANCHEZ resides in Philadelphia and is professor emerita of English at Temple University. She is the author of numerous collections of poetry, including *Collected Poems, Morning Haiku*, and *Shake Loose My Skin*, among others. She is the recipient of the 2022 Ruth Lilly Poetry Prize. Her collection *Does Your House Have Lions?* was a finalist for the National Book Critics Circle Award. soniasanchez.net

JUDITH SANDERS's poetry collection *In Deep* was published by Kelsay Books. Her work appears in numerous journals, including *Pleiades, CALYX, American Scholar*, and *Modern Language Studies*; on the websites Vox Populi, Humor Darling, and Full Grown People; and in the *Pittsburgh Post-Gazette*. She taught English at universities, in independent schools, and in France on a Fulbright Fellowship. She lives with her family in Pittsburgh.

NICOLE SANTALUCIA is the author of *The Book of Dirt* (NYQ Books, 2020), *Spoiled Meat* (Headmistress Press, 2018), and *Because I Did Not Die* (Bordighera Press, 2015). Her work has appeared or is forthcoming in publications such as *Colorado Review, Palette Poetry*, and *Best American Poetry*. She is a recipient of the Charlotte Mew Chapbook Prize, the Edna St. Vincent Millay Poetry Prize, and the *Arkana Literary Review* Editor's Choice Award. At Shippensburg University in Pennsylvania, she is an associate professor, director of first-year writing, and co-chair of the LGBTQ+ Advisory Council, and she serves on the steering committee of the Institute for Social Inclusion. She has led poetry workshops in the Cumberland County Prison, Shippensburg and Harrisburg Public Libraries, the Boys & Girls Club, and nursing homes, and she's the founder of The Binghamton Poetry Project. Santalucia received her MFA from The New School and her PhD from Binghamton University.

HAYDEN SAUNIER is the author of six poetry collections, most recently *Wheel* (Terrapin Books, 2024). Her awards include a 2023 Pushcart Prize, the 2013 Gell Poetry Prize, the 2011 *Rattle* Poetry Grand Prize, and the 2011 Pablo Neruda Award. Her work has been published in such journals as *Beloit Poetry Journal*, *Nimrod*, *Southern Poetry Review*, *The Sun*, and *Virginia Quarterly Review* and has also been featured on *Poetry Daily*, *The Writer's Almanac*, and *Verse Daily*. She lives on a farm in Bucks County. Learn more at haydensaunier.com.

JANETTE SCHAFER holds an MFA in creative writing from Chatham University and is a freelance writer, nature photographer, part-time rock singer, and full-time realtor living in Pittsburgh. She has been published numerous times in print and online. She is the author of three chapbooks: *Other Names and Places* (LBF Books); *Something Here Will Grow* (Main Street Rag); and *Mother's Unbearable Itch* (Alien Buddha Press). She is the chief editor of two anthologies, *The Dreamers Anthology: Writing Inspired by the Lives of Dr. Martin Luther King Jr. and Anne Frank* and *Is It Hot in Here or Is It Just Me? Women Over Forty Write on Aging*. Also a playwright, Janette was the winner of the Pittsburgh Original Short Play Series for her work *Mad Virginia* and also won the Pittsburgh Fringe Festival for her collaboration with five other playwrights for their production of *northeastsouthwest*. Janette lives in Stowe Township, Pennsylvania, with her husband, Garth.

MELANIE SIMMS is a former poet laureate of Perry County. She currently resides in New Bloomfield, Pennsylvania. She has a BA in creative writing from Bloomsburg University and is the author of four books of poetry, including *Remember the Sun: Poems on Nature and Inspiration* (Sunbury Press) and *Waking the Muse* (Outskirts Press). Her book *Life Signs and Fortune Cookies* (Brown Poesy Press) is a collection of poems and short stories. She edited *Poets with Masks On: A Pandemic Anthology* (Finishing Line Press, 2022), a collection of poetry that includes the work of New York artist Christine O'Connor. Simms also is the proud mother of an adult son who served in the US Army and currently works for TSA. poetmelaniesimms.wordpress.com

AMY SMALL-MCKINNEY is a Montgomery County poet laureate emeritus (2011). Small-McKinney's second full-length book of poems, *Walking Toward Cranes*, won the Kithara Book Prize (Glass Lyre Press, 2017). Her chapbook, *One Day I Am a Field*, was written during COVID-19 in 2020 and is about her husband's death (Glass Lyre Press, 2022). Her poems have been published in numerous journals, including *American Poetry Review*, the *Indianapolis Review*, *Tiferet*, *Baltimore Review*, *Connotation*, *Literary Mama*, *Pedestal Magazine*, *Philadelphia Stories*, *SWWIM*, *Vox Populi*, and *Verse Daily*, and have been translated into Romanian and Korean. Her third full-length book of poems *& You Think It Ends* is forthcoming from Glass Lyre Press. Small-McKinney has a degree in clinical neuropsychology from Drexel University and an MFA in poetry from Drew University. She resides in Philadelphia. Learn more at amysmallmckinney.com.

JUDITH SORNBERGER is the author of four full-length poetry collections: *I Call to You from Time* (Wipf & Stock, 2019), *Angel Chimes: Poems of Advent and Christmas* (Shanti Arts, 2020), *Practicing the World* (CavanKerry, 2018), and *Open Heart* (CALYX Books, 1993). Her six chapbooks include *The Book of Muses* (Finishing Line Press, 2023) and the award-winning *Wal-Mart Orchid* (Evening Street Press, 2011). Her poetry has been nominated four times for the Pushcart Prize. Sornberger's nonfiction prose memoir, *The Accidental Pilgrim: Finding God and His Mother in Tuscany*, is from Shanti Arts (2015). A professor emerita of Mansfield University (now part of Commonwealth University), she taught English and founded the women's studies program. She lives on the side of a mountain outside Wellsboro, Pennsylvania. judithsornberger.net

SHEILA SQUILLANTE is a writer and visual artist living in the Hazelwood neighborhood of Pittsburgh. She is the author of the poetry collections *Mostly Human*, winner of the 2020 Wicked Woman Book Prize from Brick House Books, and *Beautiful Nerve* as well as four chapbooks of poetry. Her *The Brightest Days: New and Selected* is forthcoming with Braddock Avenue Books. Her debut essay collection, *All Things Edible, Random and Odd: Essays on Grief, Love and Food*, was published by CLASH Books in 2023. With Sandra L. Faulkner, she is coauthor of the writing craft book *Writing the Personal: Getting Your Stories onto the Page*. Her abstract paintings have been featured in numerous literary journals, including *Brevity*, *A-Minor*, and (as cover art) a forthcoming issue of *Dogwood: A Journal of Poetry and Prose*. She directs and teaches in the MFA program in creative writing at Chatham University, where she is executive editor of *The Fourth River*. She serves as an editor-at-large for *Barrelhouse Magazine*. sheilasquillante.com

JULIE STANDIG'S poetry has recently appeared in *Schuylkill Journal Review*, *US1 Poets / Del Val*, *Gyroscope Review*, and *Crone Editions* as well as many others. She has a full collection of poems, *The Forsaken Little Black Book*, and a chapbook, *Memsahib Memoir*. A board member of the Arts and Cultural Council of Bucks County, she is currently working on a new collection of poems. Once a lifelong New Yorker, she now happily resides in Bucks County, Pennsylvania, with her husband and their springer spaniel. juliestandig.com

DAVID STAUDT has been publishing poetry, fiction, and essays in literary journals and anthologies for more than forty-five years, mostly recently in *Epoch* and *Deep Wild*. His book is *The Gifts and Thefts* (Backwaters Press, 2001). A native of Lehighton, Carbon County, he has lived much of his life there and in York between service in the Gulf War, earning his MFA at Cornell, and practicing law in Harrisburg, York, and Baltimore. He recently retired after twenty-three years of federal service in the Navy and the US Equal Employment Opportunity Commission.

GERALD STERN was a native of Pittsburgh and a poet strongly associated with a city that has produced a great number of American poets from the twentieth century into this one. Stern is the author of dozens of books and the recipient of numerous prizes and awards, including the National Book Award for Poetry. His most recent collection is *Blessed as We Were: Late Selected and New Poems* (Norton, 2020). He died on October 27, 2022.

SHIRLEY STEVENS was a member of the first graduating class of Quaker Valley in 1957 and went on to teach there from 1961 to 2001. She was awarded the Teacher of Excellence Silver Award. She was a member of St. David's Christian Writers Association, the Pittsburgh Literary Society, and the Squirrel Hill Poetry Group. Her poetry appeared in *Poet Lore* and *Time of Singing*. She is the author of the chapbook *Pronouncing What We Wish to Keep*. She passed away on April 25, 2022.

ANNE DYER STUART'S publications include *Pleiades*, *North American Review*, *AGNI*, *American Journal of Poetry*, *Raleigh Review*, *Cherry Tree*, *Sugar House Review*, *Texas Review*, *Louisiana Literature*, *New World Writing Quarterly*, and *Louisville Review*. Her work won a Henfield Prize and a *New South Journal* Prose Contest, was anthologized in Best of the Web, and was nominated for Best New Poets. *What Girls Learn*, a finalist for *Comstock Review's* 2020 Chapbook Contest, was published by Finishing Line Press in 2021. She edits *IMPOST: A*

Journal of Creative and Critical Work and teaches at Commonwealth University of Pennsylvania–Bloomsburg.

ALISON CARB SUSSMAN, a Pushcart Prize nominee, has garnered numerous awards and publications throughout her writing career. Sussman is the author of *Black Wool Cape* and *On the Edge*, a poetry collection and a poetry chapbook, respectively. Her poem "Gone Mom, 2023" was chosen as "highly commended" by Hannah Sullivan for the 2024 international Moth Poetry Prize. She also won the Abroad Writers' Conference / Finishing Line Press Authors Poetry Contest and read her winning poems as their guest in Dublin in 2015. She was a 2016 finalist in *Bellingham Review*'s 49th Parallel Award for Poetry and a finalist in *Naugatuck River Review*'s 11th Annual Narrative Poetry Contest. Her poems have appeared in *Atlanta Review*, *Gargoyle*, the *New York Times*, *Rattle*, *Southword* (Ireland), and other publications. She lives and writes in New York City.

DAVID SWERDLOW is the author of three full-length collections of poetry, including *Nightstand* (Broadstone Books, 2023). His work has appeared in *Poetry*, *American Poetry Review*, *Iowa Review*, *West Branch*, and many other distinguished journals and anthologies. The recipient of several awards, Swerdlow has received two grants from the Pennsylvania Council on the Arts. He served as a Fulbright Professor of American Literature in Peru, as a National Endowment for the Humanities Fellow, and as visiting faculty on two Semester at Sea voyages. Since 1990, he has taught literature and creative writing at Westminster College in New Wilmington, Pennsylvania.

MARY SZYBIST grew up in Pennsylvania. Her first collection of poetry, *Granted* (2003), was a finalist for the National Book Critics Circle Award, and her second book, *Incarnadine* (2013), won the National Book Award for Poetry. Her poetry has appeared in *Iowa Review*, *Denver Quarterly*, and was featured in *Best American Poetry*. maryszybist.net/about.html

PHILIP TERMAN's books include *This Crazy Devotion* (Broadstone, 2020), *Our Portion: New and Selected Poems* (Autumn House, 2015), and, as co-translator, *Tango Below a Narrow Ceiling: The Selected Poems of Riad Saleh Hussein* (Bitter Oleander, 2021). Published in 2024 are *My Blossoming Everything* (Saddle Road Press) and *The Whole Mishpocha* (Ben Yehuda Press). A selection of his poems, *My Dear Friend Kafka* (Nimwa Press, Damascus), was translated into Arabic by Saleh Razzouk. His poems and essays appear in many journals and anthologies, such as *Poetry Magazine*, *Kenyon Review*, *Poetry International*, and *The Sun*. He co-directed the James Wright Poetry Festival in 2023; directs The Bridge Literary

Arts Center, a regional writer's organization in western Pennsylvania; and is co-curator of the Jewish Poetry Reading Series, sponsored by the Jewish Community Center of Buffalo. Terman conducts poetry workshops and coaches writing hither and yon. He's collaborated with composers, visual artists, and performs his poetry with the jazz band Catro. philipterman.my.canva.site

ELAINE TERRANOVA grew up in a working-class neighborhood in Philadelphia and has held a variety of jobs: factory worker, office temp, preschool teacher, and editor. Now retired, she previously taught at the Community College of Philadelphia, Temple University, the University of Delaware, and in the Rutgers–Camden MFA Program. She is the author of eight collections of poetry, two poetry chapbooks, a memoir, and a translation. Terranova's first book, *The Cult of the Right Hand*, won the 1990 Walt Whitman Award. *Rinse* (2023) is her most recent book. Her poems have appeared in the *New Yorker*, *American Poetry Review*, *Pleiades*, *Ploughshares*, and other magazines and anthologies. Among her awards are the Pushcart Prize, the Margaret Banister residency at Sweet Briar, the Judah L. Magnes Gold Medal, and fellowships from the National Endowment for the Arts and the Pew Center. Her memoir, *The Diamond Cutter's Daughter: A Poet's Memoir*, was released in 2021.

HEATHER H. THOMAS is the author of *Vortex Street* (FutureCycle Press, 2018) and eight other poetry books, including two bilingual collections. Her poems won honors in the 2022 Joy Harjo Prize and the 2014 Rita Dove Prize from the Pennsylvania Council on the Arts and the Academy of American Poets. Her work, also published under the name H. T. Harrison, has appeared in publications including *About Place Journal*; *American Letters and Commentary*; *Barrow Street*; *Interim*; *Mizna: Prose, Poetry, Art Exploring Arab America*; *The Pedestal*; *Talisman*; *Wallace Stevens Journal*; *Women's Studies Quarterly*; and *Undocumented: Great Lakes Poets Laureate for Social Justice* (Michigan State University Press). Her poems have been translated into six languages, including Arabic. An emerita professor of English, Kutztown University, Heather also taught at Cedar Crest College. She is a former Berks County poet laureate and lives along the Schuylkill River in Reading. Her website is HeatherHThomas.com.

PATRICIA THRUSHART writes poetry and biographies from her home in the Pennsylvania Wilds. Her fifth and latest book of poems, *Goddesses I Have Known*, was put out by QPC Publishing with proceeds benefiting a local domestic violence shelter. Her previous collection, *Inspired by Their Voices: Poetry from Underground Railroad Testimony*, was published by Mammoth Books and benefits social justice causes. Patricia's poems have been published in numerous journals.

She is coeditor of the blog and anthology series for North/South Appalachia and cofounder of the group Poets Against Racism & Hate USA. In 2021, her work was chosen for an award-winning anthology of Ohio Appalachian voices, *I Thought I Heard a Cardinal Sing*. She's had poems included in the Women of Appalachia Project: Women Speak series, and her narrative nonfiction book, *Cursed: The Life and Tragic Death of Marion Alsobrook Stahlman*, was published in December 2021 by Adelaide Books. patriciathrushart.com

J. C. TODD is the author of two poetry collections, including *Beyond Repair*, a special selection for the Able Muse Book Award (2019), and three chapbooks, including *The Damages of Morning* (Moonstone Press, 2018), an Eric Hoffer Award finalist. She has held fellowships from the Pew Center for Arts and Heritage, Pennsylvania Council on the Arts, and the Bemis Center, and has had a VCCA International arts residency. Winner of the 2016 International Literary Awards' Rita Dove Poetry Prize, her poems have appeared in *Baltimore Review*, *Paris Review*, *Prairie Schooner*, *One Art*, *Virginia Quarterly Review*, and other journals. jc-todd.com

JACK TROY is a potter, teacher, and writer from Huntingdon, Pennsylvania, where he taught at Juniata College for thirty-nine years. He is the author of *Calling the Planet Home* (2003) and *Giving It Up to the Wind*. His writing awards include two Craft Fellowships and a Fellowship in Literature from the Pennsylvania Council on the Arts. jacktroy.net

LEE UPTON'S most recent book of poetry is *The Day Every Day Is*, from Saturnalia Books. She is a novelist and essayist as well as a poet. Her comic novel, *Tabitha, Get Up*, came out in 2024. leeupton.com

MATTHEW USSIA is director of Duquesne University's first year writing program in spite of the fact that he got a C- in freshman writing and was rejected from Duquesne's MA program. He is also an editor, podcaster, post-doom thereminist, softcore punk, postpunk backup singer, social media burnout, and sentient organic matter. His first book, *The Red Glass Cat*, was published by Alien Buddha Press in 2021. His writings have appeared in *Mister Rogers and Philosophy*, *Future Humans in Fiction and Film*, *North of Oxford*, *Trailer Park Quarterly*, *Anti-Heroin Chic*, the *Open Mic of the Air Podcast*, and elsewhere. More information can be found at matthewussia.com.

ANTONIO VALLONE was associate professor of English, English coordinator, and co-coordinator of the two- and four-year multidisciplinary studies programs at Penn State DuBois. He was the founding publisher of MAMMOTH books, copublisher of the *Watershed Journal* Publishing Cooperative, and former poetry editor of *Pennsylvania English*. He has published several collections: *The Blackbird's Applause, Grass Saxophones, Golden Carp,* and the chapbook-length poem *Chinese Bats.* A respected and much loved colleague and mentor, Tony Vallone died on Sunday, January 5th, 2025. His forthcoming (posthumous) collections include *American Zen* (2025) and *Blackberry Alleys: Collected Poems and Prose* (2026).

JUDITH VOLLMER'S sixth book of poetry, *The Sound Boat: New and Selected Poems*, was awarded the 2022 University of Wisconsin Press Four Lakes Prize. A reading and conversation with poet Mihaela Moscaliuc, about the book and both poets' work, can be viewed via Pittsburgh Arts and Lectures (pittsburghlectures .org). Vollmer is a recipient of poetry fellowships from the National Endowment for the Arts and the Pennsylvania Council on the Arts as well as artist residencies from the Corporation of Yaddo, the Centrum Foundation, and the American Academy in Rome, among others. Her poetry, reviews, and essays have been published in *Plume, Rhino, Barrow Street, Georgia Review, Women's Review of Books, AGNI, Prairie Schooner, Pleiades,* and elsewhere. She is professor emerita of the University of Pittsburgh–Greensburg and recipient of the Chancellor's Distinguished Teaching Award of the University of Pittsburgh. For three decades, Vollmer coedited the international poetry journal *5 AM.* Vollmer teaches poetry privately and in Carlow University's low-residency MFA Program. She lives in Pittsburgh's Nine Mile Run watershed. judithvollmer.com

G. C. WALDREP'S most recent books are *feast gently* (Tupelo, 2018), winner of the William Carlos Williams Award from the Poetry Society of America; *The Earliest Witnesses* (Tupelo/Carcanet, 2021); and *The Opening Ritual* (Tupelo, 2024). His recent work has appeared in *American Poetry Review, Poetry, Paris Review, Ploughshares, New England Review, Yale Review, The Nation, New American Writing, Conjunctions,* and other journals. Waldrep lives in Lewisburg, Pennsylvania, where he teaches at Bucknell University. gcwaldrep.com/about

JEANNE MURRAY WALKER is a writer, teacher, and poet. She has published nine volumes of poetry, including *Helping the Morning: New and Selected Poems.* She has also published two memoirs: *Leaping from the Burning Train: A Poet's Journey of Faith* and *The Geography of Memory: A Pilgrimage Through Alzheimer's.* jeannemurraywalker.com

VIRGINIA WATTS is the author of poetry and stories found in *Epiphany, CRAFT, Florida Review, Reed Magazine, Pithead Chapel, Words & Whispers, Sky Island Journal,* and elsewhere. She has been nominated four times for a Pushcart Prize and four times for Best of the Net. Her debut short story collection, *Echoes from the Hocker House,* won third place in the 2024 Feathered Quill Book Awards. Please visit her at virginiawatts.com.

SUSAN WEAVER is the editor of the literary journal *Ribbons*, the journal of the Tanka Society of America. She writes free verse, tanka, and tanka prose. She lives in Allentown, Pennsylvania.

GABRIEL WELSCH is the author of a collection of short stories, *Groundscratchers* (Tolsun Books, 2021), and four collections of poems, the latest of which is *The Four Horsepersons of a Disappointing Apocalypse* (Steel Toe Books, 2013). He lives in Pittsburgh and works as a vice president for marketing and communications at Duquesne University.

A Pennsylvania native, JERRY WEMPLE is a poet, nonfiction writer, and editor. He has published four poetry collections, mostly recently *We Always Wondered What Became of You* from Broadstone Books. In addition to *Keystone Poetry*, he also coedited, with Marjorie Maddox, *Common Wealth: Contemporary Poets on Pennsylvania.* Wemple's poetry and essays have been published in numerous journals and anthologies as well as internationally in Ireland, Sweden, and Chile. He teaches at Commonwealth University–Bloomsburg.

PATRICIA JABBEH WESLEY is the author/editor of eight critically acclaimed books of poetry, including *Praise Song for My Children: New and Selected Poems* (winner of the 2022 Theodore Roethke Memorial Poetry Prize), *Becoming Ebony*, and *Breaking the Silence: Anthology of Liberian Poetry.* Her work has appeared in *Prairie Schooner*, the *New York Times Magazine, Harvard Review,* and elsewhere. She also is the winner of the 2022 Levinson Prize from Poetry Foundation, the Edward Stanley Poetry Prize, and a 2002 Crab Orchard Award, among others. She is a professor of English and creative writing at Penn State Altoona. patriciajabbeh wesley.com

KAREN J. WEYANT'S poems have been published in *Chautauqua, Crab Orchard Review, Cold Mountain Review, Copper Nickel, Fourth River, Harpur Palate, New Plains Review, Poetry East, Lake Effect, Slipstream, Spillway, Rattle,* and *Whiskey Island.* Her poems have also appeared in *American Life in Poetry* and the Sundance Best of the Net series. The author of two poetry chapbooks, her first full-length collection, *Avoiding the Rapture,* was published in October 2023. She is an associate professor of English at Jamestown Community College in Jamestown, New York. She lives, reads, and writes in Warren, Pennsylvania. Her website is karenjweyant.com.

Native to Clinton County, Pennsylvania, SHANNA POWLUS WHEELER is the author of two books of poetry, *Evensong for Shadow* (Resource Publications/Wipf & Stock, 2018) and *Lo & Behold* (Finishing Line Press, 2009). Since studying creative writing at Susquehanna University (BA) and Penn State University (MFA), she has worked in higher education as an administrator of academic support services and as a writing instructor. She lives in the Williamsport, Pennsylvania, area with her family and now teaches at Pennsylvania College of Technology. Visit her website at shannapowluswheeler.com.

CEE WILLIAMS spends an inordinate amount of time watching baseball and complaining about the kids in his driveway. Sometimes, he writes poems. His work has appeared in various chapbooks and publications, including the *2 Bridges Review* and *Composing Poetry: A Guide to Writing Poems and Thinking Lyrically* (Kendall Hunt). He is a helpful neighbor, an avid gardener, a devoted dad to a Treeing Walker Coonhound named Ella, a proud uncle, and a grateful son. Sown, grown, and setting roots in Erie, Pennsylvania.

MARTIN WILLITTS JR. is an editor of *Comstock Review*. He won the 2014 Dylan Thomas International Poetry Award; Stephen A. DiBiase Poetry Prize (2018); Editor's Choice, *Rattle* Ekphrastic Challenge (2020); and the 17th Annual Sejong Writing Competition (2022). His twenty-one full-length collections include *The Temporary World*, which won the Blue Light Award (2019). His recent books are *Harvest Time* (Deerbrook Editions, 2021); *All Wars Are the Same War* (FutureCycle Press, 2022); *Not Only the Extraordinary Are Exiting the Dream World* (Flowstone Press, 2022); *Ethereal Flowers* (Shanti Arts Press, 2023); *Rain Followed Me Home* (Glass Lyre Press, 2023); and *Leaving Nothing Behind* (Fernwood Press, 2023). In 2024, he published *The Thirty-Six Views of Mount Fuji*, including all thirty-six color pictures (Shanti Arts Press), and *All Beautiful Things Need Not Fly* (Silver Bowl Press).

Poet, musician, educator, and curator YOLANDA WISHER is the author of *Monk Eats an Afro* (Hanging Loose Press, 2014). Wisher was named inaugural poet laureate of Montgomery County, Pennsylvania, in 1999 and third poet laureate of Philadelphia for 2016 and 2017. A Pew and Cave Canem Fellow, Wisher received the Leeway Foundation's Transformation Award in 2019 for her commitment to art for social change and was named a Philadelphia Cultural Treasures Artist Fellow in 2022. Wisher performs a blend of poetry and song with her band Yolanda Wisher & The Afroeaters; their debut album *Doublehanded Suite* was released in 2022. Along with Trapeta B. Mayson, Wisher is the founder of ConsenSIS (consensisphl .com), an initiative that seeks to count, gather, and memorialize Black femme poets in the Philadelphia area. Wisher works as the senior curator at Monument Lab. yolandawisher.com

MARJORIE WONNER was born in McKean Township near Erie, Pennsylvania. She writes in several genres, including poetry and history. Her poetry has been published in the *Pittsburgh Quarterly*, *Spoon River Quarterly*, *Second Tuesday* anthologies, *Time of Singing*, and elsewhere. She has been a member of Mercyhurst Collect Second Tuesday, now called Poet's Hall, since 1986. She received a Lifetime Poetry Award in 2017 from the group.

ANDRENA ZAWINSKI'S poems have received accolades for free verse, lyricism, spirituality, and social concern, and they have appeared in publications including *Blue Collar Review*, *Artemis Journal*, *Rattle*, and *Progressive Magazine*, with work online at *Women's Voices for Change*, *Writing in a Woman's Voice*, *Verse Daily*, and elsewhere. Her fourth full-length collection of poetry is *Born Under the Influence* (WordTech Communications, 2022). Born and raised in Pittsburgh, she now makes her home in the San Francisco Bay area.

COREY ZELLER is the author of *You and Other Pieces* (2015) and *Man vs. Sky* (2013) and coauthor, with Sophie Klahr, of *There Is Only One Ghost in the World* (2023). His work has appeared in the *Kenyon Review*, *Colorado Review*, *Indiana Review*, and *Puerto del Sol*, among others. coreyzeller.squarespace.com

index

Adair, Allison, "Gettysburg," 58

Alleghenies: Shanna Powlus Wheeler, "Glacier Pools Preserve," 121; Barbara Sabol, "I'm from a one-way bus ticket," 158. *See also* section V, "The Allegheny Highlands"

Allegheny (train stop): Robbi Nester, "The Frankford Elevated Train," 33

Allegheny River: Todd Davis, "Until Darkness Comes," 168; Joseph Bathanti, "Requiem for the Living," 185; Jeff Oaks, "The Allegheny River," 208; Richard Krohn, "Fog Off the Allegheny," 235

Allentown: Susan Weaver, "In the Allentown Shelter Kitchen," 84

Altoona: Heather Myers, "Up Myers' Lane, Altoona, PA," 153; Erin Murphy, "Fall, Central Pennsylvania," 154; Gabriel Welsch, "The Oldest Roller Coaster in the World," 154

Amish and Mennonites: Sarah Russell, "In Amish Country," 49; Alison Carb Sussman, "Lost Brother, 2019," 54; Gerald Stern, "No Wind," 56; Cynthia Hogue, "Election," 66; Martin Willitts Jr., "Why Grandfather Counted the Stars," 68; Jerry Wemple, "Wilkes-Barre," 97; Shara McCallum, "Susquehanna (Excerpts)," 109; Ann Hostetler, "Settlers in the Valley," 143

Anderson, Maggie, "Heart Fire," 174

Anderson, Nathalie F., "Sweat," 30

animals: Eileen Daly Moeller, "Philadelphia: Early Summer," 9; Robin Becker, "Elegy for the Science Teacher," 19; G. C. Waldrep, "Mütter Museum with Owl," 24; Jacqueline Osherow, "Breezeway, circa 1964," 31; Amy Small-McKinney, "Walking Toward Cranes," 32; Michael Quinn, "Home,"

36; Sandy Feinstein, "In Reading," 54; Allison Adair, "Gettysburg," 58; Katy Giebenhain, "Taxidermy in South Central Pennsylvania," 61; Martin Willitts Jr., "Why Grandfather Counted the Stars," 68; Ann E. Michael, "The Invader Alters Everything," 81; David Staudt, "Packerton," 84; Shanna Powlus Wheeler, "Glacier Pools Preserve," 121; James Brasfield, "The Ritual," 136; Julie Swarstad Johnson, "Greener Than," 139; Jack Troy, "Migration at Jacks Narrows," 148; Noah Davis, "Skins," 151; Ed Ochester, "Two Women Watched by Geese," 165; Kristin Kovacic, "Dioramas," 188; Helen Ruggieri, "Bird Watching in Bradford," 219; David Swerdlow, "Migration," 221; Lisa M. Dougherty, "Saw Again the Infamous Owl," 232; John Repp, "The Field Mice of Arneman Road," 237

anthracite: Catherine Chandler, "Harrowing," 63; Christine Gelineau, "Christmas in Public Square," 99. *See also* Anthracite Valley

Anthracite Valley: Julie L. Moore, "Nurse in Need," 132

Appalachian Mountains: Jack Chielli, "Spring Delivers Us," 87; Michael Hardin, "Sodom School, Northumberland County, PA," 114; Julie L. Moore, "Nurse in Need," 132

Appalachian Trail: Nicole Santalucia, "Keystone Ode with Jane Doe in it," 64

Armstrong County: Ed Ochester, "Two Women Watched by Geese," 165

Ashland: Stanton Hancock, "Coal Ghosts (Excerpts)," 95

autumn: Ross Gay, "To the Fig Tree on 9th and Christian," 10; Nicole Miyashiro,

"Linvilla," 37; Robert Fillman, "All Day Long There'd Been Papers," 50; Maria James-Thiaw, "White Shore, 1963," 74; Jerry Wemple, "Wilkes-Barre," 97; Erin Murphy, "Fall, Central Pennsylvania," 154; Maggie Anderson, "Heart Fire," 174; Marjorie Wonner, "October Echo," 233

Bakken, Christopher, "Eclogue (Winter)," 238
Bald Eagle Mountain: Micah James Bauman and David J. Bauman, "Alvira," 118; Gloria Heffernan, "Sunrise on a Back Porch in Pennsylvania," 124
baseball. *See* sports
basta, nicole v, "the next field over," 96
Bathanti, Joseph, "Requiem for the Living," 185
Batykefer, Erinn, "The Jailer's Wife's Epithalamium," 201
Bauer, Grace, "You've Got a Friend In . . . ," 86
Bauman, Micah James, and David J. Bauman, "Alvira," 118
Beatty, Jan, "Dreaming Door," 179
Becker, Robin, "Elegy for the Science Teacher," 19
Bensel, Alyse, "'Swans first, now a fountain,'" 57
Bernstein, Carole, "Quaker Memorial Service for a Young Girl, Germantown," 39
Bessemer: Eric Potter, "Grove City Morning," 220
Bethlehem: Joseph Dorazio, "The Ruins of Bethlehem Steel," 83
birds: Vernita Hall, "Winter Melon Soup," 20; G. C. Waldrep, "Mütter Museum with Owl," 24; Allison Adair, "Gettysburg," 58; Anne Dyer Stuart, "Still April and No Spring," 119; Julie Swarstad Johnson, "Greener Than," 139; Jack Troy, "Migration at Jacks Narrows," 148; Ed Ochester, "Two Women Watched by Geese," 165; Todd Davis "Until Darkness Comes" 168; Helen Ruggieri, "Bird Watching in Bradford," 219; David Swerdlow, "Migration," 221; Laura Rutland, "Wind on the Bay," 228; Lisa M. Dougherty, "Saw Again the Infamous Owl," 232

Blomain, Thomas Kielty, "Agnes 1972," 100
Bloomsburg: Stanton Hancock, "Coal Ghosts (Excerpts)," 95
Blue Mountain: Judith A. Kennedy, "Longfellow Pine," 65
body: G. C. Waldrep, "Mütter Museum with Owl," 24; Michael Quinn, "Home," 36; Catherine Chandler, "Harrowing," 63; Nicole Santalucia, "Keystone Ode with Jane Doe in It," 64; Judith A. Kennedy, "Longfellow Pine," 65; Marianne Peel, "Huckleberries and Homebrewed Boilo," 89; nicole v basta, "the next field over," 96; Elaine Terranova, "Susquehanna River Bathers," 103; K. A. Hays, "Lines written in the Walmart Supercenter parking lot, Lewisburg, Pennsylvania," 117; Noah Davis, "Skins," 151; Karen J. Weyant, "Where Girls Still Ride the Beds of Pickup Trucks," 217; Patricia Thrushart, "Antlers," 218; Corey Zeller, "Sometimes I Forget You Lived in This City," 225; Deborah Burnham, "August: Erie," 225
Bohince, Paula, "First Day of the Hunt," 212
Bond, Bruce, "North: 1991," 134
Bonta, Dave, "Blast Area," 150
Bradford: Helen Ruggieri, "Bird Watching in Bradford," 219
Brandywine: Grant Clauser, "A Map of Valley Forge," 45
Brandywine River: Jan Freeman, "At the Crest of the Meadow," 34
Brasfield, James, "The Ritual," 136
Brighton Beach: Julie Standig, "New Hope," 41
Brown, Jayne Relaford, "Dirt," 49
Bucks County: Hayden Saunier, "Kitchen Table," 40; Julie Standig, "New Hope," 41
Bullard, Chris, "At Schuylkill Park," 8
Burnham, Deborah, "August: Erie," 225

Camden Ferry: Eileen Daly Moeller, "Philadelphia: Early Summer," 9
Carlisle: Katy Giebenhain, "Taxidermy in South Central Pennsylvania," 61
Carnegie Museum of Natural History: Kristin Kovacic, "Dioramas," 188
Cathedral of Hope: Janette Schafer, "At the Cathedral of Hope," 197

Centralia: Amanda Hodes, "When they say to leave, she says:," 93; Faith Ellington, "Centralia, PA," 94; Stanton Hancock, "Coal Ghosts (Excerpts)," 95

Centre County: James Brasfield, "The Ritual," 136

Chandler, Catherine, "Harrowing," 63

Chelius, Joseph A., "Halfball," 26

Chielli, Jack, "Spring Delivers Us," 87

childhood: Steve Pollack, "December 26, 1960," 16; Peter Krok, "Plinkies," 18; Robin Becker, "Elegy for the Science Teacher," 19; Chloe Martinez, "Giant Heart," 23; Yolanda Wisher, "5 South 43rd Street, Floor 2," 28; Lisa Toth Salinas, "Litany of Dyings," 90; David Chin, "American Water (Excerpts)," 101; Brian Fanelli, "The Sky Above My House on Johler Avenue," 106; Lilace Mellin Guignard, "Lullaby in Fracktown," 131; Barbara Sabol, "I'm from a one-way bus ticket," 158; Sandee Gertz, "Steeltown Girls," 161; Nathaniel Ricketts, "Rivers," 176; Jim Daniels, "Good Friday, Schenley Park, Pittsburgh, 2020," 186; Cortney Davis, "Then It Was Simple," 190; Shirley Stevens, "Dear Mr. Rogers Revisited," 200

Chin, David, "American Water (Excerpts)," 101

Civil War: Matt Perakovich, "Letter to Wemple from Gettysburg," 58; Abby Minor, "Gettysburg Poem #3," 59

Clarington: Patricia Thrushart, "Antlers," 218

Clauser, Grant, "A Map of Valley Forge," 45

Clifton, Charles, "Somewhere in Pennsylvania," 164

Clinton County: Bruce Bond, "North: 1991," 134

coal: Angela Alaimo O'Donnell, "Immigrant Song," 100. See also anthracite, Anthracite Valley, mines

Cohen, Joshua P., "The Quaker Delegate from Pennsylvania," 14

Conemaugh Valley: Rachel Roupp, "In the Johnstown Flood Museum," 160

Connolly, Geraldine, "River of Mantises," 213

Corso, Paola, "On the Way Up: Pittsburgh StepTrek," 179

COVID-19 Pandemic: Chris Bullard, "At Schuylkill Park," 8; Shanna Powlus Wheeler, "Glacier Pools Preserve," 121; Judith Sanders, "Walking in Homewood Cemetery During the Pandemic," 202; Chuck Joy, "O! Erie!," 224

Crawford County: Tammy Robacker, "Amphibians," 233

Crawford Township: John Repp, "The Field Mice of Arneman Road," 237; Christopher Bakken, "Eclogue (Winter)," 238

crime: Ross Gay, "To the Fig Tree on 9th and Christian," 10; Lynn Levin, "Sleepless Johnston," 42; Alyse Bensel, "'Swans first, now a fountain,'" 57; Nicole Santalucia, "Keystone Ode with Jane Doe in it," 64; Michael Garrigan, "Bully Pulpit," 71; Susan Weaver, "In the Allentown Shelter Kitchen," 84; Jerry Wemple, "Wilkes-Barre," 97; Julia Spicher Kasdorf, "Waking Up with Jerry Sandusky," 138; Philip Terman, "A Minyan Plus One," 198; Shirley Stevens, "Dear Mr. Rogers Revisited," 200

Cromwell Drive, Pittsburgh: Sharon Fagan McDermott, "Tuesday Morning," 189

Crooker, Barbara, "Worlds End," 127

Czury, Craig, "Evening Sky Diesel Blue purple tinge," 105

dancing: J. C. Todd, "At the Polish-American Festival, Penn's Landing," 17; Mary Rohrer-Dann, "Before He Fell, or Jumped," 21; G. C. Waldrep, "Mütter Museum with Owl," 24; Nathalie F. Anderson, "Sweat," 30; Julie Standig, "New Hope," 41; Maria James-Thiaw, "White Shore, 1963," 74

Daniels, Jim, "Good Friday, Schenley Park, Pittsburgh, 2020," 186

Danowsky, Mark, "Passing Through Southeastern Pennsylvania Towns in Winter," 37

Dauphin (train stop): Robbi Nester, "The Frankford Elevated Train," 33

Davis, Cortney, "Then It Was Simple," 190

Davis, Noah, "Skins," 151

Davis, Todd, "Until Darkness Comes," 168

death: Chris Bullard, "At Schuylkill Park," 8; Vernita Hall, "Winter Melon Soup," 20; Mary Rohrer-Dann, "Before He Fell, or Jumped," 21; Leonard Kress,

"Bridesburg," 29; Michael Quinn, "Home," 36; Carole Bernstein, "Quaker Memorial Service for a Young Girl, Germantown," 39; Hayden Saunier, "Kitchen Table," 40; Alison Carb Sussman, "Lost Brother, 2019," 54; Nicole Santalucia, "Keystone Ode with Jane Doe in it," 64; Judith A. Kennedy, "Longfellow Pine," 65; Susan Weaver, "In the Allentown Shelter Kitchen," 84; James Najarian, "Kempton, PA: After My Death," 87; Jack Chielli, "Spring Delivers Us," 87; Marianne Peel, "Huckleberries and Homebrewed Boilo," 89; Lisa Toth Salinas, "Litany of Dyings," 90; S. E. Gilman, "The Urge to Bury," 112; Melanie Simms, "At the Riverview Cemetery, Northumberland, PA," 113; Barbara Crooker, "Worlds End," 127; Ann Hostetler, "Settlers in the Valley," 143; Gabriel Welsch, "The Oldest Roller Coaster in the World," 154; Rachel Roupp, "In the Johnstown Flood Museum," 160; Matthew Ussia, "Arriving in Westmont," 163; Maggie Anderson, "Heart Fire," 174; Joseph Bathanti, "Requiem for the Living," 185; Shirley Stevens, "Dear Mr. Rogers Revisited," 200; Judith Sanders, "Walking in Homewood Cemetery During the Pandemic," 202; Jeff Oaks, "The Allegheny River," 208; David Swerdlow, "Migration," 221

Delaware River: J. C. Todd, "At the Polish-American Festival, Penn's Landing," 17; Robbi Nester, "The Frankford Elevated Train," 33

Derricotte, Toi, "The Great Beauty," 193

Dimock: Craig Czury, "Evening Sky Diesel Blue purple tinge," 105

Djanikian, Gregory, "Stepping Stones," 122

Donaghy, Daniel, "What Cement Is Made of," 7

Dorazio, Joseph, "The Ruins of Bethlehem Steel," 83

Dougherty, Lisa M., "Saw Again the Infamous Owl," 232

Dougherty, Sean Thomas, "At the Rib Fest in Erie, PA," 228

DuBois: Antonio Vallone, "The Dairy Queen in DuBois, Pennsylvania Opens for Spring," 155

Easton: Lee Upton, "The Naming of Bars," 82

El (train), Philadelphia. *See* public transportation

Elk County: Karen J. Weyant, "Where Girls Still Ride the Beds of Pickup Trucks," 217; Byron Hoot, "Sanctuary of Fog," 218

Ellington, Faith, "Centralia, PA," 94

Emanuel, Lynn, "Homage to Sharon Stone," 191

Erie: Chuck Joy, "O! Erie!," 224; Corey Zeller, "Sometimes I Forget You Lived in This City," 225; Deborah Burnham, "August: Erie," 225; Berwyn Moore, "Rapture," 226; Laura Rutland, "Wind on the Bay," 228; Sean Thomas Dougherty, "At the Rib Fest in Erie, PA," 228; Cee Williams, "The Catcher and the Sighs," 230; Lisa M. Dougherty, "Saw Again the Infamous Owl," 232

Erie SeaWolves. *See* sports

Fanelli, Brian, "The Sky Above My House on Johler Avenue," 106

farms/farming: Hayden Saunier, "Kitchen Table," 40; Julie Standig, "New Hope," 41; Grant Clauser, "A Map of Valley Forge," 45; Sarah Russell, "In Amish Country," 49; Alison Carb Sussman, "Lost Brother, 2019," 54; Allison Adair, "Gettysburg," 58; Catherine Chandler, "Harrowing," 63; Cynthia Hogue, "Election," 66; Martin Willitts Jr., "Why Grandfather Counted the Stars," 68; Craig Czury, "Evening Sky Diesel Blue purple tinge," 105; Shara McCallum, "Susquehanna (Excerpts)," 109; Joanne Growney, "Life on the Farm: Things to Count On," 166

Feinstein, Sandy, "In Reading," 54

Fifer, Ken, "Shiners," 120

Fillman, Robert, "All Day Long There'd Been Papers," 50

Fincke, Gary, "The Lost Continents," 204

Fishtown: Valerie Fox, "One day," 22

flora/fauna: Elaine Terranova, "Susquehanna River Bathers," 103; Micah James Bauman and David J. Bauman, "Alvira," 118; Sharon Fagan McDermott, "Tuesday Morning," 189; Janette Schafer, "At the Cathedral of

flora/fauna (*continued*)
Hope," 197; Sheila Squillante, "Garlic Mustard," 207; Paula Bohince, "First Day of the Hunt," 212

football. *See* sports

Fox, Valerie, "One day," 22

Franklin Field: Steve Pollack, "December 26, 1960," 16

Franklin Institute: Chloe Martinez, "Giant Heart," 23

Freeman, Jan, "At the Crest of the Meadow," 34

Gamble, Robbie, "Tioga County, PA," 130

Garrigan, Michael, "Bully Pulpit," 71

Gay, Ross, "To the Fig Tree on 9th and Christian," 10

Gelineau, Christine, "Christmas in Public Square," 99

Germantown: Carole Bernstein, "Quaker Memorial Service for a Young Girl, Germantown," 39

Gertz, Sandee, "Steeltown Girls," 161

Gettysburg: Allison Adair, "Gettysburg," 58; Matt Perakovich, "Letter to Wemple from Gettysburg," 58; Abby Minor, "Gettysburg Poem #3," 59

Giebenhain, Katy, "Taxidermy in South Central Pennsylvania," 61

Gilman, S. E., "The Urge to Bury," 112

Girardville: Harry Humes, "My Father's Hands," 92

Good, Mike, "D++ Dek Hockey League Champions (2012)," 209

Great Depression: Martin Willitts Jr., "Why Grandfather Counted the Stars," 68; Erin Hoover, "Retail Requiem," 76; David Chin, "American Water (Excerpts)," 101

Greenfield, Pittsburgh: Terrance Hayes, "Some Maps to Indicate Pittsburgh," 177

Grove City: Eric Potter, "Grove City Morning," 220

Growney, JoAnne, "Life on the Farm: Things to Count On," 166

Guevara, Mauricio Kilwein, "John Kane," 182

Guignard, Lilace Mellin, "Lullaby in Fracktown," 131

Hall, Vernita, "Winter Melon Soup," 20

Hancock, Stanton, "Coal Ghosts (Excerpts)," 95

Hardin, Michael, "Sodom School, Northumberland County, PA," 114

Harrisburg: Maria James-Thiaw, "White Shore, 1963," 74; Erin Hoover, "Retail Requiem," 76

Harvey, Yona, "Ink," 195

Hayes, Terrance, "Some Maps to Indicate Pittsburgh," 177

Hays, K. A., "Lines written in the Walmart Supercenter parking lot, Lewisburg, Pennsylvania," 117

Heath, Jocelyn, "Nine Irenes," 184

Heffernan, Gloria, "Sunrise on a Back Porch in Pennsylvania," 124

Hershey Park: Virginia Watts, "Pennsylvania's Governor Advises Voluntary Evacuation," 72

Hilbert, Ernest, "Walnut Street," 27

Hill District, Pittsburgh: Terrance Hayes, "Some Maps to Indicate Pittsburgh," 177; Yona Harvey, "Ink," 195

Hinton, Le, "Wintergreen," 70

Hirsch, Edward, "Windber Field," 157

hockey. *See* sports

Hodes, Amanda, "When they say to leave, she says:," 93

Hogue, Cynthia, "Election," 66

Hohner, Matt, "Toward Pittsburgh," 156

Homewood: Judith Sanders, "Walking in Homewood Cemetery During the Pandemic," 202

Hoot, Byron, "Sanctuary of Fog," 218

Hoover, Erin, "Retail Requiem," 76

Hostetler, Ann, "Settlers in the Valley," 143

Hughesville: Shanna Powlus Wheeler, "Glacier Pools Preserve," 121

Humes, Harry, "My Father's Hands," 92

hunting: Paula Bohince, "First Day of the Hunt," 212; Eric Potter, "Grove City Morning," 220; George Looney, "With Latin Filling the Lake," 222

Huntington (train stop): Robbi Nester, "The Frankford Elevated Train," 33

illness/injury: Paul Martin, "Turning Over," 91; Harry Humes, "My Father's Hands," 92; Barbara Crooker, "Worlds End," 127; Mike Good, "D++ Dek Hockey League Champions (2012)," 209

immigration: Ross Gay, "To the Fig Tree on 9th and Christian," 10; Robin Becker, "Elegy for the Science Teacher," 19;

Vernita Hall, "Winter Melon Soup," 20; Angela Alaimo O'Donnell, "Immigrant Song," 100; David Chin, "American Water (Excerpts)," 101; Patricia Jabbeh Wesley, "Pittsburgh," 173; Paola Corso, "On the Way Up: Pittsburgh StepTrek," 179; Jocelyn Heath, "Nine Irenes," 184; Mauricio Kilwein Guevara, "John Kane," 182

Indiana County: Joanne Growney, "Life on the Farm: Things to Count On," 166

Iroquois: David Staudt, "Packerton," 84

Irwin, Westmoreland County: Geraldine Connolly, "River of Mantises," 213

Isle of Que, Snyder County: Rebecca Lauren, "Gedachtniss Tag: Remembrance Day," 111

Jacks Mountain: Emily Miller Mlčák, "Jacks Mountain," 144

Jacks Narrows: Emily Miller Mlčák, "Jacks Mountain," 144; Jack Troy, "Migration at Jacks Narrows," 148

James-Thiaw, Maria, "White Shore, 1963," 74

Jerseytown: Anne Dyer Stuart, "Still April and No Spring," 119

Johnson, Julie Swarstad, "Greener Than," 139

Johnstown: Edward Hirsch, "Windber Field," 157; Barbara Sabol, "I'm from a one-way bus ticket," 158; Rachel Roupp, "In the Johnstown Flood Museum," 160; Sandee Gertz, "Steeltown Girls," 161

Joy, Chuck, "O! Erie!," 224

Judaism: Steve Pollack, "December 26, 1960," 16; Robin Becker, "Elegy for the Science Teacher," 19; Gerald Stern, "No Wind," 56; Maria James-Thiaw, "White Shore, 1963," 74; Philip Terman, "A Minyan Plus One," 198; Shirley Stevens, "Dear Mr. Rogers Revisited," 200

Juniata River: Emily Miller Mlčák, "Jacks Mountain," 144

Kasdorf, Julia Spicher, "Waking Up with Jerry Sandusky," 138

Kempton: James Najarian, "Kempton, PA: After My Death," 87

Kennedy, Judith A., "Longfellow Pine," 65

Kensington: David Livewell, "Our Fathers in Philadelphia," 15

Kishacoquillas Valley: Ann Hostetler, "Settlers in the Valley," 143

Kittatinny Mountains: Jack Chielli, "Spring Delivers Us," 87

Kiwanis Lake: Alyse Bensel, "'Swans first, now a fountain,'" 57

Knox Mine: Christine Gelineau, "Christmas in Public Square," 99

Kovacic, Kristin, "Dioramas," 188

Kress, Leonard, "Bridesburg," 29

Krohn, Richard, "Fog Off the Allegheny," 235

Krok, Peter, "Plinkies," 18

Lakemont Park: Gabriel Welsch, "The Oldest Roller Coaster in the World," 154

Lancaster County: Martin Willitts Jr., "Why Grandfather Counted the Stars," 68; Le Hinton, "Wintergreen," 70; Michael Garrigan, "Bully Pulpit," 71

Lancaster station: Alison Carb Sussman, "Lost Brother, 2019," 54

Laurelton Village: Deirdre O'Connor, "At the Site of the Laurelton Village for Feeble-minded Girls of Childbearing Age," 115

Lauren, Rebecca, "Gedachtniss Tag: Remembrance Day," 111

Lawrenceville, Pittsburgh: Terrance Hayes, "Some Maps to Indicate Pittsburgh," 177

Leas, Dawn, "Independence," 120

Lehigh Valley: Ann E. Michael, "The Invader Alters Everything," 81; Grace Bauer, "You've Got a Friend In . . . ," 86; Paul Martin, "Turning Over," 91

Levin, Lynn, "Sleepless Johnston," 42

Lewisburg: Shara McCallum, "Susquehanna (Excerpts)," 109; K. A. Hays, "Lines written in the Walmart Supercenter parking lot, Lewisburg, Pennsylvania," 117

Linvilla: Nicole Miyashiro, "Linvilla," 37

Livewell, David, "Our Fathers in Philadelphia," 15

Looney, George, "With Latin Filling the Lake," 222

Lycoming County: Shanna Powlus Wheeler, "Glacier Pools Preserve," 121; Gregory Djanikian, "Stepping Stones," 122; Gloria Heffernan, "Sunrise on a Back

Lycoming County (*continued*)
Porch in Pennsylvania," 124; Marjorie
Maddox, "Throwing like a Girl,"
125; Mary Szybist, "Here, there are
Blueberries," 126
Lyon, Rachael, "First Rain of Spring," 137

Maddox, Marjorie, "Throwing like a Girl," 125
Mahanoy City: Marianne Peel,
"Huckleberries and Homebrewed
Boilo," 89
Martin, Paul, "Turning Over," 91
Martinez, Chloe, "Giant Heart," 23
McCallum, Shara, "Susquehanna
(Excerpts)," 109
McDermott, Sharon Fagan, "Tuesday
Morning," 189
McKean: Marjorie Wonner, "October Echo,"
233
Meadville: Tammy Robacker, "Amphibians,"
233
Mennonites. *See* Amish and Mennonites
Meshoppen: Thomas Kielty Blomain, "Agnes
1972," 100
Michael, Ann E., "The Invader Alters
Everything," 81
Miller, Jonson, "Flight 93 National
Memorial," 167
mills: David Chin, "American Water
(Excerpts)," 101; Joseph Dorazio, "The
Ruins of Bethlehem Steel," 83. *See
also* steel
mines/miners: Jay Parini, "A Pennsylvania
Journal," 3; Harry Humes, "My
Father's Hands," 92; nicole v basta,
"the next field over," 96; Christine
Gelineau, "Christmas in Public
Square," 99; Angela Alaimo O'Donnell,
"Immigrant Song," 100; Emily Miller
Mlčák, "Jacks Mountain," 144; Edward
Hirsch, "Windber Field," 157
Minor, Abby, "Gettysburg Poem #3," 59
Miyashiro, Nicole, "Linvilla," 37
Mlčák, Emily Miller, "Jacks Mountain," 144
Moeller, Eileen Daly, "Philadelphia: Early
Summer," 9
Monroe Township: S. E Gilman, "The Urge
to Bury," 112
Montoursville: Gregory Djanikian,
"Stepping Stones," 122; Gloria
Heffernan, "Sunrise on a Back Porch in
Pennsylvania," 124

Moore, Berwyn, "Rapture," 226
Moore, Julie L., "Nurse in Need," 132
Morgantown: Sonia Sanchez, "On Passing
thru Morgantown, Pa," 52
Moss, MJ, "Gracie's Run," 104
Mount Carbon: Lisa Toth Salinas, "Litany of
Dyings," 90
Mount Carmel: Linda Pennisi, "The
Viaduct," 95
mountains: Judith A. Kennedy, "Longfellow
Pine," 65; David Staudt, "Packerton,"
84; James Najarian, "Kempton, PA:
After My Death," 87; Jack Chielli,
"Spring Delivers Us," 87; Micah
James Bauman and David J. Bauman,
"Alvira," 118; Julie Swarstad Johnson,
"Greener Than," 139; Emily Miller
Mlčák, "Jacks Mountain," 144
Murphy, Erin, "Fall, Central Pennsylvania,"
154
museums: Chloe Martinez, "Giant Heart,"
23; G. C. Waldrep, "Mütter Museum
with Owl," 24; Rachel Roupp, "In
the Johnstown Flood Museum," 160;
Kristin Kovacic, "Dioramas," 188
Myers, Heather, "Up Myers' Lane, Altoona,
PA," 153
Myers, Steve, "Runoff," 236

Najarian, James, "Kempton, PA: After My
Death," 87
Nantmeal Township: Mark Danowsky,
"Passing Through Southeastern
Pennsylvania Towns in Winter," 37
Native American history: Ann Hostetler,
"Settlers in the Valley," 143
Nester, Robbi, "The Frankford Elevated
Train," 33
Neversink Bike Trail: Sandy Feinstein, "In
Reading," 54
New Wilmington: David Swerdlow,
"Migration," 221
Northside, Pittsburgh: Terrance Hayes, "Some
Maps to Indicate Pittsburgh," 177
Northumberland: Melanie Simms, "At the
Riverview Cemetery, Northumberland,
PA," 113; Michael Hardin, "Sodom School,
Northumberland County, PA," 114

O'Connor, Deirdre, "At the Site of the
Laurelton Village for Feeble-minded
Girls of Childbearing Age," 115

O'Donnell, Angela Alaimo, "Immigrant Song," 100
Oaks, Jeff, "The Allegheny River," 208
Ochester, Ed, "Two Women Watched by Geese," 165
Ohio River: Nathaniel Ricketts, "Rivers," 176
Osherow, Jacqueline, "Breezeway, circa 1964," 31

Parini, Jay, "A Pennsylvania Journal," 3
Peel, Marianne, "Huckleberries and Homebrewed Boilo," 89
Peninsula Drive, Erie: Corey Zeller, "Sometimes I Forget You Lived in This City," 225
Penn Hills: Mike Good, "D++ Dek Hockey League Champions (2012)," 209
Pennisi, Linda, "The Viaduct," 95
Penn's Landing: J. C. Todd, "At the Polish-American Festival, Penn's Landing," 17
Perakovich, Matt, "Letter to Wemple from Gettysburg," 58
Philadelphia. *See* section I, "Beginnings: Philadelphia and Its Suburbs"
Pierce, Richard, "Father Rodney," 210
Pine Street, Grove City: Eric Potter, "Grove City Morning," 220
Pittsburgh: Matt Hohner, "Toward Pittsburgh," 156. *See also* section VI, "Three Rivers and Old Mills"
Plum: Paula Bohince, "First Day of the Hunt," 212
Pollack, Steve, "December 26, 1960," 16
Potter, Eric, "Grove City Morning," 220
prayer: Martin Willitts Jr., "Why Grandfather Counted the Stars," 68; Judith Sornberger, "Prayer Flags," 128; Barbara Sabol, "I'm from a one-way bus ticket," 158; Joseph Bathanti, "Requiem for the Living," 185; Philip Terman, "A Minyan Plus One," 198; Richard Pierce, "Father Rodney," 210
public transportation: Robbi Nester, "The Frankford Elevated Train," 33

Quakers: Joshua P. Cohen, "The Quaker Delegate from Pennsylvania," 14; Robin Becker, "Elegy for the Science Teacher," 19; Jan Freeman, "At the Crest of the Meadow," 34; Carole Bernstein, "Quaker Memorial Service for a Young Girl, Germantown," 39

Quinn, Michael, "Home," 36

race relations and racism: Maria James-Thiaw, "White Shore, 1963," 74; Jerry Wemple, "Wilkes-Barre," 97; Yona Harvey, "Ink," 195; Philip Terman, "A Minyan Plus One," 198; Shirley Stevens, "Dear Mr. Rogers Revisited," 200
Reading: Heather H. Thomas, "A Girl, Reading," 52; Sandy Feinstein, "In Reading," 54
Repp, John, "The Field Mice of Arneman Road," 237
Revolutionary War: Joshua P. Cohen, "The Quaker Delegate from Pennsylvania," 14; Grant Clauser, "A Map of Valley Forge," 45
Ricketts Glen State Park: Ken Fifer, "Shiners," 120
Ricketts, Nathaniel, "Rivers," 176
rivers: Chris Bullard, "At Schuylkill Park," 8; J. C. Todd, "At the Polish-American Festival, Penn's Landing," 17; David Staudt, "Packerton," 84; Barbara Crooker, "Worlds End," 127; Nathaniel Ricketts, "Rivers," 176; Jeff Oaks, "The Allegheny River," 208; Richard Krohn, "Fog Off the Allegheny," 235. *See also* Susquehanna River
Robacker, Tammy, "Amphibians," 233
Rohrer-Dann, Mary, "Before He Fell, or Jumped," 21
Roupp, Rachel, "In the Johnstown Flood Museum," 160
Route 15: Shara McCallum, "Susquehanna (Excerpts)," 109; K. A. Hays, "Lines written in the Walmart Supercenter parking lot, Lewisburg, Pennsylvania," 117
Route 30: Gerald Stern, "No Wind," 56
Route 52: Mark Danowsky, "Passing Through Southeastern Pennsylvania Towns in Winter," 37
Ruggieri, Helen, "Bird Watching in Bradford," 219
Russell, Sarah, "In Amish Country," 49
Rutland, Laura, "Wind on the Bay," 228

Saba, Mark, "Family Reunions," 181
Sabol, Barbara, "I'm from a one-way bus ticket," 158

Salinas, Lisa Toth, "Litany of Dyings," 90
Sanchez, Sonia, "On Passing thru Morgantown, Pa," 52
Sanders, Judith, "Walking in Homewood Cemetery During the Pandemic," 202
Santalucia, Nicole, "Keystone Ode with Jane Doe in It," 64
Saunier, Hayden, "Kitchen Table," 40
Schafer, Janette, "At the Cathedral of Hope," 197
Schenley Park: Jim Daniels, "Good Friday, Schenley Park, Pittsburgh, 2020," 186
Schuylkill Park: Chris Bullard, "At Schuylkill Park," 8
Scranton: Brian Fanelli, "The Sky Above My House on Johler Avenue," 106
Shippensburg: Nicole Santalucia, "Keystone Ode with Jane Doe in it," 64
Simms, Melanie, "At the Riverview Cemetery, Northumberland, PA," 113
Small-McKinney, Amy, "Walking Toward Cranes," 32
Somerset (train stop): Robbi Nester, "The Frankford Elevated Train," 33
Sornberger, Judith, "Prayer Flags," 128
South Side, Pittsburgh: Terrance Hayes, "Some Maps to Indicate Pittsburgh," 177; Jan Beatty, "Dreaming Door," 179
spirituality: Cynthia Hogue, "Election," 66; Martin Willitts Jr., "Why Grandfather Counted the Stars," 68; Michael Garrigan, "Bully Pulpit," 71; Michael Hardin, "Sodom School, Northumberland County, PA," 114; Judith Sornberger, "Prayer Flags," 128; Joseph Bathanti, "Requiem for the Living," 185; Philip Terman, "A Minyan Plus One," 198; Judith Sanders, "Walking in Homewood Cemetery During the Pandemic," 202; Richard Pierce, "Father Rodney," 210; Byron Hoot, "Sanctuary of Fog," 218; George Looney, "With Latin Filling the Lake," 222
sports: Steve Pollack, "December 26, 1960," 16; Joseph A. Chelius, "Halfball," 26; Leonard Kress, "Bridesburg," 29; Nathalie F. Anderson, "Sweat," 30; Allison Adair, "Gettysburg," 58; Marjorie Maddox, "Throwing like a Girl," 125; Erin Murphy, "Fall, Central Pennsylvania," 154; Mike Good, "D++

Dek Hockey League Champions (2012)," 209; Eric Potter, "Grove City Morning," 220; Cee Williams, "The Catcher and the Sighs," 230
spring: Sarah Russell, "In Amish Country," 49; James Najarian, "Kempton, PA: After My Death," 87; Jack Chielli, "Spring Delivers Us," 87; Anne Dyer Stuart, "Still April and No Spring," 119; Shanna Powlus Wheeler, "Glacier Pools Preserve," 121; Rachael Lyon, "First Rain of Spring," 137; Antonio Vallone, "The Dairy Queen in DuBois, Pennsylvania Opens for Spring," 155; Joseph Bathanti, "Requiem for the Living," 185; Janette Schafer, "At the Cathedral of Hope," 197; Chuck Joy, "O! Erie!," 224
Squillante, Sheila, "Garlic Mustard," 207
Squirrel Hill: Sheila Squillante, "Garlic Mustard," 207
Standig, Julie, "New Hope," 41
State College: Rachael Lyon, "First Rain of Spring," 137; Julie Swarstad Johnson, "Greener Than," 139
Staudt, David, "Packerton," 84
steel mills: Joseph Dorazio, "The Ruins of Bethlehem Steel," 83; Todd Davis, "Until Darkness Comes," 168; Patricia Jabbeh Wesley, "Pittsburgh," 173; Cortney Davis, "Then It Was Simple," 190
StepTrek, Pittsburgh: Paola Corso, "On the Way Up: Pittsburgh StepTrek," 179
Stern, Gerald, "No Wind," 56
Stevens, Shirley, "Dear Mr. Rogers Revisited," 200
Strip District, Pittsburgh: Patricia Jabbeh Wesley, "Pittsburgh," 173
Stuart, Anne Dyer, "Still April and No Spring," 119
summer: Eileen Daly Moeller, "Philadelphia: Early Summer," 9; Ernest Hilbert, "Walnut Street," 27; Jacqueline Osherow, "Breezeway, circa 1964," 31; Robbi Nester, "The Frankford Elevated Train," 33; Matt Perakovich, "Letter to Wemple from Gettysburg," 74; Lisa Toth Salinas, "Litany of Dyings," 90; Dawn Leas, "Independence," 120
Susquehanna River: Maria James-Thiaw, "White Shore, 1963," 74; Linda

Pennisi, "The Viaduct," 95; nicole v basta, "the next field over," 96; Thomas Kielty Blomain, "Agnes 1972," 100; Elaine Terranova, "Susquehanna River Bathers," 103; MJ Moss, "Gracie's Run," 104; Shara McCallum, "Susquehanna (Excerpts)," 109; Rebecca Lauren, "Gedachtniss Tag: Remembrance Day," 111. *See also* section IV, "North Central: The Susquehanna Valleys and the Upstate Region"

Sussman, Alison Carb, "Lost Brother, 2019," 54

Swerdlow, David, "Migration," 221

swimming: Eileen Daly Moeller, "Philadelphia: Early Summer," 9; Ernest Hilbert, "Walnut Street," 27; Heather H. Thomas, "A Girl, Reading," 52; Elaine Terranova, "Susquehanna River Bathers," 103; MJ Moss, "Gracie's Run," 104; Nathaniel Ricketts, "Rivers," 176

Szybist, Mary, "Here, there are Blueberries," 126

Terman, Philip, "A Minyan Plus One," 198

Terranova, Elaine, "Susquehanna River Bathers," 103

Thomas, Heather H., "A Girl, Reading," 52

Thrushart, Patricia, "Antlers," 218

Tioga (train stop): Robbi Nester, "The Frankford Elevated Train," 33

Tioga County: Judith Sornberger, "Prayer Flags," 128; Robbie Gamble, "Tioga County, PA," 130; Lilace Mellin Guignard, "Lullaby in Fracktown," 131

Tipton: Noah Davis, "Skins," 151

Todd, J. C., "At the Polish-American Festival, Penn's Landing," 17

trees: Eileen Daly Moeller, "Philadelphia: Early Summer," 9; Ross Gay, "To the Fig Tree on 9th and Christian," 10; Nicole Miyashiro, "Linvilla," 37; Grant Clauser, "A Map of Valley Forge," 45; Judith A. Kennedy, "Longfellow Pine," 65; Le Hinton, "Wintergreen," 70; Christine Gelineau, "Christmas in Public Square," 99; Shara McCallum, "Susquehanna (Excerpts)," 109; Mary Szybist, "Here, there are Blueberries," 126; Bruce Bond, "North: 1991," 134

Troy, Jack, "Migration at Jacks Narrows," 148

Tyrone: Dave Bonta, "Blast Area," 150

Upper Yoder, Cambria County: Charles Clifton, "Somewhere in Pennsylvania," 164

Upton, Lee, "The Naming of Bars," 82

Ussia, Matthew, "Arriving in Westmont," 162

Valley Forge: Grant Clauser, "A Map of Valley Forge," 45

Vallone, Antonio, "The Dairy Queen in DuBois, Pennsylvania Opens for Spring," 155

Venango County: Richard Krohn, "Fog Off the Allegheny," 235; Steve Myers, "Runoff," 236

Villanova: Michael Quinn, "Home," 36

Vollmer, Judith, "Doppelgänger," 194

Waldrep, G. C., "Mütter Museum with Owl," 24

Walker, Jeanne Murray, "Poem about the Environment," 148

water. *See* rivers, swimming

Watts, Virginia, "Pennsylvania's Governor Advises Voluntary Evacuation," 72

Weaver, Susan, "In the Allentown Shelter Kitchen," 84

Welsch, Gabriel, "The Oldest Roller Coaster in the World," 154

Wemple, Jerry, "Wilkes-Barre," 97

Wesley, Patricia Jabbeh, "Pittsburgh," 173

Westmont: Matthew Ussia, "Arriving in Westmont," 162

Weyant, Karen J., "Where Girls Still Ride the Beds of Pickup Trucks," 217

Wheeler, Shanna Powlus, "Glacier Pools Preserve," 121

Wilkes-Barre: Stanton Hancock, "Coal Ghosts (Excerpts)," 95; nicole v basta, "the next field over," 96; Jerry Wemple, "Wilkes-Barre," 97; Christine Gelineau, "Christmas in Public Square," 99

Williams, Cee, "The Catcher and the Sighs," 230

Williamsport: Marjorie Maddox, "Throwing like a Girl," 125

Willitts, Martin, Jr., "Why Grandfather Counted the Stars," 68

Windber Field: Edward Hirsch, "Windber Field," 157

winter: Steve Pollack, "December 26, 1960," 16; Nathalie F. Anderson, "Sweat," 30; Mark Danowsky, "Passing Through Southeastern Pennsylvania Towns in Winter," 37; Sarah Russell, "In Amish Country," 49; Sandy Feinstein, "In Reading," 54; Alison Carb Sussman, "Lost Brother, 2019," 54; Erin Hoover, "Retail Requiem," 76; Susan Weaver, "In the Allentown Shelter Kitchen," 84; Lisa Toth Salinas, "Litany of Dyings," 90; Paul Martin, "Turning Over," 91; Christine Gelineau, "Christmas in Public Square," 99; Brian Fanelli, "The Sky Above My House on Johler Avenue," 106; Bruce Bond, "North: 1991," 134; John Repp, "The Field Mice of Arneman Road," 237

Wisher, Yolanda, "5 South 43rd Street, Floor 2," 28

Wonner, Marjorie, "October Echo," 233

work/workers: Daniel Donaghy, "What Cement Is Made of," 7; Hayden Saunier, "Kitchen Table," 40; Martin Willitts Jr., "Why Grandfather Counted the Stars," 68; Thomas Kielty Blomain,

"Agnes 1972," 100; David Chin, "American Water (Excerpts)," 101; Emily Miller Mlčák, "Jacks Mountain," 144; Barbara Sabol, "I'm from a one-way bus ticket," 158; Matthew Ussia, "Arriving in Westmont," 162; Todd Davis, "Until Darkness Comes," 168; Paola Corso, "On the Way Up: Pittsburgh StepTrek," 179; Mauricio Kilwein Guevara, "John Kane," 182; Andrena Zawinski, "Cinderman," 183; Sean Thomas Dougherty, "At the Rib Fest in Erie, PA," 228

writing: Jay Parini, "A Pennsylvania Journal," 3; Allison Adair, "Gettysburg," 58; Lynn Emanuel, "Homage to Sharon Stone," 191; Yona Harvey, "Ink," 195

York: Alyse Bensel, "'Swans first, now a fountain,'" 57

York (train stop): Robbi Nester, "The Frankford Elevated Train," 33

Zawinski, Andrena, "Cinderman," 183

Zeller, Corey, "Sometimes I Forget You Lived in This City," 225